Surviving
Coastal and Open
Water

SIMPLY
Survival

Greg Davenport's Books for the Wilderness

Gregory J. Davenport

STACKPOLE
BOOKS

0 11557 02815 7

This book is dedicated to the U.S. Coast Guard Search and Rescue organization and especially the Helicopter Rescue Swimmer. They risk their lives so that others might survive.

I'd like to give a special thanks to my friend and rescue swimmer Alan Auricchio, whose help was greatly appreciated throughout this project.

Copyright © 2003 by Gregory J. Davenport

For further information about Greg Davenport and Simply Survival, visit the website www.simplysurvival.com.

Published by
STACKPOLE BOOKS
5067 Ritter Road
Mechanicsburg, PA 17055
www.stackpolebooks.com

Printed in the United States

First edition

10 9 8 7 6 5 4 3 2 1

Cover photograph by the author
Cover design by Caroline Stover
Illustrations by Steven A. Davenport

Library of Congress Cataloging-in-Publication Data

Davenport, Gregory J.
    Surviving coastal and open water / by Gregory J. Davenport.—1st ed.
        p. cm.—(Greg Davenport's books for the wilderness)
    Includes index.
    ISBN 0-8117-2815-3 (pbk.)
    1. Boats and boating—Safety measures—Handbooks, manuals, etc.
2. Wilderness survival—Handbooks, manuals, etc. I. Title.

GV777.55.D38 2003
797.1'028'9—dc21
                                                            2002155841

Contents

1

Introduction

Global survival has many variables that dictate a person's success or failure. Each environment—from open-water to desert situations—presents its unique challenges. Regardless of the environment, however, the same basic principles apply. Wilderness survival is a logical process, and using the following three-step approach to global wilderness survival will help you keep a clear head and proceed with meeting your needs—even under the most adverse conditions. (For more details, read my book *Wilderness Survival.*) This process is the key to survival in any environment. The only thing that differs is the order in which you meet your needs and the methods you use to meet them.

THE THREE-STEP APPROACH
TO GLOBAL WILDERNESS SURVIVAL

1. Stop and recognize the situation for what it is.

    Often, when people realize they are in a legitimate survival situation, they panic and begin to wander aimlessly. This makes it harder for search-and-rescue teams to find them, and valuable time is lost that they could have spent meeting their needs. If you stop and deal with the situation—evaluating it and taking appropriate steps—your odds of survival are greatly increased.

2. Identify your five survival essentials, and prioritize them for the environment that you are in.

    1. Personal protection (clothing, shelter, fire).
    2. Signaling (man-made and improvised).
    3. Sustenance (identifying and procuring water and food).
    4. Travel (with and without a map and compass).
    5. Health (mental, traumatic, and environmental injuries).

1

The exact order and methods of meeting these needs will depend on the environment you are in. Regardless of the order or method you choose, these needs must be met. Various methods of meeting these needs in an open-water or coastal environment are covered throughout this text.

3. Improvise to meet your needs, using both man-made and natural resources.

Once you've identified and prioritized your five survival essentials, you can begin to improvise to meet those needs. Sometimes the answer is straightforward, and sometimes it isn't. If you need some help deciding how to best meet one of your needs, use the following approach:

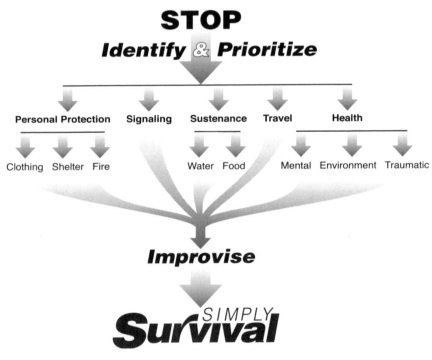

Greg Davenport's three-step approach to global survival

1. Determine your need.
2. Inventory your available man-made and natural materials.
3. Consider the different options of how you might meet your need.
4. Pick the one that best uses your time, energy, and materials.
5. Proceed with the plan, ensuring that the final outcome is safe and durable.

Being able to improvise is the key to a comfortable wilderness visit instead of an ordeal that pushes the limits of mortality. The only limiting factor is your imagination!

BEFORE YOU GO

Before departing on any trip, take the time to review your watercraft and understand its capabilities in relation to the area you intend to travel into. Can it handle the traffic, tides, and waves? If you are uncertain about your craft's capabilities, it may be best to stay home. If you intend to have passengers, evaluate their skills. Would they help or hinder you in the event something goes wrong? Take the time to review the craft and emergency procedures with your passengers. Make sure they know emergency procedures and where emergency gear is located. Areas you should cover include, but are not limited to, the following:

- How to operate the vessel, including engine use and anchor deployment.
- Location of emergency gear, including fire extinguishers, personal floatation devices, first aid and abandon-ship kits, and Emergency Position Indicating Radio Beacon (EPIRB).
- How to operate the radio and EPIRB, including the procedure for a Mayday call.
- Man overboard procedures.
- How to launch the raft.
- Your destination as well as your intended route.

During the review, assign emergency duties to everyone, and make sure they know how to accomplish their tasks.

Finally, before you depart, take the time to perform a predeparture checklist and prepare a float plan. The float plan should be left with a reliable friend whom you can count on to contact the U.S. Coast Guard (USCG) in case you do not return on time. To avoid unnecessary rescue efforts, be sure to notify this person if your return time changes. For specifics on a predeparture checklist and float plan, refer to chapter 17.

FEDERAL REQUIREMENTS FOR BOATING SAFETY

RECREATIONAL VESSELS: FEDERAL REQUIREMENTS AND SAFETY RECOMMENDATIONS

The minimal federal requirements for recreational boaters are a conservative guideline and do not guarantee the safety of a vessel or its passengers. In most cases, additional gear is advised. A number of states have additional regulations beyond these federal requirements that must be met. To see if you are in compliance with state laws, check with the boating authority for the area you plan to boat in. The following USCG quick reference chart shows the minimal requirements for recreational boats.

USCG REFERENCE CHART
FEDERAL REQUIREMENTS AND SAFETY TIPS
FOR RECREATIONAL BOATS

Vessel Length (in feet)				Equipment	Requirement
<16	16–26	26–40	40–65		
X	X	X	X	Certificate of number (state registration)	All undocumented vessels equipped with propulsion machinery must be registered with the state where they are located. Certificate of number must be on board when the vessel is in use. Note that some states require all vessels to be registered.
X	X	X	X	State numbering	(a) Plain block letters/numbers at least 3 inches in height must be affixed on each side of the forward half of the vessel in a color that contrasts with the boat's exterior. (b) State validation sticker must be affixed within 6 inches of the registration number.
	X	X	X	Certificate of documentation	Applies only to "documented" vessels: (a) Original and current certificates must be on board.

Vessel Length (in feet)				Equipment	Requirement
<16	16–26	26–40	40–65		
					(b) Vessel name/hailing port is marked on exterior part of hull in letters at least 4 inches in height. Official number is permanently affixed on interior structure in numbers at least 3 inches in height.
X	X	X	X	Life jackets (PFDs)	(a) One Type I, II, III, or V wearable USCG-approved PFD for each person on board.
	X	X	X		(b) Must carry one Type IV (throwable) PFD.
X				Visual distress signal (VDS)	(a) One electric distress light or three combination (day/night) red flares. Note: These are only required to be carried on board when operating between sunset and sunrise.
	X	X	X		(b) One orange distress flag and one electric distress light *or* three handheld or floating orange smoke signals and one electric distress light *or* three combination (day/night) red flares: handheld, meteor, or parachute-type.
X	X			Fire extinguishers	(a) One B-I (when enclosed compartment).
		X			(b) One B-II or two B-I. (Note: A fixed system equals one B-I.)
			X		(c) One B-II and one B-I or three B-I. (Note: A fixed system equals one B-I or two B-II.)
X	X	X	X	Ventilation	(a) All vessels built after April 25, 1940, that use gasoline for fuel with an enclosed engine and/or fuel tank compartments must have natural ventilation (at least two ducts fitted with cowls). (b) In addition to paragraph (a), a vessel built after July 31, 1980, must have rated power exhaust blower.

Vessel Length (in feet)				Equipment	Requirement
<16	16–26	26–40	40–65		
X	X	X		Sound-producing devices	(a) A vessel 39.4 feet in length must, at a minimum, have some means of making an "efficient" sound signal (i.e., a handheld air horn or athletic whistle. Human voice/sound is not acceptable).
		X	X		(b) A vessel 39.4 feet (12 meters) or greater in length must have a sound-signaling appliance capable of producing an efficient sound signal, audible for a half-mile with a four- to six- second duration. In addition, the vessel must carry on board a bell with a clapper (bell size not less than 7.9 inches, based on the diameter of the mouth).
X	X	X	X	Backfire flame arrestor	Required on gasoline engines installed after April 25, 1940, except for outboard motors.
X	X	X	X	Navigational lights	Required to be displayed from sunset to sunrise and in or near areas of reduced visibility.
		X	X	Oil pollution placard	(a) Placard must be at least 5 × 8 inches in size and made of durable material. (b) Placard must be posted in the machinery space or at the bilge station.
		X	X	Garbage placard	(a) Placard must be at least 4 × 9 inches in size and made of durable material. (b) Displayed in a conspicuous place notifying all on board about the discharge restrictions.
X	X	X	X	Marine sanitation device	If installed, the vessel must have an operable marine sanitation device Type I, II, or III toilet.
		X	X	Navigation rules (inland only)	The operator of a vessel 39.4 feet (12 meters) or greater in length must have on board a copy of these rules.

The U.S. Coast Guard provides minimum standards for commercial and recreational boats.

These USCG recommendations are the minimum requirements and by no means should be considered adequate. Additional items you should consider include the following:

Communication equipment

Emergency Position Indicating Radio Beacon (EPIRB)

Navigation gear (including a GPS)

Inflatable life raft

Survival kit that accounts for your five survival essentials (reviewed earlier in this chapter)

First aid kit created with consideration given to circumstances that might arise in open and coastal waters

Immersion suit for everyone on board, if you will be in cold water

For more detailed information on gear-related items, refer to chapter 3.

2

Weather Forecasting

*The weather quickly changed into 45-degree
temperatures, 15-foot seas, and 45-knot winds when a
large wave sunk the vessel. There was no time for the
crew to get out a distress call nor did they have an ELT
on board, and therefore rescue efforts did not begin until
the craft was twenty-four hours overdue. Although
severely hypothermic, three of the four crew members
were rescued. The fourth did not survive.*

—*Aviation Survival Technician Mark Sargent
U.S. Coast Guard Helicopter Rescue Swimmer*

COASTAL/OCEANIC/MARINE TERMINOLOGY

The following list of terms relate to severe weather conditions, which
include unusual water, waves, currents, or wind.

Advisory: Provides information related to impending or present tropical cyclones. Details include the location, intensity, and movement
of the storm as well as precautions that should be taken.

Coastal flood watch/warning: A coastal flood watch reflects the
possibility of a flood. A coastal flood warning means a flood is
expected or occurring.

Heavy surf advisory: Warns of heavy (high) surf conditions that may
threaten life and property.

Small-craft advisory: Issued when winds of 18 to 33 knots (21 to 38
mph) are predicted or occurring.

Gale warning: Issued when winds of 34 to 47 knots (39 to 54 mph)
are predicted or occurring.

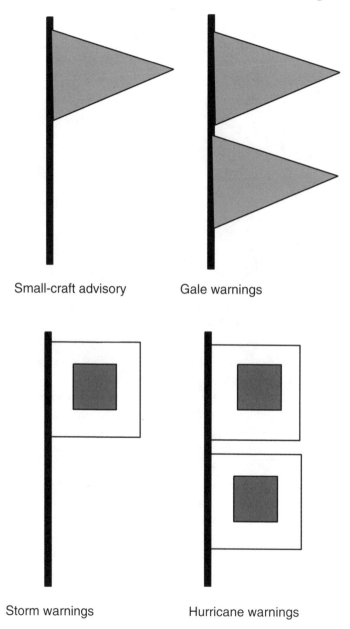

Small-craft advisory   Gale warnings

Storm warnings   Hurricane warnings

Wind advisory flags

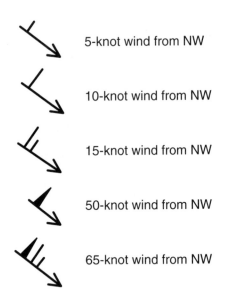

	5-knot wind from NW
	10-knot wind from NW
	15-knot wind from NW
	50-knot wind from NW
	65-knot wind from NW

Wind and wind direction symbols

Storm warning: Issued when sustained surface winds of 48 knots (55 mph) or higher are anticipated or occurring.

Tropical storm watch: Issued, usually within thirty-six hours, of when a tropical storm poses a threat in a specific location.

Tropical storm warning: Issued when sustained winds of 34 to 63 knots (39 to 73 mph) are expected to occur within twenty-four hours or less in a specific coastal area.

Hurricane watch: Issued usually within thirty-six hours of when a hurricane poses a threat to a specific location.

Hurricane warning: Issued when sustained surface winds of 64 knots (74 mph) or higher are expected to occur within twenty-four hours or less in a specific coastal area.

ABBREVIATIONS OFTEN USED

SCT	Scattered
ISOLD	Isolated
NMRS	Numerous

STNRY	Stationary
DVLPG	Developing
WKNG	Weakening
LTL	Little
FCST	Forecast
OTLK	Outlook
KT	Knots
VSBY	Visibility
CHG	Change

HOW WEATHER FORMS

Weather is a result of the sun's variable heat along with the differences in the thermal properties of the land and ocean surfaces. When temperatures of two bordering areas become unequal, the warmer air tends to climb and flow over the colder, heavier air. Wind currents are the product of the vertical (or near-vertical) process that occurs during the natural horizontal movement of the atmosphere. For example, this process occurs at the equator where the sun's rays heat up the surrounding air. The heated air is lighter and thus rises high into the atmosphere, where it travels toward the poles, cools, becomes denser, and sinks, before it circles back toward the warmer air located at the equator. The returning cool air slides under the lighter warm air, displacing it upward, and the whole process starts over.

Wind and precipitation are often created when the cool dense air rushes back and displaces the warmer air. The earth's rotation deflects the wind from taking a direct north or south route, an effect called the Coriolis force. In the Northern Hemisphere, this force causes the air to spin clockwise around a high-pressure system and counterclockwise around a low-pressure system. The Coriolis force has the same impact on high- and low-pressure systems in the Southern Hemisphere, only in the opposite direction. The Coriolis Effect also will cause the prevailing winds (see below) in the Northern Hemisphere to deflect to the right and those in the Southern Hemisphere to deflect to the left.

WIND

Basic wind patterns consist of prevailing winds, seasonal winds, and local winds.

Prevailing winds

The prevailing winds are characterized as winds that blow more frequently from one direction than any other. Four pressure systems contribute to this process:

Doldrums: A belt of low pressure around the equator that is created when heated air expands and rises. Shifting slightly north or south depending on the season, the doldrums often produce light winds, depressing humidity, and afternoon thunderstorms and showers.

Horse latitudes: A belt of high pressure located at 30 degrees north and south latitude that is characterized by its regions of descending air.

Polar front: A belt of low pressure located at the polar fronts at 60 degrees north and south latitude.

Polar caps: A belt of high pressure located at the North and South Poles.

Prevailing winds are created when air is moved from a high-pressure region toward an adjacent low-pressure belt. Because the earth rotates, prevailing winds in the Northern Hemisphere are deflected to the right and those in the Southern Hemisphere are deflected to the left. The following are the general prevailing winds.

Trade Winds

Northeast Trades: Located between the equator and 30 degrees north of the equator (wind blows in a northeast direction).

Southeast Trades: Located between the equator and 30 degrees south of the equator (wind blows in a southeast direction).

Prevailing Westerlies

Southwest Antitrades: Located between 30 and 60 degrees north of the equator (wind blows in a southwest direction).

Roaring Forties: Located between 30 and 60 degrees south of the equator (wind blows in a northwest direction).

Polar Easterlies

Polar Easterlies: Located between 60 and 90 degrees north of the equator (wind blows in a northeast direction).

Polar Easterlies: Located between 60 and 90 degrees south of the equator (wind blows in a southeast direction).

Seasonal winds

The air located above land is warmer during the summer and colder during the winter than the air located above the ocean. Since cold air produces a higher-pressure system, wind, as a general rule, will blow inland during the summer and toward the ocean during the winter.

Local winds

Local winds are created as a result of temperature changes that occur between day and night, especially during summer months. When compared to adjoining ocean air, the air above land is warmer during the day and colder at night. Since cold air produces a higher-pressure system, wind usually will blow inland during the day and toward the ocean during the night. Mountain and valley breezes are created from a similar process. During the day when the air along the sides of mountains and at valley heads is warmer than the air below it, wind will blow up the valleys. At night, the opposite is true.

PRESSURE SYSTEMS

Atmospheric pressure at the earth's surface directly affects weather. Air located in an area of high pressure will compress and warm as it descends, thus inhibiting cloud formation. So even though a slight haze or fog might occur in a high-pressure area, most days are sunny. Just the opposite happens within an area of low atmospheric pressure.

High pressure

A high-pressure center is where the pressure has been measured to be the highest in relation to its surroundings. Air moving away from that location will result in a decrease in pressure. On a weather map, the center of a high-pressure area is shown as a blue "H." In the Northern Hemisphere, the winds will flow clockwise around these high-pressure areas, while in the Southern Hemisphere, the winds will travel in a counterclockwise direction. Air in high-pressure areas will compress and warm as it descends. This

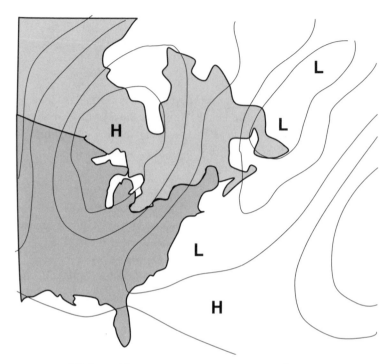

High- and low-pressure centers on a weather map

warming process inhibits the formation of clouds and often results in bright, sunny days with calm weather.

Low pressure

A low-pressure center is where the pressure has been measured to be the lowest in relation to its surroundings. Air moving away from that location will result in an increase in pressure. On a weather map, the center of a low-pressure area is shown as a red "L." In the Northern Hemisphere, winds will flow counterclockwise around these low-pressure areas, and in the Southern Hemisphere, the winds will travel in a clockwise direction. In low-pressure areas, the light warm air tends to rise, cool, condensate, and form clouds, which often leads to precipitation.

FRONTS

When two air masses of different density meet, they seldom mix. Instead, the lighter, warmer air mass is pushed up and over the more dense, cooler air. The resulting boundary between the two is called a front. The four basic fronts are warm, cold, stationary, and occluded.

Warm front

A warm front is the boundary between warm and cold air where the warm air is advancing and replacing cold air. Most warm fronts form on the east side of a low-pressure center as a result of the southerly winds that push the warm air northward. The advancing warm air rides above the colder, heavier air where its water vapor commonly condenses into clouds that can produce rain, snow, sleet, or freezing rain. The weather map symbol for a warm front is a red line with half-circles pointing in the direction the cold air is moving.

Cold front

A cold front is the boundary between warm and cool air where the cool air is arriving and replacing warm air. Winds preceding a cold front typically approach from a southerly direction, while cool winds behind the front tend to be northerly. The advancing dense cold air rides below the warm light air

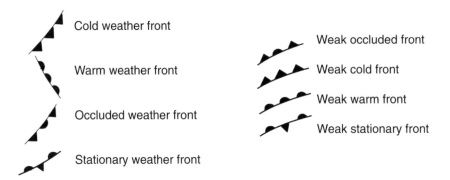

How various fronts appear on a weather map

it is replacing. The warm air cools while rising, often resulting in precipitation, depending on humidity. The weather map symbol for a cold front is a blue line with triangles pointing in the same direction that the cold air is moving.

Stationary fronts

A stationary front occurs when the meeting between cool and warm air results in a standoff. Often several days of cloudy, wet weather occur. Stationary fronts are breeding grounds for new low-pressure areas to form, some of which have been known to grow into storms. The weather map symbol for a stationary front combines the cold and warm front symbols by alternating blue triangles that point away from the cold air and red half-circles that point away from the warm air.

Occluded fronts

Often seen when a storm advances, a frontal occlusion results from warm air being lifted off of the ground. Both cold and warm occluded fronts can occur. A cold occlusion develops when the air behind the front is colder than the air ahead of it. The colder dense air undercuts the cool air and produces results similar to a cold front. A warm occlusion develops when the air behind the front is warmer than the air ahead of it. The lighter, less cold air rises up and over the colder air and produces results similar to a warm front. Both occluded fronts have well-defined boundaries between the coldest air, the cool air, and the warm air.

PREDICTING THE WEATHER

BEAUFORT WIND SCALE

The Beaufort wind scale has been used to predict wind velocity since Francis Beaufort created it in 1805. Although slightly modified since its invention, it remains a great tool to help you understand the present wind conditions for your area.

BEAUFORT WIND SCALE

Force	Wind (Knots)	*WMO Classification	Appearance of Wind Effects	
			On the Water	On Land
0	Less than 1	Calm	Sea surface smooth and mirror-like	Calm; smoke rises vertically
1	1–3	Light air	Scaly ripples; no foam crests	Still wind vanes; smoke drift indicates wind direction
2	4–6	Light breeze	Small wavelets; crests glassy; no breaking	Wind felt on face; leaves rustle; vanes begin to move
3	7–10	Gentle breeze	Large wavelets; crests begin to break; scattered whitecaps	Leaves and small twigs constantly moving; light flags extended
4	11–16	Moderate breeze	Small waves 1–4 feet, becoming longer; numerous whitecaps	Dust, leaves, and loose paper lifted; small tree branches move
5	17–21	Fresh breeze	Moderate waves 4–8 feet, taking longer form; many whitecaps; some spray	Small trees in leaf begin to sway
6	22–27	Strong breeze	Larger waves 8–13 feet; whitecaps common; more spray	Larger tree branches moving; whistling in wires
7	28–33	Near gale	Sea heaps up; waves 13–20 feet; white foam streaks off breakers	Whole trees moving; resistance felt walking against wind
8	34–40	Gale	Moderately high (13–20 feet) waves of greater length; edges of crests begin to break into spindrift; foam blown in streaks	Whole trees in motion; resistance felt walking against wind
9	41–47	Strong gale	High waves 20 feet; sea begins to roll; dense streaks of foam; spray may reduce visibility	Slight structural damage occurs; slate blows off roofs

BEAUFORT WIND SCALE (Continued)

Force	Wind (Knots)	*WMO Classification	Appearance of Wind Effects	
			On the Water	On Land
10	48–55	Storm	Very high waves 20–30 feet with overhanging crests; sea white with densely blown foam; heavy rolling; lowered visibility	Seldom experienced on land; trees broken or uprooted; consider able structural damage
11	56–63	Violent storm	Exceptionally high (30–45 feet) waves; foam patches cover sea; visibility more reduced	
12	64+	Hurricane	Air filled with foam; waves over 45 feet; sea completely white with driving spray, visibility greatly reduced	

*World Meteorological Organization

USING BAROMETRIC PRESSURE TO FORECAST WEATHER

Before the technical revolution, a barometer was used to predict weather patterns. Atmospheric pressure is affected by high- and low-pressure systems and the elevation where you are (air pressure decreases as you gain altitude). An aneroid (without fluid) barometer measures atmospheric pressure. The instrument's pointer will rise or fall as the pressure of the atmosphere increases or decreases. Air pressure at sea level is normally 29.92 inches of mercury, and as a general rule, when the air pressure drops, bad weather is imminent.

USING BAROMETRIC PRESSURE AND WIND DIRECTION TO FORECAST WEATHER

The National Weather Service provides a guideline for predicting weather in the United States based on wind direction and barometric readings (sea-level pressure). To use this guideline to predict the weather for your area, you will need to convert the barometric pressure so that it is based on sea level at your present location. A simple way to calculate this difference is to subtract about 1 inch of mercury for every 1,000 feet of altitude over sea level.

For example, a barometric pressure of 30 at sea is roughly equal to a barometric pressure of 32 at a 2,000-foot elevation. In order to use the following guide, you must convert the barometric pressure to its sea-level reading. Subtracting 1 inch for every 1,000 feet above sea level gives you 30 inches of mercury and a reading relevant to the National Weather Service Guidelines.

Wind Direction	Barometric Reading	Predicted Weather
SW to NW	30.10 to 30.20 and steady	Fair with slight temperature change for one to two days
SW to NW	30.10 to 30.20 and rising rapidly	Fair, followed by rain within two days
SW to NW	30.20 and above and stationary	Continued fair, with no decided temperature changes
SW to NW	30.20 and above and falling slowly	Slowly rising temperatures and fair for two days
S to SE	30.10 to 30.20 and falling slowly	Rain within twenty-four hours
S to SE	30.10 to 30.20 and falling rapidly	Wind increasing in force, with rain within twelve to twenty-four hours
SE to NE	30.10 to 30.20 and falling slowly	Rain in twelve to eighteen hours
SE to NE	30.10 to 30.20 and falling rapidly	Increasing wind and rain within twelve hours
E to NE	30.10 and above and falling slowly	During summer and times of light winds, rain may not fall for several days; in winter, rain within twenty-four hours
E to NE	30.10 and above and falling rapidly	During summer, rain is probable within twelve to twenty-four hours; in winter, rain or snow with increasing winds

Wind Direction	Barometric Reading	Predicted Weather
SE to NE	30.00 or below and falling slowly	Rain will continue for one to two days
SE to NE	30.00 or below and falling rapidly	Rain with high wind, followed (usually within thirty-six hours) by clearing (and colder conditions in winter)
S to SW	30.00 or below and rising slowly	Clearing within a few hours, followed by several days of fair weather
S to E	29.80 or below and falling rapidly	Severe storm imminent, followed within twenty-four hours by clearing (and colder conditions in winter)
E to N	29.80 or below and falling rapidly	Severe northeast gale and heavy precipitation; in winter, often heavy snow followed by a cold wave
West wind	29.80 or below and rising rapidly	Clearing and colder

USING CLOUDS TO FORECAST WEATHER

Clouds have a direct role in our weather and can provide valuable clues about what type of weather to expect. In addition to bringing precipitation, clouds warm the earth by preventing its radiant heat from escaping and cool the earth by blocking it from the sun. Clouds are usually classified by height and type.

Cloud terminology

Prefix "cirro"

Clouds above 20,000 feet (high-level) have the prefix "cirro" assigned to their name. Cirrus clouds usually contain ice crystals and are typically very thin and translucent.

Prefix "alto"
Clouds at 6,500 to 23,000 feet (mid-level) have the prefix "alto" assigned to their name. These clouds usually contain liquid water droplets in summer and a liquid droplet–ice crystal mix during the winter.

Prefix "nimbo"
Clouds that produce precipitation often have the prefix "nimbo" assigned to their name. Nimbus clouds will typically be big and black with ragged dark edges.

Types of clouds and their meaning

Stratus clouds
Stratus clouds, which look similar to a high fog, often cover most of the sky with their gray uniform appearance. These clouds are associated with warm, mild weather that will often have a mist or drizzle.

Cirrostratus: Thin high-level (above 20,000 feet) stratus clouds that form a milky, white sheet covering the entire sky. These clouds are so thin that the light rays from the sun and moon pass through them and form a visible halo around the sun and moon. Cirrostratus clouds often indicate the arrival of rain or snowfall within twenty-four hours of an approaching warm or occluded front.

Altostratus: Thin mid-level (between 6,500 and 23,000 feet) stratus clouds that form a gray sheet covering the sky. The sun can be seen under thin sections of altostratus clouds as a dim round disc often referred to as a watery sun. Although the sun might be seen, the clouds will not allow enough rays to pass through to produce a visible shadow on the ground. Altostratus clouds often indicate an impending storm with heavy precipitation.

Nimbostratus: Low-level (below 6,500 feet) stratus clouds are dark gray and usually associated with continuous light to moderate precipitation. This cloud formation provides no information about impending weather since it has already arrived. The sun and moon will not be visible through these clouds.

Stratocumulus: Low-level (below 6,500 feet) stratus clouds are white to dark gray and can be seen in rows or patches or as rounded masses with blue sky in between individual cloud formations. Although these clouds can be associated with strong winds, precipitation is rarely seen.

Cumulus clouds

Cumulus clouds are an isolated group of clouds that look similar to a cotton ball with a flat base and a fluffy top. These clouds typically have large areas of blue sky between each cloud and are normally, but not always, associated with fair weather.

> *Altocumulus:* Mid-level (between 6,000 and 20,000 feet) isolated groups of cumulus clouds with the typical flat-based cotton ball appearance, often found in parallel waves or bands. These clouds typically have a darkened area (often at their flat base) that sets them apart from the higher cirrocumulus clouds. Although these clouds usually indicate good weather, when they appear as "little castles" in the sky, especially on a warm humid summer morning, afternoon thunderstorms have been known to follow.

> *Cirrocumulus:* High-level (above 18,000 feet) isolated groups of cumulus clouds that look like rippled sand or globular masses of cotton (without shadows). As with most cumulus clouds, fair weather is often present or expected when these clouds are prominent in the sky, although a storm may be approaching.

> *Cumulonimbus:* These high mountainous clouds are more commonly known as thunderstorms. The towering clouds will often look like the top of an anvil, which is a classic appearance for thunderstorms, and when present, bad weather can be expected in the immediate area.

3

Gear

*One of the most obvious and effective pieces of life-
saving equipment around the water is the life jacket. On
a day during a bad storm, I recovered three deceased
fishermen who drowned within 200 yards from shore.
They were not wearing life jackets. Later that same day,
I rescued three individuals whose vessel sank at nearly
the same location. In the second instance, all three had
life jackets.*
—*Aviation Survival Technician Eric Forslund*
U.S. Coast Guard Helicopter Rescue Swimmer

When deciding what gear to take with you on your trip to sea, try to select
items that provide multiple uses. For example, a durable space blanket can
be used as an extension of your clothing and also as a signal (orange side in
winter, silver side in summer), a water collection device, or a shelter. A
military poncho, thick-ply garbage bag, and parachute line are other examples of multiuse items. To protect battery-operated equipment from cold
soaking, moisture, salt corrosion, and sand, wrap them in a good insulating
material and carry them between the layers of your clothing to take advantage of your radiant heat.

While not all-inclusive, this chapter covers the basic items you might
consider taking on a trip to sea. Many additional items can be found refer-
enced throughout this book or within the recommended abandon-ship, survival, and medical kits.

GEAR AT SEA

The coast guard has established minimum standards for recreational vessels and associated safety equipment. These standards require most equipment to meet coast guard–approval guidelines for performance and construction.

SURVIVAL CRAFTS

If you are a recreational boater, you should have a buoyant apparatus, an inflatable buoyant apparatus, or a life raft.

Buoyant apparatus

A buoyant apparatus is a quick-response lifesaving device that comes in a variety of shapes, sizes, and styles. Its rigid double-sided reversible design allows for rapid manual launching—with minimal preparation—during a

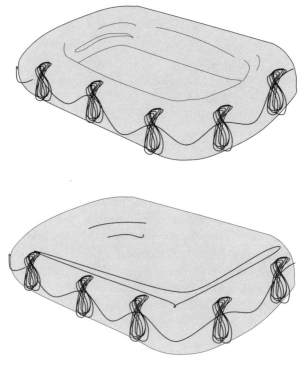

Buoyant apparatus

crisis. A buoyant apparatus can be used as a lifeline during a rescue or to keep you afloat in case your vessel is sinking. Often rectangular in shape, the apparatus has either a solid platform or a solid outer ring with a central compartment that can be used to keep gear afloat. Lifelines attached to the outside of the apparatus are designed so that someone immersed in the water can hold on to them to stay afloat.

Inflatable buoyant apparatus
Although better than a buoyant apparatus, an inflatable buoyant apparatus falls short of a life raft. The inflatable buoyant apparatus is intended for use

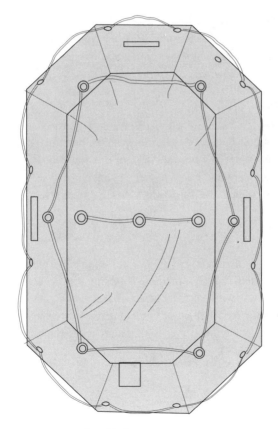

Inflatable buoyant apparatus

aboard vessels operating close to shore. This device comes in various shapes and sizes, and unlike a buoyancy apparatus, it will support you and a varying number of occupants out of the water. Normally these devices have only one buoyancy tube and do not have an inflatable floor or canopy. Like a life raft, they can be stored in a valise or hard deck-mount type of container.

Life raft

The inflatable life raft is an extremely important lifesaving device that all boats should have. Life rafts vary greatly from manufacturer to manufacturer and from one style to another. Take the time to become familiar with the raft you carry before it is time to use it. Since your raft is packed, ask your vendor or servicing representative to demonstrate how to inflate your particular raft. You should also make sure to have the raft serviced in accordance with the manufacturer's recommendations. When purchasing a life raft, consider the following.

Size and shape

Inflatable life rafts, which must be coast guard approved, come in round, oval, octagonal, or boat shapes. Raft capacities normally range from four to twenty-six people. The type and size of raft you choose for your vessel will depend on many factors: Are you staying close to the coastline? Are you heading into international waters? How many people will be on board the vessel, and what is their experience?

Inflation tubes

The ideal raft will have two separate inflation tubes (buoyancy tubes) located on its outer edge. For increased stability and decreased tube bending, tubes need to be at least 12 inches in diameter when inflated. A cylinder of carbon dioxide (CO_2) alone or in combination with nitrogen is used to inflate the raft. The cylinder is normally attached to the bottom of the raft and can be activated by sharply pulling the line, usually a 100-foot-long operating cord, attached to it.

Pressure relief valves

Most rafts have a pressure relief valve located in the inflation tubes that allows excess gas to escape. The valves will also allow air to escape during

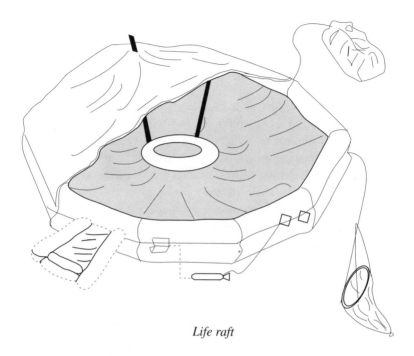

Life raft

warm days when the gas in the tube expands. On the flip side, in the evening when cooler temperatures cause the air to contract, you may have to manually pump more air into the chambers. While it is normal for pressure relief valves to hiss while gas escapes right after the raft is inflated, this process should last only a few minutes. On occasion, pressure relief valves will fail and continue to leak gas. If that happens, you will have to plug the valve using one of the plugs in your life raft repair kit.

Raft floor
Most life rafts have a double floor that can be inflated with a hand pump. In cold weather, inflating the floor will keep you warmer by creating an insulating dead air space between you and the cold water. In hot weather, however, keeping the floor deflated allows the cooler seawater to keep you cool.

Arches

Most rafts have an inflatable arch, and some have two or three. The arches support a canopy that can be used to protect you from rain, wind, and sun.

Stabilizers

A life raft is stabilized by its ballasts and sea anchor. Ballasts are water pockets located under the life raft that allow seawater inside when the raft is launched. In addition to stabilizing the raft by making it less likely to capsize, the ballasts also help slow the raft's drift. The number and size of ballasts on a raft vary from one manufacturer to another. Like the ballasts, a sea anchor is used to help stabilize the raft, especially in rough seas when waves are coming from the same direction as the wind. Make sure the anchor is made of a strong durable material and is big enough to make a difference in rough water. Refer to chapter 12 for further details on how to use a sea anchor.

Survival kit

USCG-approved life rafts provide a survival kit. Be sure to check its contents and talk to your vendor about adding any other materials when the raft is packed or serviced. For more details on life raft survival kits, refer to chapter 15.

Life raft storage

If your life raft is kept in a canister, it will probably sit on a cradle that is secured on top of the open deck. The greatest benefit of this storage method is easy access. Another benefit to this system is that the canister will float free of the vessel in case it would sink before you can manually launch the raft. The canister is made of two compartments that create a watertight seal when combined. The two compartments are held together by bands that break when the raft is inflated. Holes on the bottom of the canister allow condensation drainage and air circulation, and the words "this side up" on the top of the container will help you make sure the holes are down. Tie-down straps, which often are used to secure a container to the cradle, support a hydrostatic release that can be kicked to free the canister from the cradle. Other releases are used, so be sure to familiarize yourself with your system. Often, a cleat is located near the cradle and can

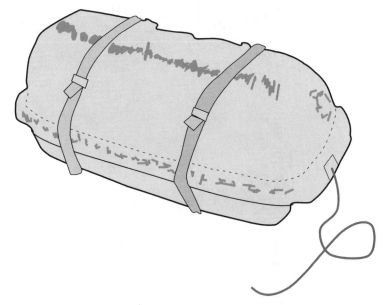

Life rafts are often stored in a canister that sits on a cradle located on the deck.

be used to tie a retaining line when manually launching the raft. Since most inflation lanyards separate from the raft when activated, don't mistake them for a retaining line. Life rafts that are stored in a valise are often stowed below deck and out of the way. During an emergency, these rafts must be brought to the surface for launching.

Life raft paddles
Life raft paddles come in many designs, and the exact type of paddle you have will depend on your life raft. While these paddles are helpful near land, when trying to make landfall, and when moving away from a sinking vessel, they are seldom used otherwise. This is because paddling a raft uses up precious energy that should be conserved during a life-threatening situation. If you decide to move the raft by paddling, pull in the sea anchors, empty the ballast pockets, and place one paddler at each side of the raft.

A smaller life raft without the canopy

The same raft with the canopy up

LIFE RAFT REPAIR KITS

If your life raft would develop a hole, you would be glad you packed a repair kit. Don't be fooled into thinking that a kit containing rubber tube patches and cement will fix your problem. Not only do these patches require a dry work area and are only useful for extremely small holes, but you cannot completely inflate the raft until the patch has had twenty-four hours to dry. If you do decide to use these patches, be sure to cut the patch at least 1 inch larger than the hole it is covering. Next, apply cement to both the patch and the area around the hole, and allow both to completely dry before applying a second coat to both. Once the second coating reaches a tacky texture, press the patch on the hole. Do not completely inflate the raft until the patch has had twenty-four hours to dry.

A better way to seal raft holes is to carry raft repair clamps. Unlike the patches, clamps provide an immediate fix to your problem. Repair clamps come in small, medium, and large sizes (3, 5, and 8 inches), allowing you to choose the size that best fits the needed repair. The clamp is made of two pieces of convex metal, with outer rubber edges, that are connected by a post and wing nut that run through the center of each. When using a clamp, loop its cord around your wrist to prevent the accidental loss of the clamp overboard. Next, get the clamp wet so that it will be easier to insert inside the hole. Push the clamp's bottom plate through the hole, and pull it up against the inner surface of the tube. If the hole is too small, enlarge it

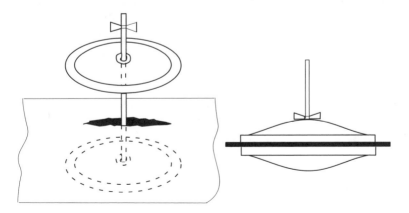

Raft repair clamps are ideal for sealing a hole in your raft.

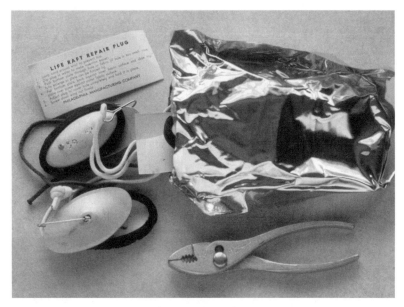

Life raft repair clamps

enough so that the clamp barely slides through. Next, slide the top part of the clamp over the bottom portion and adjust the clamp so that it completely covers the hole. Holding the clamp in place, screw the wing nut tight, and either wrap the wire around the nut or break it off.

Another item to consider packing in case you need to repair raft leaks is a roll of sail-mending tape or duct tape. Sail-mending and duct tape are effective for sealing small leaks that occur above the waterline. Not all sail-mending and duct tape brands are the same, so make sure the one you select sticks when wet. Leaks can also occur at pressure release and topping valves. Be sure to know whether your raft has a plug for these devices and to carry several spares of each in case one is lost.

ABANDON-SHIP BAGS

An abandon-ship bag is simply a survival and first aid kit that floats. The contents of each kit will depend upon many variables, including your sport, the length of your outing, and the time of year. These bags are great for storing emergency gear and should be placed in an easily accessible location. You should also tie a lanyard line to the bag's D-ring with a carabiner at the other end that could easily be attached to your raft or PFD harness. While most commercial abandon-ship bags will float, only the more expensive dry bags are waterproof. The Landfall Navigation Abandon Ship Dri-Bag, the leader in this arena, can keep approximately 100 pounds of gear afloat and dry. The bag is 21 inches wide and 13.5 inches tall with ³⁄₁₆-inch-thick closed-cell foam padding covering its bottom and sides. Its exterior is made from heavily reinforced 1,000-denier Antron nylon cloth, and its interior is welded polyurethane-coated 420-denier nylon. Its zipper provides a positive seal and extends 4.5 inches down the sides. The bag's handles are made of heavy-duty webbing and come with two stainless steel D-rings for attaching such items as a float-free automatic strobe.

RELIEFBAND MEDICAL DEVICE
The ReliefBand Device has been approved by the Food and Drug Administration as a treatment for nausea and vomiting related to motion sickness. Worn like a wristwatch, the device emits an electrical signal on the underside of the wrist that somehow interferes with the nerves that cause nausea. The band has five settings that allow you to adjust it to the amount of relief you need for your nausea. The best part about using the ReliefBand is avoiding the drowsiness caused by oral antiseasickness medications.

SEA KAYAKS
A sea kayak, which is made for directional stability, allows the kayaker to expend a minimal amount of effort to maintain a cruising speed. When selecting a kayak that meets your needs, you may have to choose between speed and stability. Consider the following when selecting a kayak.

Material
Most kayaks are made from either polyethylene plastic or fiberglass. If you are just discovering the sport, start with the more affordable polyethylene plastic kayak. And if you decide to stick with kayaking, the inexpensive plastic kayak has an outstanding resale value that makes it easier for you to go out and purchase another kayak—if you choose—once you become more proficient in the sport.

Sea kayak

Speed and maneuverability
Longer kayaks are faster but less maneuverable than shorter kayaks. A kayak that is 15 to 17 feet long is considered an appropriate length for general all-purpose use.

Stability
Wider kayaks are more stable than narrow kayaks, and in anything but calm seas, kayaks with V- or round-shaped hulls are more stable than those

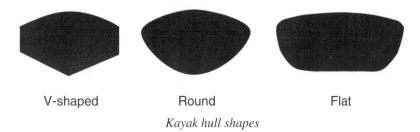

V-shaped   Round   Flat

Kayak hull shapes

with U-shaped hulls. A kayak that is 23 to 25 inches wide is considered an appropriate width for general all-purpose use.

Storage capacity
When considering the storage capacity of a kayak, take the time to ponder its intended use. Will you be going on trips that last one day, two weeks, or perhaps a month? Based on this answer, you should be able to decide how much storage space you need. As a general rule, a medium-volume kayak will provide enough storage space for a two-week trip.

Convenience issues
Do you often kayak with another person? If so, perhaps a double-seat kayak would be best. Although far more affordable than two individual kayaks, the larger double-seat kayak is not as responsive and does not have the storage capacity that two separate boats would have. If storage or transport of the kayak is an issue, perhaps a collapsible kayak would be a good choice.

PADDLES
For kayakers, paddles provide added stability and are the main source of propulsion and steering for the boat. When deciding which paddle to purchase, consider its material, weight, length, shaft and blade style, and whether it has feathered or nonfeathered blades. Buy a spare just in case you lose or break your primary paddle.

Material
Kayak paddles can be found in fiberglass (the best choice), wood (a good choice), plastic (a bad option), and various combinations of these materials. On the higher end of performance and cost, you will find paddles made of fiberglass that has been made stronger and lighter by reinforcement with carbon fiber, graphite, or Kevlar. On the lower end of cost and performance are paddles made with an aluminum shaft and plastic blades.

Weight
While paddles come in many weights, the average paddle weighs about 2½ pounds. Paddles weighing more than 3 pounds are too heavy and will tire

you during a long day in the water. Paddles under 2 pounds are nice but extremely expensive.

Length

The optimal paddle length allows your blade to properly contact the water without disturbing your natural stroke. Two things to consider when selecting a paddle are your height while sitting in your vessel and the width of the boat at that point. If you sit low in the boat or if your kayak is fairly wide, you will need a longer paddle to contact the water and decrease body strain. A shorter paddle is best for those who either sit high or have a narrow boat.

Shaft and blade style

Shafts can be found with oval or round shapes, and both have advantages and disadvantages. An oval shaft helps keep your hands on the shaft so that its blades are properly aligned with the water. However, if you change the angle of your paddle, the fit of your hand on the shaft can become uncomfortable. If this is an issue, a round shaft may be more suitable. The blade style you choose will depend on your intended use. Blades come curved or flat and symmetrical or asymmetrical. Sea kayakers usually prefer a flat asymmetrical blade. This blade doesn't allow quick turns or acceleration, but it requires less energy to maintain a constant speed.

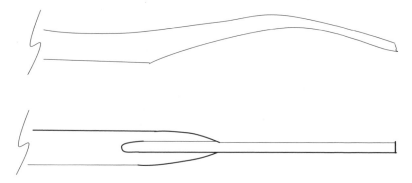

Curved and flat kayak paddle blades

The kayak paddle

Feathered or nonfeathered paddles
A feathered paddle has blades offset at 60 to 90 degrees to each other and, depending on how the power side of the blade is oriented, is designated either a right- or left-handed control. A nonfeathered paddle has the power side of both blades on the same plane and side. Both types of paddles have advantages and disadvantages. The best way to determine which type meets your needs is from experience. It might be worthwhile to purchase a paddle that you can break down and set at each of the various positions. Once you decide which type meets your needs, keep that paddle as your spare.

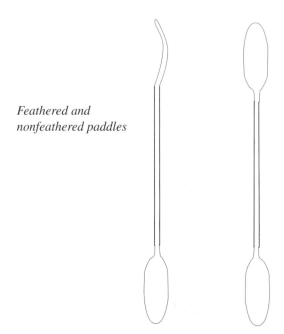

*Feathered and
nonfeathered paddles*

The paddle float

PADDLE FLOAT

A paddle float helps a kayaker to reenter a capsized boat. To use the paddle float, which will be either a foam block or an inflatable float, inflate the float, slip it over one end of the paddle, and slide the other end of the paddle onto the kayak behind the cockpit. Before entering the water, you might consider rigging some line behind the cockpit since it can help hold the paddle in place. Once in place, the paddle float helps stabilize the kayak, thereby making it easier for you to climb back in the boat.

PERSONAL FLOTATION DEVICES (PFDs)

All recreational vessels are required to carry one wearable PFD (Type I, II, III, or V PFD) for each person aboard. Boats 16 feet and longer, except canoes and kayaks, must also carry one throwable PFD (Type IV). All PFD devices must be in good serviceable condition, meet coast guard approval, and fit the intended user. For best results, a PFD should be worn at all times, but if you are not wearing the device, it should be easily accessible and you should know how to put it on quickly in case of an emergency. The throwable device also should be visible and ready for immediate use. Although federal law does not require PFDs on racing shells, rowing sculls, racing canoes, and racing kayaks, state laws vary greatly and may mandate otherwise.

Three basic designs for personal flotation devices

Inherently buoyant

Mostly made of foam, this very reliable wearable and throwable PFD comes in all sizes and is made for both swimmers and nonswimmers.

Inflatable

This wearable PFD is made for the adult swimmer at least sixteen years old. Its compact design makes it easy to wear and perform routine tasks without getting in the way. To meet coast guard requirements, this PFD must have a full cylinder, and all status indicators on the inflator must be green.

Hybrid

Foam and inflatable combined, this reliable wearable PFD comes in all sizes and is made for both swimmers and nonswimmers.

Types of personal flotation devices

Type I

Type I is created for offshore use and is effective in all waters, including rough seas, or where rescue may be delayed. This extremely buoyant PFD is designed to turn an unconscious wearer face up in the water.

Type II

Type II is created for near-shore use and is effective in calm inland waters or where a quick rescue can be expected. This PFD will also turn an unconscious wearer face up in the water, but not as often or with the same ease as type I.

Type III

Type III is created for use in calm, inland water where a quick rescue can be expected. The wearer must actively maintain a face-up position and must therefore be conscious for the PFD to work.

Type IV

This throwable PFD is for use in calm, inland waters where help is always available. Not intended as a wearable PFD, this device is thrown into the water so that the person overboard can grasp it and be pulled to the vessel.

Type V

This special-use PFD comes in many formats depending on the type of activity it was made to be used with. It can be carried instead of another PFD, but only if it is used in accordance with its labeling. Because some of these devices provide hypothermia protection, they make excellent multi-use items.

Purchasing a PFD

When purchasing a personal floatation device, be sure it is coast guard approved. Try it on. The PFD should fit snuggly to your body yet allow you to freely move your arms. To make sure it fits right, zip it up, tighten down the straps, and raise your arms over your head. Are you able to move them freely while the device is tightened down? Next, have someone raise the

PFD straight up your shoulders. If the zipper reaches your nose or higher, get a smaller PFD. If you are able, test the PFD in water to make sure that it keeps your mouth and nose above the waterline when your head is tilted back. The optimal PFD includes pockets and clips capable of storing emergency gear like whistles, mirrors, strobes, and flares.

BILGE PUMP
The bilge is that part of a vessel that sits below the waterline. Given time, most vessels will get water in this area, and the bilge pump allows you to easily remove the water from your boat. These pumps come in manual and electric options. Before deciding on a pump, consider your vessel and how it might be used. Be sure the pump you choose will meet your needs. If you decide to get an electric pump, carry a manual backup just in case it stops working.

CAMELBAK
The CamelBak is a great innovation that helps you stay hydrated while allowing you to carry additional emergency gear. I have several sizes, all of which allow me to carry 100 ounces of water that I can easily access through a drinking nozzle located over the shoulder strap. Whether boating on the water or camping on land, I always wear a CamelBak. If on the trail, the device is securely placed on top of my large pack, and the water bladder's hose is draped over my pack's shoulder strap. By doing this, I continue to have easy access to my water and can quickly get into my emergency gear when I stop. The HAWG CamelBak costs approximately $100 and can carry 1,203 cubic inches (1,020 in the cargo pocket). It weighs 1.9 pounds empty and approximately 8.2 pounds when its 100-ounce water reservoir is filled. It measures 9 by 7 by 19 inches in size.

KNIVES
A knife has many uses and is probably one of the most versatile tools a survivor can carry. However, using a knife can cause injury, and thus every precaution should be taken to reduce this risk. Cutting away from yourself and maintaining a sharp knife will substantially reduce your risk of injury. I use the acronym SCOLD (sharp, clean, oiled, lanyard, and dry) to help me remember the proper care and use of my knives.

S—Sharp. A sharp knife is easier to control and use, which helps to decrease the chance for injury. Two methods for sharpening a knife are outlined below.

Push and pull
In a slicing fashion, repeatedly push and pull the knife's blade across a flat sharpening stone. (If a commercial sharpening stone isn't available, use a flat, gray sandstone.) For best results, start with the base of the blade on the long edge of the stone, and pull it across the length of the stone so that when you're done, its tip has reached the center of the stone. To obtain an even angle, push the other side of the blade across the stone in the same manner. Each side should be done the same number of times.

Circular
In a circular fashion, repeatedly move the knife blade across a circular sharpening stone or gray sandstone. Starting with the base of the blade at the edge of the stone, move the knife in a circular pattern across the stone. To obtain an even angle, turn the blade over and do the same on the other side. Each side should be done the same number of times.

To establish the best sharpening angle for either method, lay the knife blade flat onto the sharpening stone and raise the back of the blade up until the distance between it and the stone is equal to the thickness of the blade's back side.

C—Clean. Grit and dirt that get into the joint where the knife folds can destroy the joint and cause it to either freeze closed (or open) or even break. Depending on the type of knife you are using, dirt is also harmful to the blade's steel and can lead to its deterioration. When cleaning a knife, use a rag and wipe it from the backside to avoid cutting yourself. Never run it across your pants or shirt since that will transfer the dirt into the pores of your clothing and you might cut yourself.

O—Oiled. Keeping the blade and joint of your knife oiled will help protect the joint and steel and decrease the chances of rust.

L—Lanyard. Before even thinking of using a knife, make sure you tie it to your body. The lanyard's length should allow you to hold the knife in

Benchmade Knife makes the 100SH20-H20, a partially serrated fixed blade that is 100 percent corrosion resistant.

your hand, with six inches to spare, when your arm is fully extended over your head. This length allows you full use of the knife and, because the lanyard is long enough, decreases the risk of cuts.

D—Dry. Keep your knife dry to prevent rust and corrosion that can affect the blade and its joint.

Folding Blade Knives

I consider a folding pocketknife one of my most important tools. When purchasing a knife, consider that the weakest part is its lock—the part that keeps the blade open and prevents it from closing on your fingers. Look for a good lock that will secure the blade tightly to the handle when it is open. I prefer a blade length of 3 inches. A serrated blade works best for cutting wet rope and line and is a better choice for use at sea.

Fixed-Blade Knives

A large fixed-blade knife is used for most of my big outdoor projects, from cutting down 2-inch-diameter dead trees to prepping the larger stages of my firewood. A simple blade is all you need. Avoid knives that have multiple modifications to the blade, which supposedly allow you to do the unimaginable; it is just marketing hype. I prefer a 7- to 9-inch blade with the total length measuring between 15 and 17 inches. A large knife should be safely handled and cared for using the SCOLD acronym previously discussed.

GEAR ON SHORE

BACKPACKS

Most likely, you will not have a backpack with you when you reach shore in a life raft or disabled kayak. Don't let this discourage you. Instead, improvise. To make an improvised backpack, find a forked branch (sapling or bough) and cut it 1 foot below the fork and 3 feet above. Trim off excess twigs. Cut notches about 1 inch from each of the three ends, and tie rope or line around the notches of the two forked branches. Bring the two lines together and tie them to the notch on the single end of the sapling to make the pack's shoulder straps. Make sure the gap between the line and branch is wide enough for your shoulders to fit into without being too tight or too loose. Place your gear inside a waterproof bag, and attach it to the forked branch. To make carrying this pack more comfortable, add a chest strap that runs through the shoulder straps at armpit height. This line should be long enough so that you can hold the free end in your hand and thereby control the amount of pressure exerted by the pack on your armpits and shoulders.

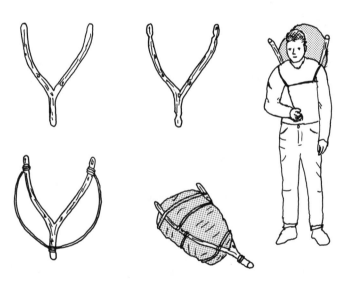

Improvised backpack

Various sleeping bag construction designs

SLEEPING BAGS

If kayaking for extended periods of time, you will probably have a sleeping bag. There are many types of sleeping bags available, and the type used varies greatly. However, there are several basic guidelines you should consider when selecting a bag. The ideal bag should be compressible, have an insulated hood, and be lightweight but still keep you warm. Most manufacturers rate their bags for summer, three-season, or winter expedition use and provide a minimum temperature at which they expect the bag to perform. This gross rating should help you select the bag that best meets your needs. A sleeping bag cover is useful for keeping your bag clean and adding an additional layer of insulating air. How well the bag will keep you warm depends on the amount and type of insulation and loft, design, and method of construction.

Design

Without question, the hooded, tapered mummy style should be your bag of choice. The hood should tighten around your face, leaving a hole big enough for you to breathe through. The foot of the bag should be somewhat circular and well insulated. Side zippers need good insulated baffles behind them.

Insulation

Sleeping bags will use either a down or synthetic insulation material.

Down

Down is very lightweight, effective, and compressible. A down bag is rated by its fill power in cubic inches per ounce. A rating of 550 is standard, with values increasing in excess of 800. The higher ratings provide greater loft, which means a warmer bag. The greatest downfall to this insulation is its inability to maintain its loft and insulating value when wet. In addition, a down bag is very expensive. These bags are not best suited for use in water sports.

Synthetic insulation

Synthetic materials provide a good alternative to the down sleeping bag. Their greatest strength is their ability to maintain most of their loft and insulation when wet and their ability to dry relatively quickly. On the flip side, synthetic insulation is heavier and doesn't compress as well as down. Although cheaper than down, synthetic insulation tends to lose its loft quicker over long-term use. Lite Loft and Polarguard are two good examples of synthetic insulation.

Method of construction

Insulation material is normally contained in baffles, which are tubes created within the bag. There are three basic construction designs for sleeping bags: slant-tube, offset quilt, and square box. Each design has its benefits, and the type you choose depends on many factors, including weight, temperature rating, and compressibility.

Understanding the basic bag design is the key to improvising a bag in a time of crisis. If you reach shore in your life raft, you can still have a sleeping bag. You will need to inventory your materials (both man-made and natural) and improvise one. I once made a bag using rip-stop parachute material, dry leaves, and moss.

SLEEPING PADS

A sleeping pad is essential for insulating you from the cold moist ground. Most commercial pads are closed-cell or open-cell foam or a combination of the two. Each style has its pros and cons.

Closed-cell foam

These types of pads provide excellent insulation and durability but are bulky to carry. They may or may not have an outer nylon shell covering.

Open-cell foam
These pads are often self-inflating and use a high-flow inflation valve. Their ability to compress and rebound makes them ideal to take on a trip when space is a concern. Open-cell foam pads are usually covered with a durable, low-slip polyester fabric.

If you do not have a pad, you can improvise one using boughs, moss, leaves, or similar dry materials. Make a mound that is 18 inches high and large enough to protect your whole body from the ground.

SAWS
The Pocket Chain Saw and Sven Saw are two great items to consider taking on any trip.

Pocket Chain Saw
The 31-inch heat-treated steel Pocket Chain Saw weighs only 6.2 ounces when stored inside a small 2¾-inch-diameter by ⅞-inch-high tin can. The saw has 140 bidirectional cutting teeth that will cut wood just like a chain saw. The manufacturer claims it can cut a 3-inch-diameter tree limb in less than ten seconds. The kit comes with two small metal rings that attach to the saw's far ends and plastic handles that slide into the rings and provide a grip for cutting. To save space, I don't carry the handles and simply insert two sturdy branches, about 6 inches long and 1 inch in diameter, into the metal rings. The Pocket Chain Saw costs around $20.

Sven Saw
The lightweight Sven Saw is made from an aluminum handle and 21-inch steel blade that folds inside the handle for easy storage. When open, the saw makes a triangle that measures 24 by 20 by 14 inches, and when closed, it measures 24 by 1½ by ½ inches. The saw, which weighs 16 ounces, costs around $22.

BACKPACKING STOVES
Kayakers who go on extended trips often carry a backpacking-style stove. These stoves provide a quick and efficient way of cooking food and boiling water. When selecting a stove, consider its weight; the altitude and temperatures of where you are going; the stove's ease of operation, especially in

cold, wet, or windy conditions; and fuel availability. The two basic styles are canister and liquid fuel. Canister designs use butane, propane, or isobutene cartridges as their fuel source. The most common types of liquid fuels used are white gas and kerosene.

Butane/propane
This canister allows for a no-spill fuel that is ready for immediate maximum output. These canisters are available throughout the United States and most of the world. I like these types of stoves because of their ease of use and unmatched performance. Keep in mind that some versions do not perform well in temperatures below freezing, and disposal of the used canisters can be a problem.

White gas
White gas has a high heat output and is easily available in the United States. Although the fuel quickly evaporates, it is highly flammable if spilled. The stove often does not require priming to start.

Kerosene
Kerosene gas has a high heat output and is available throughout the world. Unlike white gas, this fuel evaporates slowly when spilled and will not easily ignite. The stove requires priming to start.

The exact use of each stove will depend upon the manufacturer's recommendations and the type of fuel you use. As a general rule, you will need a windshield, you must preheat the stove, and you will get better performance from a stove with a pump if you pump it up. For safety purposes, don't use a stove in a tent or enclosed area unless absolutely necessary. If you have to, make sure the area is vented and do everything in your power to avoid fuel leaks. Always change canisters and lines, fill fuel tanks, and prime the stove outside of the shelter. Plan on a quarter of a quart of liquid fuel per person per day if you have to melt snow for water. Plan on an eighth of a quart of fuel per person per day if water is available.

HEADLAMPS
Headlamps, which have become a great alternative and replacement to the old handheld flashlights, free up your hands for other can uses. When

selecting a headlamp, consider its comfort, battery life history, durability, weight, water resistance, and tendency to turn on while in a pack. I personally prefer the newer headlamps with a compact profile where the battery pack is located directly behind the bulb.

COOKING POTS

A cooking pot is a luxury item often carried by kayakers, who use it to boil water and cook food. There are many types available, and the pot you choose will depend on your needs. I recommend a cookware set consisting of a frying pan that doubles as a lid, several pots, and a pot gripper or handle. Pots are available in the following four basic materials.

Aluminum

Aluminum is cheap and the most common choice for cooking pots among backpackers. However, unless you buy it with a nonstick coating on the inside of the pan, plan on scorching your food.

Stainless steel

Stainless steel is far more rugged than aluminum but weighs considerably more.

Titanium

Titanium is lighter than aluminum but expensive. Titanium pots have a tendency to blacken your food unless you constantly stir it.

Composite

Composite cooking pots combine aluminum and stainless steel to create a durable yet lightweight pot. The steel inside of the pan reduces scorching, and the aluminum on the outside decreases the weight of the pot.

4

Vessel Distress

While in 20-foot-high seas, I swam from one survivor to another. What a ride! The survivor's panic filled the air, fueling my mission. I was never more alive as each was hoisted out of the water and to safety.

—*Aviation Survival Technician Mark Bowling*
U.S. Coast Guard Helicopter Rescue Swimmer

LARGE/SMALL VESSELS

MAN OVERBOARD PROCEDURES
When someone goes overboard, hypothermia and drowning are his or her biggest threats, and a rapid recovery from the water is often the key to the person's survival. How quickly and successfully a person is recovered hinges on the training and experience of the crew and the person in the water. While training is important to a successful outcome, time is also critical, especially in cold water where hypothermia will quickly set in. The following guidelines can be used as a general rule to determine the average survivable time in cold water. It should be noted, however, that this guideline was established using young, healthy individuals and is probably overly optimistic.

Water Temperature		Average Survival Time
Less than 34° F	Less than 2° C	Less than 45 minutes
34° to 40° F	2° to 4° C	Less than 90 minutes
40° to 50° F	4° to 10° C	Less than 3 hours

Water Temperature		Average Survival Time
50° to 59° F	10° to 15° C	Less than 6 hours
59° to 69° F	15° to 20° C	Less than 12 hours
Greater than 70° F	Greater than 20° C	Indefinite (depends on physical condition)

Hypothermia, the result of an abnormally low body temperature, occurs when body heat is lost due to radiation, conduction, evaporation, convection, and respiration. While in cold water, the body loses heat twenty-five times faster than it would while in a similar air temperature. Signs and symptoms of hypothermia include uncontrollable shivering, slurred speech, abnormal behavior, fatigue and drowsiness, decreased hand and body coordination, and a weakened respiration and pulse.

Subject behavior
If you find yourself in the water, most likely the seas will be cold and rough. Not only is it doubtful that you can swim to your vessel, but the heat you would lose trying to could hasten a hypothermic state. Your best bet is to signal the vessel, use the techniques outlined here, and wait for the vessel to pick you up. Hopefully you will be dressed appropriately for the conditions and will be wearing a life jacket. As quickly as you can, try to get out of the water by getting back aboard your vessel, in a life raft, or on top of debris. Since approximately 50 percent of your body heat is lost from the head, make every effort to keep your head dry and above the waterline. If you are unable get out of the water, use the following method to increase your chances of survival.

Wearing a life jacket
In cold water, try to insulate your head, neck, sides, and groin, which are areas of high heat loss, by assuming the Heat-Escape-Lessening Position (HELP). To do this, hold your upper arms against your sides and cross your lower arms across your chest. At the same time, keep your legs close together with ankles crossed and pull your knees to your chest. Be sure to keep your head above the waterline. If there are other persons in the water, face each other in a huddle, making as much body contact as possible.

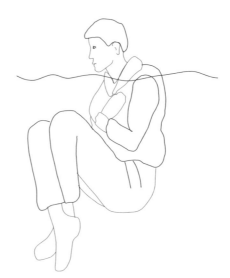

HELP position

Group huddle to retain body heat

Exercising while surviving in cold water is not recommended as this actually hastens the loss of body heat due to convection.

Without a life jacket

If for some unforeseen reason you should end up in the water without a life jacket, your biggest concern will be to prevent drowning. In cold water, this can create a dilemma as moving hastens heat loss, but if you do not move, you will drown. As best you can, keep your head dry and tread water to stay afloat. You will actually expend less energy doing this than if you perform the popular floating technique called drownproofing.

In warm water, however, drownproofing decreases the amount of energy lost when compared to treading water or swimming. The maneuver, which uses the lungs for buoyancy, can increase your chances of survival in warm water significantly. Practice the following steps of drownproofing before you need to use it in an emergency:

> *Resting position:* Take a deep breath and go limp with your face in the water. The back of your head and back should be parallel with the surface of the water.

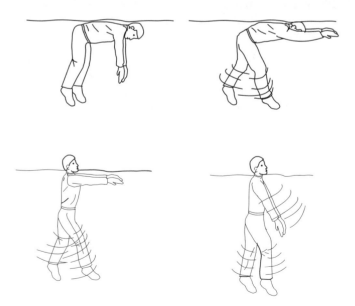

In warm water, drownproofing is an excellent option for staying afloat.

Preparing to exhale: When it is time to take another breath, slowly lift your arms to shoulder height and separate your legs into a scissors-type position.

Exhale: This step is done immediately once the arms are up and the legs are separated. Raise your head just high enough to get your mouth out of the water and exhale.

Inhale: Once you have exhaled, slowly press your arms down and bring your legs together while inhaling.

Return to rest position: Resume the resting position by relaxing your arms, allowing your legs to dangle, and placing your face back down into the water.

Crew behavior

Within 20 seconds, a vessel moving at 5 knots will be 168 feet away from the person who fell overboard. At 10 knots, the vessel will be 336 feet away. When someone goes overboard, immediate action by the remaining crew is vital to a successful rescue. The crew should take the following steps immediately upon seeing someone fall overboard:

1. Sound an alarm. Immediately begin yelling "man overboard" along with his or her position in relation to the vessel. For example, if on the right side of the vessel, yell "man overboard, starboard side!" On the left side, yell "man overboard, port side!" In front of the vessel, yell "man overboard at the bow!" and at the rear of the vessel, yell "man overboard at the stern!"

2. Mark the spot. During daylight hours, immediately throw a ring buoy or similar item toward the person, and if possible, drop a smoke float that will mark the spot where the person fell overboard. During darkness, immediately throw a life preserver or buoy ring with water lights and keep the vessel's searchlight fixed on the subject. If you have a GPS, mark your position.

3. Position the vessel. The pilot of the vessel should immediately begin maneuvering the stern side away from the subject.

4. Post a lookout. Post a lookout whose only job is to keep the subject in sight and provide a direction guide to the crew by extending an arm and pointing toward the subject. This job is crucial since even small waves will make it hard to see a bobbing head. The person who witnessed the fall is usually the best suited for this task.

Steps 2 through 4 require teamwork and should occur simultaneously. Try to practice before an actual emergency occurs.

5. Remove obstacles. Retrieve or cut free any outlying gear that interferes with how the vessel moves.

6. Vessel approach. As long as the person is still in sight, circle your vessel so that it points into the wind, which allows you to better control boat speed and position. Keep the propeller away from the person in the water. Note that this approach may not be practical for all conditions, and your situation may dictate otherwise.

7. Retrieval. Retrieving someone who has fallen overboard may be the most difficult part of this process. How successful a recovery is depends on the subject's physical condition, the number and experience of the crew members, and the type of vessel and its recovery gear. Once the vessel is alongside the subject, disengage the propeller by placing the engine in neutral. Use whatever line and equipment are available to reach the person in the water and have him or her secure the line around his or her body. Lifting the person out of the water will take exceptional skill and strength since his or her water weight will make the person extremely heavy. However, no one should enter the water unless all other options fail or don't appear to be safe. If someone must enter the water to help retrieve the subject, then that person should be secured to the vessel and wear either an antiexposure suit in cold water or a PFD in warm water.

8. First aid. Treat the patient for cold injuries. (See chapter 13.)

9. What if. If more than a few minutes have passed since you sounded the "man overboard" signal and the person is not in sight, you should notify the U.S. Coast Guard of your situation. The coast guard will want to know how many people are on board, your location, any identifying features of the vessel, and what the crisis is (see below details on contacting the coast guard).

10. Search pattern. If you cannot see the subject, begin a search pattern. The search pattern starts at the last known position of the person who is overboard and follows an ever-expanding square shape. Continue this search process until the subject is rescued or until the USCG arrives.

11. Use the alert call Pan-Pan to notify other vessels that you have a man overboard. The Pan-Pan call will alert others and allow you to notify them on how you intend to maneuver in the area.

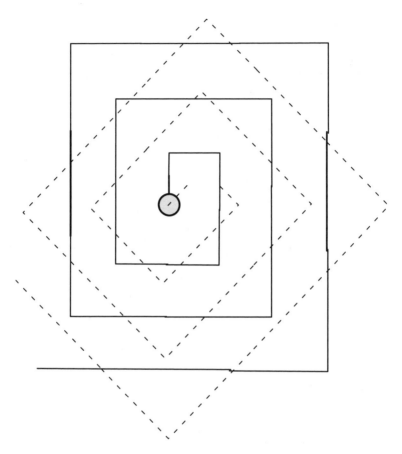

Expanding square search pattern

Prevention

Most overboard falls occur when someone is moving, standing, or leaning over the edge of a vessel. Other potential causes include poor visibility, rapid accelerations or sharp turns, large waves, and slippery surfaces. To avoid an overboard incident, use handrails, always be aware of ground obstacles, wear a lifeline when working near the edge of the vessel, and never horse around when on the deck.

ABANDON-SHIP PROCEDURES

At the first sign of a potential problem, establish communication with the U.S. Coast Guard. Don't wait until it is too late. The coast guard can provide valuable advice on improvising methods that can delay or stop a vessel from sinking. In addition, they often deliver fuel, de-water pumps, and other necessary survival items.

The key to successfully abandoning ship is proper preparation and practice. Become familiar with the abandon-ship process and your gear before a crisis occurs. Such preparation helps to control anxiety in this stressful situation. Also make sure that those on board know the abandon-ship procedure and can step in should you be unable to take charge. Leadership both on board the vessel and in the life raft plays an important role in ensuring the survival of a crew. Once the decision has been made to abandon ship and the alarm has been sounded, follow the steps below.

Step 1: Mayday

Broadcast a Mayday on channel 16 VHF or 2182-kHz SSB using MAYDAY, MAYDAY, MAYDAY. Repeat your vessel name and call sign three times. State your present location three times (give latitude and longitude if you can, along with a distance and direction from a known point), the nature of the distress, and the number of people on board. Repeat this process until you either get a response or are forced to leave your vessel.

Step 2: Dress up

If you have time and your wardrobe allows, dress in layers that will wick moisture away from your body, insulate you even when wet, and provide a degree of waterproofing. (See chapter 5 on clothing.) If you have a hat and gloves, put them on.

Step 3: Life jacket

A life jacket is a must. If you have to tread water without a life jacket, your body will lose 35 percent more heat than it would if you were wearing a life jacket. While a life jacket is important, in cold climates you are better off with a buoyant survival suit (immersion suit). If you have one, put it on.

Step 4: Survival kit
Grab the abandon-ship bag, survival and first aid kits (if separate), portable radio, EPIRB, and cell phone, if you have one. If you have extra time, take along navigation gear, food and water, medicines, blankets, line, and anything else you think you might need. However, do not delay launching the life raft to gather these extra items.

Step 5: Launch the raft
If a canister raft, release the tie-down straps by pressing on the hydrostatic release or pelican hook. Holding the canister or valise pack in the upright position, carry it to the lee (downwind) side of the vessel. Don't roll the canister. Depending on your system—be sure to know it in advance—you will need to tie the operating cord (painter/lanyard) to the vessel *above* the weak link. Be sure to do this before launching the raft. To do this, pull several feet of the painter line from the canister, and attach it to the vessel so that the weak link is beyond the knot. The weak link needs to be between the knot and the free end. Bypassing the weak link ensures a strong connection between the vessel and the life raft. The weak link is only useful during a float-free launch (see below). Leaving the bands in place, two members of the crew should throw the canister overboard. Once the life raft and canister are in the water, pull on the painter (operating cord). You may need to pull out the line until you feel resistance and then give it a sharp tug. Keep the line free of tangles. The bands will release the two halves of the container, and the life raft will inflate. Never inflate the raft on the vessel since the canister halves could fly off and cause harm or the raft could become jammed between separate areas of the vessel. For now, leave the operating cord attached to the vessel.

If you are unable to deploy the raft before your vessel sinks, you may still be in luck as long as your raft is in a canister stored on the vessel's cradle and the painter has been attached to the vessel. The hydrostatic release on the raft is set to automatically release when it reaches a depth of 10 to 15 feet. The freed container will rise to the surface, and the ship will pull on the canister's bands, causing them to part and triggering the inflation of the raft. Within approximately thirty seconds, the life raft should be fully inflated and ready to board. In time, the raft's buoyancy and the sinking ship will reach a point where the weak link (located where the painter is attached to the cradle) will break, thus freeing the raft from the vessel.

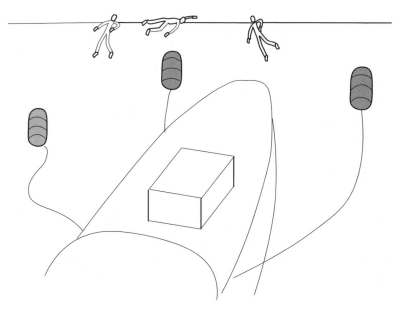

Free-floating container will rise to the surface.

As the raft inflates and the vessel sinks, the painter cord will break, freeing the raft.

Step 6: Board the raft

When boarding the raft, try to keep dry. You may be able to board directly from a ladder, line, or net. If the distance is short, you might want to jump into the canopy entrance. Some rafts allow this and some don't, so check with your vendor. If you do jump, land on the balls of your feet so that you don't fall backward into the water. Also stretch out your arms so that you land with your chest against the inflated canopy arch to decrease the chance of injuring others already on board the raft.

If you must enter the water to board the raft, do so as close to the raft as you can. Also, jump from the lowest point and hold on to the painter (line) so that you are not swept away. The line can also guide you over to the raft. To board the raft from the water, place your feet on the boarding ladder, grab the handholds or internal lifelines, and pull yourself into the raft headfirst. Life boat canopies are known to tear, so you should not use them to pull yourself into the raft. If someone is injured or needs help getting into the raft, two people can pull that person on board using the following technique:

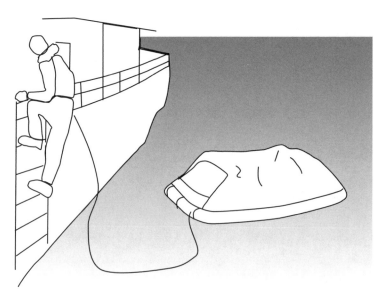

Whenever possible use a ladder to board the raft.

Jump into the canopy opening only when other options are not available.

1. Place your knee that is away from the center of the door on the top of the buoyancy tube.
2. Turn the person in the water so that his or her back is toward the life raft door.
3. Grab the subject's life jacket with your hand that is closest to the center of the door.
4. With your other hand, grab the subject's upper arm (each rescuer should take an arm) and then push the individual slightly down before pulling him or her up and over the buoyancy tubes and into the life raft.
5. While pulling the person up, fall to one side on the raft's floor and allow the subject to fall between you and the other rescuer.

If the life raft deploys upside down, one person can right the raft as long as it is done before the canopy fills with seawater. Find the raft's CO_2 cylinder, which is typically marked with the words "RIGHT HERE." Flipping the raft over from this position ensures that the CO_2 cylinder does not hit you and possibly knock you out. If there are strong winds, try to get the canister side of the raft on the downwind side, which will make the raft easier to turn. The bottom of the raft will have righting straps. Grab the straps and

Once two people are in the raft, they can help others aboard.

Pulling someone aboard the life raft

Flipping an overturned life raft

pull yourself—kicking your feet may help—up and onto the raft. Next, stand on the edge next to the cylinder, and pull on the righting straps while leaning back. If the raft lands on top of you, swim face up until you clear its edge. If you need to catch your breath during this time, simply create an air pocket by pushing your arms and head upwards against the floor of the raft. If the canopy of the capsized raft has filled with seawater, it may take two people to right the raft.

Step 7: Cut free of sinking vessel
Remove the knife that should be included in your raft, and cut the operating cord to free the life raft from the sinking ship. Keep the knife sheathed until needed, and immediately sheath it after each use. If the vessel is on fire, paddle away from it. If the vessel remains afloat, however, stay as close to the boat as long as you can. Rescue will start at that location.

Step 8: Deploy the sea anchor
Once you are away from the sinking vessel, let out the sea anchor, which will help stabilize the life raft and make it less prone to tipping over in rough seas.

Step 9: Attend to medical needs
Any life-threatening injuries, such as airway, bleeding, circulation, and shock, should be treated immediately. In cold water, treat and prevent hypothermia. Other injuries should be attended to once all life-threatening problems are treated. Avoid dehydration by taking seasickness pills.

Step 10: Inventory your materials
Review the contents of your abandon-ship bag, survival kit, and medical kit, and take the time to tie everything, including the paddles, to the raft.

Step 11: Use your signals
Make sure you know how to use the signals before you need them. If the EPIRB has not been activated, do so now. If you were able to take the VHF radio on board the raft, transmit another Mayday. If you have a cell phone, try to reach someone. Post a lookout, sweep the horizon with your signal mirror, and familiarize yourself and your crew with the signals and how they should be used. For signaling information, refer to chapter 8.

Step 12: Personal protection
Bail out any water in the raft, inflate the floor, and put up the canopy if you have one. Wring out wet clothes, and try to empty water out of immersion suits.

Step 13: Read the survival manuals
Life rafts normally come equipped with a survival manual. Read it. You may find some helpful information.

KAYAKS

Even though a kayaker is often dressed for the conditions, he or she faces the threat of hypothermia and drowning problems if the kayak capsizes. If this should happen, survival rests on knowledge, skill, and remaining calm, all of which come from practice. Take lessons from those with experience, and learn how to correct your kayak before, during, and after it capsizes.

CAPSIZED RECOVERY

Sooner or later your kayak will capsize, and when it happens, you have two choices: either exit the cockpit and do a wet reentry or perform an Eskimo roll and return the vessel to an upright position. Your experience and the situation itself will dictate which option you choose.

Eskimo roll

There are several variations of an Eskimo roll, but in this book, I am going to describe a sweep roll (also known as the screw roll). The best way to learn how to roll, however, is not from a book. Take classes from a qualified instructor and practice, practice, and practice some more. The Eskimo roll can be broken down into three movements that when done in a fluid motion will bring you into an upright position. The three movements are setup; sweeping brace stroke; and hip flick and layback.

Setup

After capsizing, get into the setup position by leaning forward and upward against the kayak's deck. Position the paddle parallel to the kayak so that your right hand is forward when the paddle is on the left side and your left hand is forward when the paddle is on the right side. The power side (front side) of the forward blade should be facing upward.

Sweeping brace stroke

Once you are in position, bring the paddle slightly out of the water and position the forward blade so that its backside is down, horizontal to the water's surface, and out and away from the vessel's bow. Arms should now be positioned so that the forward arm is almost straight and the back hand is close to the waist ready to function as a pivot point. From this position, sweep the paddle in a broad arc from front to back, allowing the forward blade to skim along the water's surface. Once the paddle is perpendicular to the vessel, stop the stroke. The strength of this maneuver comes from the entire upper body, not just your arms, and for best results your head and torso should follow the paddle's path until you are leaned back as far as you can and your head is on or near the deck. Using a knee lift on the side of the kayak you want to raise will help you to right the boat.

Hip flick

With your torso and head laid back with the sweeping stroke, you should be in the proper position to apply a hip flick to right the vessel. This movement, which uses the twisting of your torso, doesn't require a bodybuilder's physique to complete. The biggest problem that occurs with this step is raising your head too fast. If you do the Eskimo roll properly, you will come to an upright position in the following order: boat, waist, torso, and finally head. Your head should actually be on or close to the rear deck until the boat is leveling out.

Wet reentry

No matter how hard you try not to, sooner or later you will capsize the kayak and have to exit and reenter the vessel while in the water. You may have to do this as a self-rescue or an assisted process. Many people fear exiting a capsized vessel, but this fear is easily put to rest with a little practice. In fact, the biggest problem isn't getting out of the kayak but letting go of the vessel or paddle in the process.

Wet exit

To perform a wet exit from a capsized kayak, follow these steps:

1. While holding the paddle parallel to the kayak with one hand, release the spray skirt with the other hand. To free the skirt, you must pull and lift the release strap. If for some reason you cannot find the strap, lean to one side of the kayak, grab the wrinkled skirt on that side, and release it from the coaming.
2. While you continue to hold the paddle, grab the cockpit of the kayak next to your hips with your free hand.
3. Relax and straighten your legs.
4. While leaning your upper body toward the front of the kayak, use your arms to push your lower body back and free of the cockpit.
5. Never let go of the paddle or kayak.

Hopefully, your boat has been fitted with adequate flotation. The less flotation it has, the more water your kayak will probably take on. If you are close to shore, go there to empty the water out. If not, get next to the cockpit of the inverted vessel, and while keeping the paddle in one hand, use the other hand to reach under the kayak and grab the coaming on the opposite side. Quickly pull the coaming from the opposite side toward you while you push the other side up and away. When performed quickly, this maneuver will help you right the vessel so that very little water is left inside. Once back inside the cockpit, you may need to bail or pump out any remaining water. To get back in the kayak, you will need to use either a paddle-float self-rescue or, if someone else is close by, an assisted rescue or reentry.

Paddle-float self-rescue

A paddle float, either made of foam block or an inflatable material, helps a kayaker reenter a capsized boat. To perform a paddle-float self-rescue, use the following steps:

1. Move to the downwind side of your vessel.
2. Inflate the float, slip it over one end of the paddle, and slide the other end on top of the kayak behind the cockpit. If you have rigged line behind the cockpit, inserting the blade into it will make this technique much easier to do. The paddle should be at a 90 degree angle to the kayak.

The paddle float helps a kayaker reenter a capsized boat.

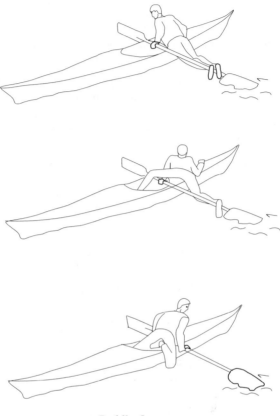

Paddle-float rescue

3. While keeping a low and flat center of gravity, pull your torso up and onto the back deck—turn your head so it is facing the back side of the kayak—and lift your upside knee to rest it on the paddle. Try to keep as much body contact with the raft as you can. Do not get up on your knees or elbows.

4. While keeping your center of gravity on the kayak's paddle side, rotate your body and place the forward leg into the cockpit. Once it is inside, your other leg on the paddle should follow. At this point, you should be lying on top of and parallel to the kayak with your head and torso on the back deck in a facedown position.

5. Rotate your body and torso until you are sitting up and facing forward. For this maneuver to be done successfully, you need to keep your weight toward the side of the kayak with the paddle.
6. Bail and pump out any remaining water and replace the kayak's skirt.
7. Remove the paddle float and reattach it to the kayak.

The paddle-float rescue is a good way to reenter a capsized boat when the shore is not close by. While it can be used in most circumstances, it will probably not be successful if used inside the surf line. If you capsize inside the surf line, swim to shore for reentry into the vessel.

Assisted rescue

If you are traveling in a group and become separated from your kayak or it sank or is damaged beyond repair, then an assisted rescue can keep you afloat and, if applicable, help to reunite you with your vessel. Drowning and hypothermia are your biggest threats once you are in the water. The sooner you get out of the water, the better your chance of survival. Often, the wisest decision is to climb aboard another kayak. To do this, the rescuing kayaker should get close to you and hold this position while you climb aboard the back deck of the vessel with your head toward the kayaker. For stability, keep a low and flat center of gravity with your head down, grab the kayaker's waist, and spread your legs so that your feet hang off the sides. Try to keep as much body contact with the raft as you can. Do not get up on your knees or elbows. If your kayak is still afloat, it is most likely drifting broadside to the wind and can be approached from the windward side. Once there, an assisted reentry can easily reunite the kayaker with his or her kayak. If the vessel is disabled, it may need to be towed to shore. If you must tow a boat, use a system that allows for a quick release of the boat and always tow the boat so that it is a safe distance, usually two to three boats, away.

Assisted reentry

An assisted reentry is easier and faster than a paddle-float rescue and often occurs after an assisted rescue has taken place. The following steps detail an assisted reentry:
1. Ideally, the rescuing kayaker should approach the vacant vessel from the windward side so that the two boats are parallel and bow to stern. Use common sense as this may not always be practical.

2. The person in the water should right the capsized kayak.
3. The rescuer should place both paddles behind his or her kayak's cockpit, perpendicular to the vessel, and position the middle of the paddles under his or her armpits so that each paddle runs between the rescuer's forearm at the bicep and his or her body. With the paddles in this position, the rescuer can lean over and grab the free kayak's coaming. The weight of the rescuer on the paddles helps to stabilize the two kayaks.
4. While keeping a low and flat center of gravity, the person in the water should pull his or her torso up and onto the back deck, turning his or her head so it is facing the back side of the kayak. This person should try to keep as much body contact with the raft as he or she can and should not get up on his or her knees or elbows.
5. The person being rescued should try to keep his or her center of gravity toward the rescuing kayak and rotate his or her body until able to place a forward leg into the cockpit. Once that leg is inside, the outside leg can follow. At this point, he or she should be lying on top of and parallel to the vessel with his or her head and torso on the back deck in a facedown position.
6. The rescued person should then rotate his or her body and torso until he or she is sitting up and facing forward. For the assisted entry to be performed successfully, he or she must keep his or her weight shifted forward toward the rescuing vessel, and the rescuer must provide a constant counterbalance.

EMERGENCY ISSUES

If you have prepared for an emergency in advance, then you should know what to do if you find yourself in such a situation. Make sure you have accessible emergency gear secured to the kayak with a lanyard. This equipment includes a VHF radio, EPIRB, and survival and medical kits. If you find yourself in the water, avoid drowning and hypothermia by boarding your kayak. If your kayak isn't with you, try to keep your head above the waterline and stay as still as you can. If you lost your kayak, how well you are able to activate a search will depend on what you have carried on your person. If a true emergency exists and the equipment is available, you should activate your EPIRB and use your VHF radio to make an emergency transmission. If you have a cell phone, try to call someone for help. Blow your rescue whistle every couple of minutes, and know how to use your other signals by reviewing them before you need them. Try to sweep the horizon with your signal mirror on a regular basis. Further details on responding to an emergency can be found in the man overboard section in this chapter.

RESCUE AT SEA

A rescue by a surface rescue is often a simple process. In most cases, the rescue craft will direct its approach so that you are on the lee side. The rescue vessel will then drift toward you. To avoid contact with the boat's propeller, be sure to pull in your sea anchor. Once contact with a rescue vessel is made, follow the guidance of the rescue crew.

A helicopter rescue may not be as simple. Movement caused by waves, wind, and the helicopter itself will make it difficult to stay balanced in the life raft. To avoid losing gear and potential damage to the helicopter's rotor system, secure all gear to the raft. A rescue basket, rescue sling, or stokes litter might be used to hoist you aboard the helicopter, and in most cases a rescue swimmer will be dropped down to help you put on the rescue device. Don't be surprised if the rescue swimmer asks you to leave the craft.

To avoid potential injury, there are several things you should know. First, the cable coming from the helicopter can have a static charge. Do not

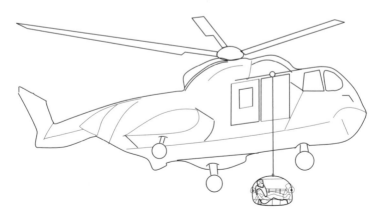

Helicopter rescue

touch the cable until it has made contact with your vessel or the water, thus allowing the static electricity to discharge. Second, if a litter or basket is dropped, it normally has a trail line that, once grounded, you can use to stabilize the basket as it gets closer to your vessel. Once the rescue swimmer has secured you to the rescue device, he or she will give vigorous thumbs up to the helicopter crew so it will know to begin the hoist process.

RESCUE BASKET

For survivors who are not injured, the U.S. Coast Guard usually uses a rescue basket, which is simple to use. Once the basket has landed in the water, the rescue swimmer will disconnect the cable, help you climb in, and direct you to sit down with your hands and arms inside. Once the cable is reattached you will be hoisted up to the helicopter door.

RESCUE SLING

A rescue sling (padded loop) is used in other countries and in some isolated rescues by the USCG. Once the sling has been lowered into the water, slip it over your body and under your armpits so that the loop goes around your back. For added security fasten the chest strap that is often affixed to the outside of the sling.

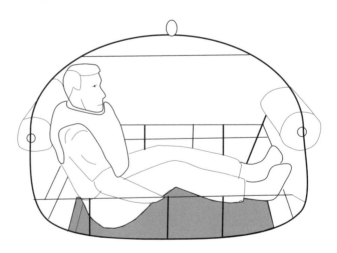

Rescue basket

Rescue sling

STOKES LITTER

A stokes litter is often used for survivors who have serious injuries or illnesses. This device requires that help be available. Once the litter has been lowered to the water, the rescue swimmer will disconnect the cable and straps, remove the blankets, place the survivor inside, cover him or her with the blankets, and refasten the straps and cable. Since the litter is hoisted at a head-up (feet-down) angle, it's important that chest straps are secured under the victim's arms. Otherwise, he or she could slide out.

The helicopter rescue

RESCUE ON LAND

Helicopter rescues on the land are becoming more common as more and more people head into the wilderness. Rescue crews may be civilian but are more likely to be either the military or coast guard. If the helicopter can land to perform a rescue, it will. If not, a member of the rescue team will be lowered to your position. At this point, you will be either hoisted to the helicopter or moved to a better location while dangling from the helicopter in a harness or basket. If you are rescued by a helicopter, be sure to secure all loose items before the helicopter lands. Otherwise, items may be blown away or worse yet sucked up into the helicopter's rotors. Once a helicopter has landed, do not approach it until signaled to do so and then only approach the front side and from downhill. This will ensure that the pilot can see you and will decrease your chances of being injured or killed by the rotor blades.

5

Clothing

*Make sure to always wear proper clothing: a wicking
layer, insulating middle layer, and a wind- and waterproof outer layer. You'll never know if you will have
enough time to build a shelter before dark.*

—*Aviation Survival Technician Rich Sansone*
U.S. Coast Guard Helicopter Rescue Swimmer

Clothing is your first line of defense against the environment. In cold
weather, your clothing insulates you and keeps you warm; in hot weather,
the proper clothing helps to keep you cool. The body is constantly regulating itself in an attempt to keep its thermostat between 97 and 99 degrees
Fahrenheit. As heat is lost through radiation, conduction, convection, evaporation, and respiration, you will need to adjust your clothing to help maintain
your body's core temperature.

HOW HEAT IS LOST

RADIATION
Heat transfers from your body into the environment through the process of
radiation. The head, neck, and hands pose the greatest threat for heat loss
due to radiation. While increased clothing will slow the radiation process,
it will not stop it from occurring.

CONDUCTION
When your body comes in contact with any cold item, heat is lost from the
body through conduction. This becomes a significant problem when your

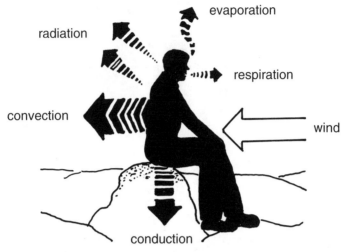

Five sources of heat loss

clothing beecomes soaking wet or you are submerged in cold water. Depending on the circumstances, try to remove and change wet clothing or wring out as much moisture as possible.

CONVECTION
Similar to radiation, convection is a process in which your body loses heat to the surrounding cold water and air. But unlike radiation, convection would not occur if you were standing completely still and there was absolutely no current or wind. The movement of the water, the wind, and your body causes you to lose heat from convection. By wearing clothes in a loose and layered fashion, you will help trap warm air next to your body, which decreases the heat loss from convection and insulates you from the environment.

EVAPORATION
Body heat is lost through the evaporative process that occurs with perspiration. To prevent this from happening, try to monitor your activity to avoid sweating. If you are inactive, your layered clothing will trap dead air, which will decrease the amount of heat lost through evaporation and actually keep you cooler.

RESPIRATION

Body heat is also lost through the normal process of breathing. To decrease the heat lost when breathing in cold air, cover or encircle your mouth with a loose cloth. By doing this, you will trap dead air and allow it to warm up slightly before you breathe it in, thereby decreasing the amount of heat lost due to respiration.

UNDERSTANDING YOUR CLOTHES' INSULATION

How well you adjust to heat loss will depend on how well your clothes insulate you. The fabric of most clothing is made of intertwined fibers, which create spaces that trap dead air. Your clothes keep you warm by trapping the heat your body loses inside this dead air space. Therefore, make sure the clothing you select not only protects you from cold and wet conditions but also provides the breathability needed to avoid overheating. Winter clothes are made from many natural and synthetic materials. When choosing clothing for wet and cold climates, you need to understand the characteristics of these materials.

NATURAL FABRICS

Cotton

Cotton has been nicknamed "death cloth" since it loses almost all of its insulating quality when wet. Wet cotton will absorb many times its weight, has extremely poor wicking qualities, and takes forever to dry.

Down

Down is a very good lightweight and natural insulating material. But like cotton, down becomes virtually worthless when wet since the feathers clump together and no longer trap dead air. This material is best used in dry climates or when you can guarantee it won't get wet.

Wool

Wool retains most of its insulating quality when wet. Wool also retains a lot of moisture, however, making it extremely heavy when wet. Because wool is fairly effective at protecting you from the wind, it is a good choice to be worn as an outer layer. Its weight and bulkiness are the main draw-backs.

SYNTHETIC FABRICS

Polyester and polypropylene
As a wicking layer, polyester and polypropylene wick well, maintain their insulating quality when wet, and dry quickly. As an insulating layer, these fabrics are lightweight and compressible. However, because these synthetic fabrics are not very effective at protecting you from the wind, you will also need to wear an outer shell. Polyester pile and fleece are common examples of polyester used for the insulating layer.

Polarguard, Hollofil, and Quallofil
Although these synthetic fibers are most often used in sleeping bags, they may also be found in heavy parkas. Polarguard is composed of sheets, Hollofil of hollow sheets, and Quallofil of hollow sheets with holes running through the fibers. Basically, Hollofil and Quallofil took Polarguard one step further by creating more insulating dead air space. As with all synthetic fabrics, these materials will dry quickly and retain most of their insulating quality when wet.

Thinsulate, Microloft, and Primaloft
These thin synthetic fibers create an outstanding lightweight insulation material by allowing more layers. Thinsulate, the heaviest of the three, is most often used in clothing. The lightweight Microloft and Primaloft are an outstanding alternative to the lightweight down sleeping bag because they retain their insulating quality when wet.

Neoprene
Neoprene is made of closed-cell foam and comes in a variety of thicknesses. The exact thickness you choose for your clothing will depend upon the air and water temperatures and your tendency to get cold.

Nylon
Nylon is a common shell material often seen in parkas, rain and wind garments, and mittens. Because nylon is not waterproof, most manufacturers

will use the special fabrication techniques or treatments reviewed below to make their nylon waterproof.

Polyurethane coatings
This inexpensive, lightweight coating will protect you from outside moisture, but since the coating is nonbreathable, inside moisture may not escape. Only use this type of outer garment if physical exertion will be minimum.

Breathable waterproof coatings
When applied to the inside of a nylon shell, this coating leaves billions of microscopic pores that are large enough for inside vapors to escape yet small enough to keep raindrops out. These coats cost more than those with polyurethane coatings but are less expensive than garments made using a breathable laminated waterproof membrane.

Breathable laminated waterproof membrane
Instead of an inner coating, these garments have a separate waterproof and breathable membrane that is laminated to the inside of the nylon. The membrane is perforated with millions of microscopic pores that work under the same principle as the waterproof coating. Gore-Tex is the most common example.

For breathable fabrics to be effective, you must keep the pores free of dirt and sweat, and only wash and dry the clothing in accordance with the tag instructions. Don't expect these breathable coats to be perfect. If your heat output is high and you begin to sweat, moisture cannot escape from these fabrics any more than the rain can get in. To prevent this, you will need to wear your clothing loose and layered.

COLDER ACRONYM
An acronym that can help you remember how to care for and wear your clothing is COLDER.

C: Clean
Clothes are made of intertwined fibers that, when clean, trap dead air that works as insulation to keep you warm. When clothes are dirty, they lose their ability to insulate you.

O: Avoid overheating

Clothes either have to absorb or repel sweat, causing them to lose their insulating quality, or make you wet. In addition, when you become overheated, you lose valuable body heat through evaporation.

L: Loose and layered

Clothing that is too tight will constrict circulation and predispose you to frostbite. By wearing multiple layers, you increase the amount of dead air space surrounding your body. You also may add or remove individual layers of clothing as necessary for the given weather conditions. The ability to take off a layer or add it back when needed helps you to avoid getting too cold or hot. I normally wear three layers: one that wicks moisture away, an insulating layer, and an outer shell.

Wicking layer

Perspiration and moisture wick through this layer to keep you dry. This is a very important layer, since having wet clothes next to your skin will cause heat loss to occur at a rate 25 times greater than with dry clothes. Polyester and polypropylene are best for this layer. Cotton is not recommended.

Insulating layer

This layer traps warm air next to the body. Multiple insulating layers may work better than one, since additional air is trapped between them. The best fabrics for this layer are wool, polyester pile, compressed polyester fleece, Hollofil, Quallofil, Polarguard, Thinsulate, Microloft, and Primaloft. Down can be used in dry climates or when you know you won't get wet.

Outer shell

This layer protects you from wind and precipitation. The ideal shell will protect you from getting wet when exposed to precipitation yet has enough ventilation for body moisture to escape. Waterproof coatings that breathe and laminated waterproof membranes that breathe, such as Gore-Tex, are the best for this layer. Because one-third to one-half of body heat loss occurs from the head and hands, headgear and gloves are

Layering clothing

a must. Depending on conditions, neoprene may be worn as both insulating and outer layers.

D: Dry
Wet clothes lose their insulation quality. To keep the inner layer dry, avoid sweating. To protect the outer layer from moisture, either avoid exposure to rain or snow or wear proper clothing for wet conditions. If your clothes do become wet, dry them by a fire or in the sun. If it's below 32 degrees F and you can't build a fire, let the clothes freeze; once frozen, break the ice out of the clothing. If snow is on your clothes, shake it off; don't brush it off, as this will force the moisture into the fibers.

E: Examine
Examine clothing daily for tears and dirt.

R: Repair
Repair any rips and tears as soon as they occur. Make sure you pack a needle and thread to make such repairs.

CLOTHING AT SEA

PARKA AND RAIN PANTS

A parka and rain pants will protect you from moisture and wind. They are normally made from nylon with a polyurethane coating, a waterproof coating that breathes, or a laminated waterproof membrane that breathes (Gore-Tex). Sometimes, a parka will come with an insulating garment that can be zipped inside. Regardless of which material you choose, your parka and rain paints should meet the following criteria.

Size

These garments should be big enough for you to comfortably add wicking and insulating layers underneath without compromising your movement. The parka's lower end also should extend beyond your hips to keep moisture away from the top of your pants.

Dual separating zippers

Look for zippers that separate at both ends.

Ventilation adjustment

The openings for parkas should be located in front, at your waist, under your arms, and at your wrist. The openings for rain pants should be located in the front and along the outside of the lower legs to about midcalf to make it easier to add or remove boots. Pants for women are available with a zipper that extends down and around the crotch. These openings can be adjusted with zippers, Velcro, or drawstrings.

Sealed seams

Seams must be taped or well bonded to prevent moisture from penetrating through the clothing.

Accessible pockets

What good is a pocket if you can't access it? Make sure the pocket opening has a protective rain baffle.

Brimmed hood

A brimmed hood will help channel moisture away from the eyes and face. In addition, a neck flap will help prevent loss of radiant body heat from the neck area.

DRY AND WET SUITS

When deciding whether to wear a wet or dry suit, consider the insulation and protective qualities of the suits. How cold is the water, and how long will you be submersed? Are you in an area where you need to protect your skin? Without an appropriate suit, long submersions in water with temperatures below 98 degrees F will decrease your body's core temperature, which could lead to hypothermia. The two types of suits available are wet and dry. When deciding which suit to buy, select one that provides the best protection from exposure and skin scrapings. A bright-colored suit is a better signal and preferred to the black versions. Consider a full body suit that has a snug fit without any compromise in arm or leg movement. Make sure the suit fits well and has good seam placement and that its wrist and ankle seals are tight but not too tight as to cut off circulation. Next, consider the thickness of the material. Use the following guide as a general rule of thumb when deciding how thick your suit should be. Recognize that thicker is probably better, and you should always err on the conservative side.

Water Temperature	Recommended Thickness
75°–85° F	$\frac{1}{16}$-inch (1.6 mm) neoprene, Lycra, Polartec
70°–85° F	$\frac{1}{8}$-inch (3 mm) neoprene
65°–75° F	$\frac{3}{16}$-inch (5 mm) neoprene
50°–70° F	$\frac{1}{4}$-inch (6.5 mm) neoprene
35°–65° F	$\frac{3}{8}$-inch (9.5 mm) neoprene, dry suit

Wet suits

Although some wet suits are used in cold water, most are created for use in cool to warm waters. Mostly made of closed-cell foam called *neoprene,* the suits come in a variety of thicknesses and are made to fit snuggly to the body. Wet suits keep you warm by decreasing the amount of heat lost from conduction (direct contact) and convection (current movement around the body). Trapped air bubbles in the neoprene help to insulate you from heat loss due to conduction, and a well-fitting suit with minimal inside water flow helps to protect you from heat loss due to convection. A polyester layer next to the skin and an outer jacket that is coated rubber or Gore-Tex will increase the insulation value of your wet suit. Because a full-body wet suit is too restrictive in the arms for some, they use a farmer john's suit (a full wet suit with no arms) instead. These suits are mostly appropriate in places with mild to moderate weather conditions most of the time.

Dry suits

Dry suits were originally created for use in cold water, but they may also be worn in places with mild to moderate temperatures. These watertight suits are made of foam neoprene, coated rubber, or Gore-Tex. Because neoprene and coated rubber don't allow body heat and moisture to escape, you will get wet from the inside. Gore-Tex, on the other hand, allows body moisture (radiant heat), not droplets of sweat, to escape while it still protects you from outside moisture. All of the options provide little to no insulation value, so to keep warm, you will need to wear an inner wicking layer and a middle insulation layer under the dry suit. The seals at the wrist, ankles, and neck of the suit must be extremely tight but not too tight to cut off your circulation. Some dry suits come with boots and hoods as part of the garment. Once you have the suit on, you will need to burp the suit to expel all of its excess inner air.

IMMERSION SUITS

Most immersion suits are full-body type V flotation devices designed to handle prolonged exposure to cold water and provide face-up flotation. These brightly colored suits often have built-in buoyancy support, adjustable spray shields, reflective tape, hoods, booties, gloves, and inflatable head rests. Adult suits are sold as one size fits all and can be worn by a person weighing anywhere from 110 to 330 pounds. Suits should be inspected at least once a year and placed in an area that you can quickly access should an

Most immersion suits are full-body type V flotation devices.

emergency occur. Because time is of the essence in an emergency when you need to put on an immersion suit, the USCG recommends that you practice until you can get the suit on in sixty seconds or less.

HEADGEAR AND NEOPRENE HOODS
Since more than 50 percent of your body heat is lost through your head, you must keep it covered. There are many styles of headgear, and your activity and the elements will dictate which style you choose. As a general rule, there are two basic types of headgear: rain hat and insulating hat.

Rain hat
A rain hat is often made from nylon or an insulation material with an outer nylon covering. For added waterproof and breathable characteristics, Gore-Tex is often used. For added protection in extreme conditions, choose a hat with earflaps. These hats perform best when worn while in the vessel or on shore.

Insulating hat

An insulating hat is made from wool, polypropylene, polyester fleece, or neoprene. The most common styles are the watch cap, the balaclava, and the neoprene hood or hooded vest. The balaclava is a great option in the vessel or on shore since it covers the head, ears, and neck yet leaves an opening for your face. Neoprene hoods and hooded vests are good choices for water wear.

Since so much heat is lost through the head, headgear *should not* be the first thing you take off when you are overheating. Mild adjustments, such as opening the zipper to your coat, will allow for the gradual changes you need to avoid sweating. In cold conditions, headgear should only be removed when other options have not cooled you down enough.

GLOVES AND MITTENS

Since a fair amount of heat is lost from the hands, you should keep them covered. Gloves encase each individual finger and allow you the dexterity to perform many of your daily tasks. Mittens, which encase the fingers together, decrease your dexterity but increase hand warmth from the captured radiant heat. Which type you decide to wear will depend on your activity. I often will wear gloves when working with my hands, and then when not working, I will insert the gloved hand inside a mitten. My gloves are made from a polyester fleece or a wool/synthetic blend. My mittens are made from a waterproof yet breathable fabric, such as Gore-Tex. When in the water, I often will wear neoprene gloves.

SHOES/BOOTS

Boots, a very important part of your clothing, should fit your needs and be broken in before your trip. When selecting boots, consider the type of travel you intend to do. I have four styles of boots, each of which serves a different purpose. They are made of leather, lightweight leather/fabric, rubber, and neoprene.

Leather boots

Leather boots are the ideal all-purpose boot. Under extreme conditions, you will need to treat them with a waterproofing material (read the manufacturer's directions on how this should be done) and wear a comfortable, protective wool-blend sock. Another popular option in leather boots is the added Thinsulate and Gore-Tex liner, which help to protect your feet from cold and moist conditions. If you decide to use Thinsulate or Gore-Tex, be sure to follow the manufacturer's directions explicitly on how to care for and treat the boots. If oils soak through the leather and into the lining, the insulating qualities of the boots will be nullified. Although leather makes a good boot for on shore, it might not be the best option for on a deck or in a kayak.

Lightweight leather/fabric boots
The lightweight boot is a popular fair-weather boot because it is lighter and dries faster than the leather boot. On the downside, moisture easily soaks through the fabric and creates less stability for your ankle. Depending on the style of boot sole, it may or may not be a good option for deck or kayak use.

Rubber boots
Rubber boots are most often used for extreme cold-weather conditions. They normally have nylon uppers with molded rubber bottoms. The felt inner boot can be easily removed and dries quickly. These boots perform well on a deck but tend to be too bulky for kayak use.

Neoprene bootie
Neoprene booties that are made for kayaking are a good option to wear both in the kayak and on the deck. They have the insulation qualities of neoprene, boast a rigid sole, and provide good support when walking.

Keeping your boots clean will help them protect you better. For leather and lightweight leather/fabric boots, wash off dirt and debris using a mild soap that doesn't damage leather. For rubber and neoprene boots, wash and dry the liners and clean all dirt and debris from the outer boots. If you decide to waterproof the leather boot, check with the manufacturer on its recommendations for what to use.

SOCKS
Socks need to provide adequate insulation, reduce friction, and wick away and absorb moisture from the skin. Most socks are made of wool, polyester, nylon, or an acrylic material. Wool tends to dry slower than the other

materials but is still a great option. Cotton should be avoided because it collapses when wet and loses its insulation qualities. For best results, wear two pairs of socks. The inner sock (often made of polyester) wicks moisture away from the foot; the outer sock (often a wool-blend material) provides insulation to keep your feet warm. During extremely wet conditions, Gore-Tex socks are often worn over the outer pair of socks. Regardless of which sock you decide to wear, be sure to keep your feet dry and change your socks at least once a day. Immediately apply moleskin to any hot spots that develop on your feet before they become blisters.

EYE PROTECTION
Goggles or sunglasses with side shields that filter out UV wavelengths are a must while traveling in open water. It doesn't take long to burn the eyes, and once this happens, you will have several days of eye pain along with light sensitivity, tearing, and a foreign body sensation. Since the symptoms of the burn usually don't show up until four to six hours after the exposure, you will get burned and not even realize it is happening. Once a burn occurs, you must get out of the light, remove contacts if you are wearing them, and cover the eyes with a sterile dressing until the light sensitivity subsides. If pain medication is available, you will probably need to use it. Once healed, be sure to protect the eyes to prevent another burn. If you do not have goggles or sunglasses, improvise some by using either a man-made or natural material to cover the eyes and provide a narrow horizontal slit for each eye.

ZIPPERS
Zippers often break or get stuck on garments and sleeping bags. While this may not present a great problem under mild conditions, you can lose a lot of body heat when you are unable to use a zipper properly in a wet and cold-weather environment. To decrease the odds of this occurring, make sure your gear has a zipper with a dual separating system (separates at both ends) and teeth made from a material, such as polyester, which won't rust or freeze. To waterproof your zippers, either use a baffle covering or apply a waterproof coating to the zipper's backing. The waterproof coating allows for lighter weight and easier access to the zipper.

SKIN PROTECTION

Ultraviolet (UV) radiation that reflects off of the water is very intense. The best way to avoid debilitating and painful sunburn during travel into a hot or cold, wet environment is to wear protective clothing. For skin that cannot be covered, use a sunscreen or sunblock. Sunscreens are available in various sun protection factor (SPF) ratings, which indicate how much longer than normal you can be exposed to UV radiation before burning. Sunscreens work by absorbing the UV radiation. Sunblock reflects the UV radiation and is most often used in sensitive areas such as the ears and nose, where intense exposure might occur. Regardless of what you use, you will need to constantly reapply it throughout the day as its effectiveness is lost over time and due to sweating.

CLOTHING ON SHORE

The same principles that apply for clothing while at sea will apply for clothing on shore. You may want to add natural materials to augment the insulation qualities of your shore clothing. Depending on where you are, various plant leaves and grasses may help to insulate and protect your body. The only limiting factor is your imagination.

6

Shelter

Building an adequate shelter can be time-consuming. It should be one of the first tasks completed in a survival situation. A good shelter should be close to natural resources such as food, fuel, and water as well as provide protection from the elements and possible predators.

—*Aviation Survival Technician Dave Kroll*
U.S. Coast Guard Helicopter Rescue Swimmer

After clothing, a shelter is your next line of personal protection. A shelter protects you from the elements of cold, heat, wet, and wind. The type of shelter you use will be determined by your circumstances, available material, and the climate.

OPEN WATER

In the open water, your shelter options are extremely limited. At sea, you will want to protect yourself from sea water and precipitation, wind, and heat. If you are in a life raft, the raft's canopy will provide protection from the sun, wind, and precipitation. How to put up your canopy will differ among the various raft manufacturers, so read the directions. In cold climates, you should close the doors to retain heat inside the raft. Inflating the floor of the raft and bailing out standing water will decrease heat loss through conduction. If your raft does not have a canopy or inflatable floor, you might need to improvise. Try rigging a space blanket as a canopy and sitting on gear that is tied to the raft to protect you from the cold floor.

ON LAND

SELECTING A CAMPSITE

When selecting a campsite, make sure its location allows you to easily meet your other survival needs. The environment, materials on hand, and the amount of time available will determine the type of shelter you choose. The ideal site will meet the following conditions.

Location and size

Your site should be level and big enough for both you and your equipment. If close to shore, make sure it is above the high-tide mark and at least one dune shoreward beyond the sea.

Optimize the sun's warmth

Position the shelter for a southern exposure if it's north of the equator or a northern exposure if south of it. This allows for optimal light and heat from the sun throughout the day. Try to position the door so that it faces east, since an east-side opening will allow for the best early-morning sun exposure.

Avoid wind problems

Since wind can wrap over the top of a tent and through its opening, do not place the door in the path of or on the opposite side of the wind's travel. Instead, position the door 90 degrees to the prevailing wind. Avoid shelter on ridgetops and open areas. When setting up your tent, secure it in place by staking it down. It doesn't take much of a wind to move or destroy your shelter.

Use the snow's insulation

If you are in snow, dig down to bare ground whenever possible. The ground's radiant heat will help keep you warmer at night.

Water source

To avoid having to melt snow or traveling for water, build your shelter 100 feet or so from a stream or lake, if you can find one.

Safety first

Avoid sites with potential environmental hazards that can wipe out all your hard work in just a matter of seconds. Examples include avalanche slopes; drainage and dry riverbeds with a potential for flash floods; rock formations that might collapse; dead trees that might blow down; overhanging dead limbs; and large animal trails. If you are near bodies of water, stay above the high-tide mark.

Survival

During an emergency, make sure your camp is located next to a signal and recovery site.

TENTS

If you have a tent, use it. More than likely, however, you will have to improvise a shelter by using man-made and natural materials.

When on long trips, a kayaker will often carry a tent. In an emergency situation, a tent is a welcome addition once shore has been reached. The majority of tents are made of nylon and held up with aluminum poles. Tents need to be waterproof to prevent moisture from entering from the outside and breathable to avoid condensation forming on the inside. Because nylon is not waterproof, some tent manufacturers use a breathable waterproof coating or a breathable laminated waterproof membrane for the tent's inner wall. Both of these options allow inside moisture to escape and prevent outside moisture from entering. If an outer wall is used, this inner wall treatment is not necessary. To make the outer wall water-repellant, a polyurethane coating is often added. Some tents come with UV protection and even have a fire-retardant finish. The tent's seams will either have a tape-weld or require that you apply a seam sealant before its first use. Follow the manufacturer's recommendations on what to do to seal the tent's seams. A tent's poles must be durable enough to handle the wind and snow without bending or breaking. For general use, get poles with a diameter of 8.5 mm. For extreme conditions, use a 9.0-mm-diameter or greater pole to add more durability to the tent's frame.

A tent's size, strength, and weight all factor into your decision on which tent to use. A balance between weight and strength is often foremost in people's minds. When choosing a tent, you will have to decide which is more important: less weight on your back or more durability and comfort in camp. I advise against a single-walled tent, unless it has multiple vents that can be opened to decrease inner condensation moisture. A double-walled tent provides a breathable inner wall and an outer waterproof rain fly. Since moisture from inside the tent will escape through the breathable wall and collect on the inside of the rain fly, make sure the two walls do not touch. If they do touch, the moisture will not escape and condensation will form inside the tent. The ideal rain fly will allow for a small area of protection between the door and outside, commonly called a vestibule. This area allows for extra storage, boot removal, and cooking. Information on zippers can be found in chapter 5.

Most tents are classified as either three-season or four-season tents. There are also combo tents that can be used for either three or four seasons.

Three-season tents
Three-season tents are normally lighter and often have see-through mesh panels that provide ventilation.

Four-season tents
Four-season tents are made from solid panels and are usually heavier and stronger. Typically they have stronger poles and reinforced seams.

Combo tents
Some tents are marketed to be used in either three or four seasons. They are constructed of a solid panel that can be zipped shut over the ventilating mesh.

BIVOUAC BAGS
The original concept of the bivouac bag was to provide the backpacker and mountaineer with an emergency lightweight shelter. However, many water enthusiasts now carry one as their primary three-season shelter. A good bag is made from a waterproof and breathable fabric, such as Gore-Tex or Tetra-Tex, with a coated nylon floor. Look for a hoop or flexible wire sewn across the head area of the upper bag and nonremovable mosquito netting

Bivouac bag

that allows venting. The bag should also have a dual separating zipper with baffles and a waterproof coating along the teeth, which should be made from polyester or a similar material.

EMERGENCY TARP SHELTERS

If no other options are available, make an emergency shelter using your canopy or a tarp. The exact type of shelter you build will depend on the environment, available materials, and time. Your shelter site should be large enough for you and your equipment and located close to your resources, but away from potential safety hazards. Regardless of the type of tarp shelter you build, try to have a 45- to 60-degree angle on all sides. If you have two tarps, erect a rain fly over the first to increase your protection from the elements. If you use line, attach it to the tarp's grommet or a makeshift button created from a rock, grass, or other malleable substance that will not tear or cut the tarp. By balling up the material inside a corner of the tarp and securing it with a slip knot, you can fasten the shelter piece to the ground using the free end of the line and tying it to vegetation, rocks, big logs, or an improvised stake. If using an improvised stake, pound it into the ground so it is leaning away from the tarp at a 90-degree angle to the wrinkles in the material. To avoid breaking your hand when pounding the stake into the ground, hold the stake so that your palm is facing up. Holding it this way allows a missed strike to hit the forgiving palm instead of the unforgiving back of the hand.

A-tent design
The A-tent is used most often in warm temperate and snow environments. To construct, tightly secure a ridgeline 3 to 4 feet above the ground and between two objects approximately 7 feet apart. Drape the tarp over the stretched line, and use trees, boulders, tent poles, or twigs to tightly secure its sides at a 45- to 60-degree angle to the ground.

A-frame
An A-frame is also used in winter and snow environments. Find a tree with a forked branch about 3 to 4 feet high on the trunk of the tree. Break away any other branches that pose a safety threat or would interfere with the construction of your A-frame. Place a ridgepole into the forked branch,

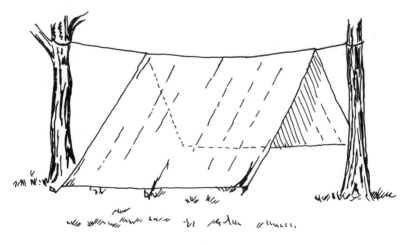

Tarp A-tent

Tarp A-frame

forming a 30-degree angle between the pole and the ground. The ridgepole should be 12 to 15 feet long and the diameter of your wrist. If you are unable to find a tree with a forked branch, lash the ridgepole to the tree. Other options include finding a fallen tree that forms an appropriate 30-degree angle between the tree and the ground or laying a strong ridgepole against a 3- to 4-foot-high stump. Drape the tarp over the pole, and use trees, boulders, tent poles, or twigs to tightly secure both sides of the tarp at a 45- to 60-degree angle to the ground.

Lean-to

Like the A-tent and A-frame, a lean-to is used most often in warm temperate and snow environments. To construct, find two trees about 7 feet apart with forked branches 4 to 5 feet high on the trunk. Break away any other branches that pose a safety threat or would interfere with the construction of your lean-to. Place a ridgepole (a fallen tree approximately 10 feet long and the diameter of your wrist) into the forked branches. If you are unable to find two trees with forked branches, lash the ridgepole to the trees. Another option is to tie a line tightly between the two trees and use the line in the same fashion as you would the pole. Lay three or more support poles across the ridgepole at a 45- to 60-degree angle to the ground. Support poles should be about 10 feet long and placed 1 to 2 feet apart. If using a

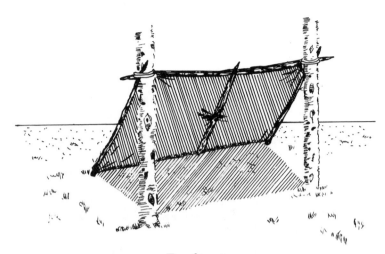

Tarp lean-to

line instead of the ridgepole, you may not need to use support poles. Drape the tarp over the support poles and attach the top to the ridgepole. Using trees, boulders, tent poles, or twigs, tightly secure the tarp over the support poles and to the ground. You may want to draw the excess tarp underneath the shelter to provide a ground cloth to sleep on.

Improvised lean-to using a life raft and tarp

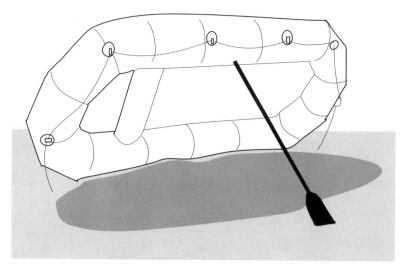

Desert/shade shelter made from a raft and paddle

If you have a life raft and a tarp, you can make a quick and easy lean-to on a sandy shore beyond the reach of high tide. To construct, bury approximately one-fifth of the raft perpendicular to the ground, attach a tarp to the top of the raft, and secure the tarp to the ground, forming a 45- to 60-degree angle between the tarp and the ground.

Desert/shade shelter
A desert/shade shelter is used in dry environments. Ideally, you need to locate an area with an 18- to 24-inch depression between rocks or dunes. Another option is to dig an 18- to 24-inch deep trench that is large enough for you to comfortably lie down in. If a trench is dug, pile the removed sand around three of the four sides. Provide for an adequate entryway by removing additional sand from the remaining open area. Cover the trench with your tarp or poncho, and secure it in place by weighing down its edges with sand or rocks. If you have a second tarp or poncho, place it 12 to 18 inches above the first. (Layering the material reduces the inside temperature even more.) If you have a raft and paddle or solid branch, a shade shelter can be made by propping the raft up with the paddle.

A desert/shade shelter will reduce midday heat by as much as 30 to 40 degrees. To avoid sweating or dehydration, build this shelter during the morning or evening hours. Until then, get out of the heat by attaching a tarp to your raft (see above), an elevated rock, or a sand dune and stretching it out so that a 45- to 60-degree angle is formed between the tarp and the ground.

EMERGENCY NATURAL SHELTER

A natural shelter can be made of materials found in the wilderness. (Please note that the use of natural shelter materials is recommended only in an actual survival situation.) As with any shelter, the sole purpose of a natural shelter is to protect you and your equipment from the elements. Construction techniques for several natural shelters are outlined below.

Cave

A cave, the ultimate natural shelter, can be found along many shorelines. With very little effort, it can provide protection from the various elements. However, caves are not without risk. Some of these risks include, but are not limited to, animals, rodents, reptiles, and insects; bad air; slippery slopes, rocks, and crevasses; floods or high-water issues; and combustible gases (most common where excessive bat droppings are noted). When using a cave as a shelter, you should follow some basic rules:

1. Never light a fire inside a small cave. It may use up oxygen or cause an explosion if enough bat droppings are present. Fires should be lit near the entrance to the cave, where adequate ventilation is available.
2. To avoid slipping into crevasses, getting lost, or breathing bad gas, never venture too far into the cave.
3. Make sure the entrance is above high tide.
4. Be constantly aware of water movement within the cave. If the cave appears to be prone to flooding, look for another shelter.
5. Never enter or use old mines as a shelter. The risk is not worth it. Collapsing passages and vertical mine shafts are just a few of the potential deadly problems.
6. If possible, use a cave where the entrance is facing the sun (south entrance if north of the equator; north entrance if south of the equator). If you take shelter in a cave, build a wall at the cave entrance by leaning

support poles against the entrance and covering them with natural materials. Be sure to leave open an area large enough to build a fire and provide adequate ventilation within the shelter.

Hobo shelter

A hobo shelter can be used in temperate oceanic environments where a more stable long-term shelter is necessary. To construct, you will need to find several pieces of driftwood or boards that have washed ashore. Next, locate a sand dune beyond the reach of high tide, and on the land side of the dune, dig out a rectangular space big enough to fit both you and your equipment. Place the removed sand close by so that it can be used later. Gather as much driftwood and boards as you can find, and using any available line, build a strong frame inside the rectangular dugout. Create a roof and walls by attaching driftwood and boards to the frame, leaving a doorway. If your wood supply is limited, don't place support walls at the back or on two sides of the structure. Some sand may fall into the shelter, but the design will still meet your needs. If you have a poncho or tarp that is not necessary for meeting any other needs, consider placing it over the roof. Insulate the shelter by covering the roof with 6 to 8 inches of sand.

Hobo shelter

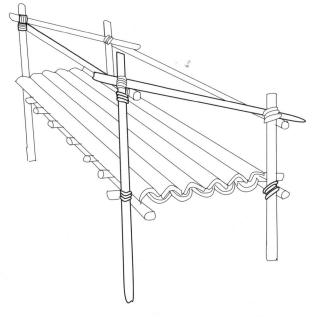

Tropical hut

Tropical hut

These huts are used in tropical regions, swamps, or areas that have excessive amounts of rain. The elevated bed/floor provides protection from the moist or water-covered ground while the overhead roof keeps you dry. To construct a small tropical hut, pound four poles (8 to 12 feet long) 8 to 12 inches into the ground at each of the shelter's four corners. Tap dirt around them to make more secure. Create the floor by lashing a strong pole 2 feet off the ground on each side of the shelter so that the poles connect to form a square or rectangle. Next, create a solid platform by laying additional poles on top of and perpendicular to the side poles. Make sure that all the poles are strong enough to support your weight. Finish the floor with moss, grass, leaves, or branches.

To create the roof, use the same support poles that you used to build the floor. A lean-to roof is quick and easy. Attach two support poles to the front and back of the shelter so that they are horizontal to the ground and perpendicular to the shelter's sides. The front support pole should be higher than the back support pole so that a 45- to 60-degree downward angle forms when the roof poles are placed. Lay roof poles on top of and perpendicular to the roof's support poles, and lash them in place. Cover the roof with a tarp, large overlapping leaves, or another appropriate shingling material.

Emergency tree pit

A tree pit shelter is a quick, immediate-action shelter used in most forested environments. The optimal tree will have a number of lower branches—such as a Douglas or grand fir—that protect its base from the snow, rain, and sun. Pine trees provide little protection and are not a good choice. In snow environments, the snow level rises around the tree to provide excellent insulation for your shelter. To make a tree pit, remove any lower dead

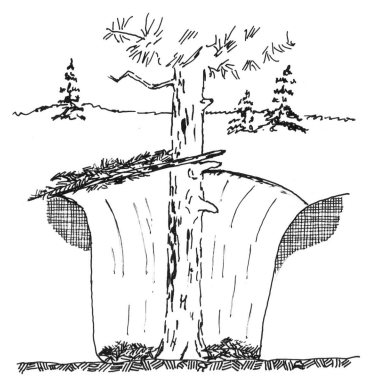

Tree pit

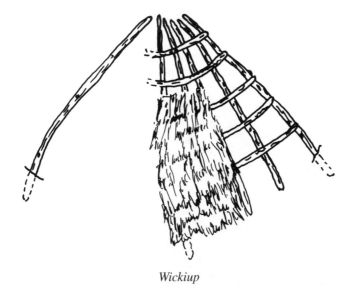

Wickiup

branches and snow from the tree's base, making an area large enough for you and your equipment. If snow is present, dig until you reach bare ground and remove obstructive branches, which can used for added overhead cover to protect you from the elements.

Wickiup

The wickiup shelter is most common in areas where building materials are scarce, but this shelter can be used anywhere that poles, brush, leaves, grass, and boughs are found. The wickiup is not the ideal shelter in areas with prolonged rains, but if you heap on thick the insulation material, this shelter will provide adequate protection from most elements.

To make it, gather three strong 10- to 15-foot poles and use a shear lash to connect them together at the top. Note that if one or more of the three poles has a fork at its top, it may not be necessary to lash the poles together. Spread the poles out until they can stand without support to form a tripod at approximately a 60-degree angle. Using additional poles, fill in all the sides by leaning them against the top of the tripod. Don't discard shorter poles as they can be used in the roof. Make sure you leave a small entrance that later can be covered with a hide or other appropriate material.

To use immediately, cover the shelter with brush, leaves, reeds, or bark. For additional protection, layer the roofing materials in the following design: Starting at the bottom, cover the framework with boughs, grass, or plant stalks. Next, cover the shelter, from bottom to top, with mulch and dirt. Finally, to hold the roof material in place, lay poles on top and around the wickiup. Be sure to leave a vent hole at the top if you plan on having fires inside the shelter.

A-frame

An A-frame is used most often in warm temperate and snow environments. Find a tree with a forked branch 3 to 4 feet above the base of the trunk. Break away any other branches that pose a threat or would interfere with the construction of your A-frame. Place a ridgepole—a fallen tree 12 to 15 feet long and the diameter of your wrist—into the forked branch to form a 30-degree angle between the pole and the ground. If you are unable to find a tree with a forked branch, lash the ridgepole to the tree. Other options include finding a fallen tree that's at an appropriate 30-degree angle to the ground or laying a strong ridgepole against a 3- to 4-foot-high stump. Lay support poles across the ridgepole, on both sides, at a 60-degree angle to the ground. Support poles must be long enough to extend above the ridgepole slightly, and they should be placed approximately 1 to 1½ feet apart. Do not have the support poles end above the roof material as moisture will run down them and into your shelter. Crisscross small branches into the support

A-frame

Opposing lean-to

poles. Cover the framework with any available grass, moss, or boughs. Start at the bottom, and layer the material. If snow is available, throw a minimum of 8 inches over the top of the shelter. Cover the door opening with your pack or a similar item.

Lean-to

A lean-to can be built with natural materials found in most environments. Find two trees approximately 7 to 8 feet apart with forked branches 5 to 6 feet high on each trunk. Break away any of the branches that pose a safety threat or would interfere with the construction process. Also clear away any saplings, duff, or wood between the two trees that may interfere with the lean-to's construction. Place a ridgepole (a strong pole the diamater of your wrist) between the two trees into the forked branches. If you are unable to find two trees with forked branches, use a square lash to attach the ridgepole to the trees.

Lay several support poles across the ridgepole at a 45- to 60-degree angle to the ground. Support poles must be long enough to provide this angle and yet barely extend beyond the top of the ridgepole. Weave small saplings into and perpendicular to the support poles. Then cover the entire shelter with 12 to 18 inches of boughs, bark, duff, and snow in that order, depending on availability of resources. The material should be placed in a layered fashion starting at the bottom. If snow is available, throw a minimum of 8 inches over the top of the shelter. The lean-to allows you to build a fire in front of the shelter as long as the fire is safely spaced away from you and your gear. To help heat your shelter, build a fire reflector behind the fire. In cold climates, create an opposing lean-to by making a front wall in the same fashion as the back wall. Be sure to incorporate the sides into the framework, and leave enough room for a small doorway on either side. The doorway can be covered with your pack or a snow block when needed. For an opposing lean-to, make a vent hole in top if you plan to have a small fire inside. As always when using snow, don't let the temperature inside your shelter go above 32 degrees Fahrenheit or the snow will start to melt.

Snow cave
Used most often in winter and snow environments, a snow cave is a quick and easily constructed one- or two-man shelter. When using this type of shelter, the outside temperature must be well below freezing to ensure that the walls of the cave will stay firm and the snow will not melt. Once the snow shelter is built, never let the inside temperature go above freezing. If this happens, the snow cave will lose its insulation quality, and you will get wet from the subsequent moisture. Therefore, these shelters are not designed for large groups since the radiant heat of many people will actually raise the temperature above freezing and make the shelter a dangerous environment. As a general rule of thumb, if you cannot see your breath, the shelter is too warm. When constructing the cave, use the COLDER principle and take care not to get wet or overheated.

To construct a snow cave, find an area with firm snow at least 6 feet deep. A steep slope such as a snowdrift will work as long as there is no risk of an avalanche. Dig an entryway into the slope deep enough to start a tunnel and wide enough for you to fit into (approximately 3 feet). Since cold air sinks, you must construct a snow platform 2 to 3 feet above the entryway. The platform should be flat, level, and large enough for you to comfortably lie down on. Use the entryway as a starting point, and hollow out a domed area large enough for you and your equipment. To keep the ceiling from settling or

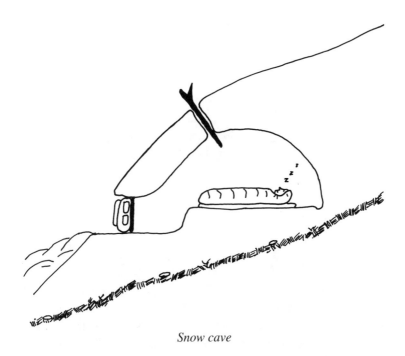

Snow cave

falling in, create a high domed roof. To prevent asphyxiation, make a ventilation hole in the roof. For best results, the ventilation hole should be at a 45-degree angle to your sleeping platform, creating an imaginary triangle between the platform, the door, and the ventilation hole. Insert a stick or pole, if available, through the ventilation hole so that it can be cleared periodically. To further protect the shelter from the elements, place a block of snow or your pack in the entryway. Since you will be oblivious to the conditions outside, you should check the entrance periodically to make sure it is clear of snow.

Snow A-frame shelter
A snow A-frame is used most often in winter, snow, and ice environments where the snow has been wind blown and firmly packed. To make a snow A-frame, find an 8-by-4-foot flat area that is clear of trees and underbrush. (The snow must be at least 3 to 4 feet deep.) Stomp out a rectangular platform wide and long enough to accommodate your body, and let it harden

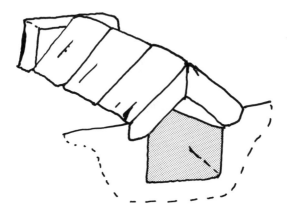

Snow A-frame

for at least thirty minutes. Dig a 3-feet-deep entryway just in front of the rectangular area. Evacuate the compacted snow by cutting multiple 3-foot-square blocks that are 8 to 10 inches wide. You will need an instrument such as a snow saw, large machete, stick, or ski. Once the blocks have been removed, place them against each other to form an A-frame above the trench. For best results, cut one of the first opposing blocks in half lengthwise. This makes it easier to place the additional blocks on one at a time instead of trying to continually lay two against one another. Fill in any gaps with surrounding snow and cover the doorway.

If the snow is not wind packed and a snow cave is not an option, you can make a variation of the snow A-frame shelter. Simply dig a trench (as described above but with one side higher than the other), cover it with a framework (lean-to design) of branches or similar material, and then add a thick layer of snow roofing.

Molded dome
The molded dome, a variation of the snow cave and igloo, is used where the snow is not wind packed and a snow cave is not an option. Using your gear, boughs, or similar material, create a cone that will serve as the foundation to your shelter. You could build this shelter without doing this step, but it will require more work. Pile snow on top of the cone until you have a

Molded dome

dome that is approximately 5 feet high and has at least 3 feet of snow covering the inner core. Smooth the outer surface, and let the snow sit for one to two hours, depending on your weather conditions, so that it can settle. Since 18 inches is an ideal insulating depth for a molded dome, gather a number of 2-foot-long branches and insert them into the dome, toward its center, leaving approximately 6 inches of the branches exposed. Decide where you'd like your entryway, and dig a 3-foot-deep entry tunnel. Keep the height of the tunnel equal to the bottom of the inner core, and dig approximately a third of the way toward the center of the molded dome or until you reach the core material. Now remove the gear and boughs from the core, and hollow out the inside using the sticks as your guide for how thick to make the inner walls.

7

Fire

*Nothing will rally your morale more than a productive
fire. It provides heat, protection, light, and is a great
improvised signal. Learn how to build a fire, and carry a
tinder kit and heat source whenever you travel into the
wilderness. It may save your life.*

> —*Aviation Survival Technician Derrick Breton*
> *U.S. Coast Guard Helicopter Rescue Swimmer*

Fire is the third line of personal protection and, in most cases, will not be
necessary if you've adequately met your clothing and shelter needs. In extreme conditions, however, fire is very beneficial for warding off hypothermia and other exposure injuries. Fire serves many other functions as well:
providing light, warmth, and comfort; a source of heat for cooking, purifying
water, and drying clothes; and a means of signaling. For some of these purposes, you might be able to use a backpacking stove, sterno stove, or solid
compressed fuel tablets instead of a fire. Finally, a fire is relaxing and may
help to reduce stress. Remember that fire is limited to survival on the shore.
Common sense dictates that fires should not be started inside a life raft.

MAN-MADE HEAT SOURCES

A man-made heat source can be used in any of your various shelter options,
as long as you have proper ventilation. However, if you are in a tent, limit
fires to the vestibule area to avoid fuel spills and burning the tent. In a natural or thermal shelter, use the breath rule—you should always be able to see
your breath—to make sure you do not get the temperature above 32 degrees
F. The following are some of the man-made heat sources you might use.

BACKPACKING STOVE

The two basic styles of backpacking stoves are canister and liquid fuel. Canister designs use butane, propane, or isobutene cartridges as their fuel source. The most common types of liquid fuels are white gas and kerosene. For more details of the various styles of backpacking stoves, see chapter 3 on gear.

STERNO

Sterno has been around for a long time and still has a place for many back-country explorers. This fuel is a jellied alcohol that comes in a 7-ounce can. Under normal conditions, sterno has a two-hour burn time. Although far inferior to a good backpacking stove for cooking, sterno is very effective at warming water and a shelter in an emergency. An inexpensive folding stove is made for use with sterno, but with a little imagination, you can create the same thing.

SOLID COMPRESSED FUEL TABLETS

Esbit, Trioxane, and Hexamine are the three basic tablets on the market. Esbit is the newest of the three, and unlike its predecessors, it is nontoxic. This nonexplosive, virtually odorless and smokeless tablet can generate up to 1,400 degrees F of intense heat and provide twelve to fifteen minutes of useable burn time per cube. When combined with a commercial or impro-vised stove, it can sometimes boil a pint of water in less than eight min-utes. Because these tablets easily light from a spark, they can also be used as a tinder to start your fire.

BUILDING A FIRE

When man-made heat sources either are not available or don't meet your needs, you may elect to build a fire. Always use a safe site, and put the fire out completely so that it is cold to the touch before you leave. Place the fire close to your fire materials and your shelter. It should be built on flat, level ground and have adequate protection from the elements. Before starting a fire, prepare the site by clearing a 3-foot fire circle and scraping away all leaves, brush, debris, and snow down to bare ground if possible. To success-fully build a fire, you need to have all three elements of the fire triangle—

heat, oxygen, and fuel—present, although your fuels will vary depending on what is on hand.

HEAT

The focus of this book is on wilderness survival, not primitive skills, and although some shorelines will provide what you need to start a fire using a natural-friction system, such as bow and drill or hand drill, most will not. (If you would like information on primitive fire-starting techniques, read my book *Wilderness Living*.) This book focuses on man-made heat sources. Heat is required to start a fire, but since matches and lighters often fail and will eventually run out, you should consider alternative sources of heat. A sparker or metal match is a good choice that will virtually never fail you.

Matches

Matches run out, get wet, and seem to never work in a time of crisis. However, if you are determined to use matches, I recommend NATO-issue survival matches, which have hand-dipped and varnished heads that are supposed to light even when wet and exposed to strong wind or rain. These matches will burn approximately twelve seconds, enough time to light most fires. To protect the match from going out, light it between cupped hands while positioning your body to block the flame from the wind and rain. Regardless of the type of matches you carry, store them in a waterproof container until ready for use.

Lighters

Lighters are a form of flint and steel with an added fuel source, which keeps the flame going. Like matches, they also have a tendency to fail when used during inclement weather and once the fuel is gone. If you understand a lighter's shortcomings and still elect to use one, I recommend a Colibri Quantum brand. These high-end lighters are water-resistant and shockproof, can ignite at high altitudes, and are marketed as wind-resistant. To use, simply place the flame directly on to the tinder.

Metal match (artificial flint)

A metal match is similar to the flints used in a cigarette lighter but a lot bigger. When stroked with an object, the friction creates a long spark that can be used to light tinder. Most metal matches are made from a mixture of metals and rare earth elements, which is alloyed at a high temperature and shaped into rods of various diameters.

To use a metal match, place it in the center of your tinder, and while holding it firmly in place with one hand, use a knife blade to strike the metal match at 90 degrees with a firm yet controlled downward stroke. The resulting spark should provide enough heat to ignite the tinder. It may take several attempts. If, after five tries, the match has not lit, then the tinder should be reworked to ensure that adequate edges are exposed and oxygen is able to flow through it. The S.O.S. Strike Force is the most popular commercial metal match available. Two one-hand-use metal matches—the Spark-Lite and the BlastMatch—are also on the market.

S.O.S. Strike Force
This metal match has a ½-inch round alloy flint attached to a hollow hard-plastic handle, which houses emergency tinder. A hardened steel striker is

Unlike matches and lighters, an artificial flint virtually never runs out.

attached to the flint cover to make this system completely self-sufficient. Although a little bulky, the system weighs slightly less than 4 ounces.

The Spark-Lite

The Spark-Lite is small and lightweight, measuring approximately 2¼ by 9/32 by 9/32 inches. It has a serrated wheel, similar to what is found on a cigarette lighter, which strikes a small flint when stroked. To make this a one-hand-use device, the flint is spring-loaded and maintains contact with the wheel at all times. The small flint is supposed to allow for approximately 1,000 strokes before it runs out. While its spark is smaller than that of the larger metal matches, this device is also a lot smaller. To use, stroke the sparking wheel with your thumb while holding the Spark-Lite's body with your fingers from the same hand.

BlastMatch

The BlastMatch is larger and weighs more than the Spark-Lite. It measures 4 by 1⅜ by ⅞ inches, and its larger molded plastic body holds a 2½-inch-long by ½-inch-diameter rod of flint. The flint is spring-loaded, and when the cap is released, the flint is propelled out. To use, place the flint tip in the center of your tinder, apply pressure to the side catch with your thumb, and push the body downward. This action will force the scraper, which is located inside the catch, down the flint to create a large spark.

Pyrotechnics

Flares should be used only as a last resort to start fires. You are better off saving these signaling devices for their intended use. However, if you are unable to start a fire and the risk of hypothermia is high, a flare is a very effective heat source. Its use is simple: After preparing the tinder, ignite it by lighting the flare and directing its flames onto the tinder. Because time is critical once you light the flare, prepare your firelay in advance and be sure to leave an opening large enough to direct the flare's flame onto the underlying tinder.

OXYGEN

Oxygen is necessary for fuel to burn, and it must be present at all stages of a fire. To ensure this, you must create a platform and a brace for your fire.

A platform and brace keep tinder dry and help ensure adequate oxygen flow to your fuel.

A platform can be any dry material, such as dry tree bark or a dry non-porous rock, that protects your fuel from the ground. Waterlogged rocks may explode when wet, so don't use them. During extremely wet conditions or when there is a heavy snow covering, a platform can be made by laying multiple green logs next to one another. Building the fire on green logs will protect the fire from the snow or moist ground. Your fuel should lean against a brace, which is usually a branch the diameter of your wrist that allows oxygen to circulate through the fuel.

FUEL
Fuel can be separated into three categories, with each type of fuel building upon the previous one. The three categories of fuel are tinder, kindling, and fuel.

Tinder
Tinder, which is any material that will light from a spark, is extremely valuable in getting the larger stages of fuel lit. There are two types of tinder: man-made and natural.

Man-made tinder
When venturing into the wilderness, always carry a man-made tinder in your survival kit. If you should become stranded during harsh weather con-

ditions, it may prove to be the key to having a fire that first night. However, you should immediately begin to gather natural tinder so that it can be dried out and prepared for use once your man-made tinder is used up. To work, natural tinder must be dry, have edges, and allow oxygen to circulate within it. Man-made tinder, on the other hand, simply requires a scraping or fluffing to catch a spark. The most common man-made forms of tinder are petroleum-based, compressed tinder tabs, and solid compressed fuel tablets, which were discussed earlier under man-made heat sources.

Petroleum-based tinder
While there are many examples of this product, the most common is the Tinder-Quik tab. It is waterproof, odorless, and made from a light compressible fiber that is impregnated with beeswax, petroleum, and silicones. To use it, simply fluff up the fiber so that it has edges to catch a spark. The tinder will burn for approximately two minutes. Although Tinder-Quik was designed for use with the Spark-Lite flint system (described above), it can be used with any heat source. Less expensive, homemade petroleum-based tinder can be made with 100 percent cotton balls that are saturated with petroleum jelly and stuffed into a 35-mm film canister. This tinder is very effective even under harsh wet and windy conditions.

Compressed tinder tabs
WetFire tinder tablets are perhaps the most common compressed tinder tablets. Each tablet is waterproof, nontoxic, odorless, and smokeless, and will burn around 1,300 degrees F for two to three minutes. Unlike the Tinder-Quik tabs, the WetFire tablets are not compressible. To use them, I prepare the tinder by making a few small shavings of the tablets to catch my metal match sparks.

Natural tinder
For natural tinder to work, it must be dry, have edges, and allow oxygen to circulate within it, although there are a few exceptions to this rule. Gather natural tinder before you need it so that you have time to dry it in the sun, between your clothing, or by a fire. Keep it dry until you need it. The three basic types of natural tinder are bark, scrapings, and grass, ferns, and lichen. If you are uncertain whether something will work as tinder, try it. Always

Cotton balls and Vaseline make excellent inexpensive tinder.

remove any wet bark or pith before breaking the tinder down, and keep the tinder off of the wet ground during and after it is prepared. Since some tinder will collect moisture from the air, always prepare it last.

Bark

To prepare layered forms of tinder, you must work them between your hands and fingers until they're light and airy. To do this, start by holding a long section of the bark with both hands. Use a back-and-forth twisting action, working the back until it becomes fibrous. Next, place the fibrous bark between the palms of your hands, and roll your hands back and forth until the bark becomes thin, light, and airy. At this point, you should be able to light them from a spark. In most cases, I prepare enough tinder to form a small bird's nest. Many types of bark will work as tinder, but my favorite is birch. Birch bark will work even when wet due to a highly flammable resin in it.

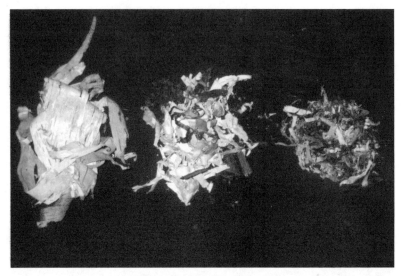

Breaking down birch bark.

Wood scrapings provide a good tinder.

Wood Scrapings

To create wood scrapings, repeatedly run your knife blade, at a 90-degree angle, across a flat section of pitch or heart wood. You will need enough scrapings to fill the palm of your hand. Like birch bark, pitch wood also will light even when wet. The high concentration of pitch in the wood's fibers makes it highly flammable.

Grass, Ferns, and Lichen

As with bark, I create a bird's nest with these materials, and depending on the situation, I may break them down further. This form of tinder must be completely dry to achieve success.

Kindling

Kindling, usually comprised of twigs or wood shavings that range in diameter from pencil lead to pencil thickness, should light easily when placed on a small flame. Sources include small, dead twigs found on dead branches at

Kindling ranges in diameter from pencil lead to pencil thickness

the bottom of many trees; shavings from larger pieces of dry dead wood; heavy cardboard; and gasoline- or oil-soaked wood.

Fuel

Any material that is thumb-size or bigger and will burn slowly and steadily once it is lit could be called fuel. Types of fuel include dry standing dead wood and branches; dead heartwood (the dry inside portion of a fallen tree trunk or large branches); green wood that is finely split; dry grasses twisted into bunches; and dry animal dung. Dead heartwood works best when obtained from a tree that died a natural death rather than one that has been cut with a chainsaw. Stumps from trees that fall down naturally tend to have pointed tops that do not allow snow and moisture to collect and eventually saturate the inner wood. Certain coniferous trees that have died from natural causes will contain large amounts of pitch, and because it lights easily even under the worst conditions, this pitch wood is a great find when you are cold and in need of a quick fire. Obtain this wood by any means available, from cutting it with an ax or big knife to using a pry pole to separate large splinters of the wood to kicking the stump. Break down the larger pieces with your knife or ax.

Fuel acquired from the dead lower tree branches

Fuel acquired from heartwood

STEPS TO BUILDING A FIRE

When building a fire, be sure you gather enough fuel to build three knee-high fires. This allows you to go back to a previous stage should the fire start to die. It also keeps the fire going while you get more material. Once the wood or other fuel is gathered, break it down from big to small, always preparing the smallest stages last. This helps to decrease the amount of moisture your tinder and kindling collect during the preparation process. If conditions are wet, strip off all lichen and bark, and split the branches in half to expose the inner dry wood. Be sure to use a platform and brace to keep your various stages of fuel off of the ground while you are breaking it down.

Once all the stages are prepared, either light the tinder or place the lit tinder on the platform next to the brace. Use the brace to place your smaller kindling directly over the flames. Spread a handful of kindling over the flame all at once instead of one stick at a time. Once flames wick up through the kindling, place another handful of kindling perpendicular across the first. When this stage is going well, advance to the next size. Continue this crisscrossing process until your fuel is burning and the fire is self-supporting. If you have leftover material, set it aside in a dry place so that it can be used to start another fire later. If you have a problem building your fire, reevaluate your heat, oxygen, and fuel to determine which one is either not present or inadequate.

8

Signaling

The weather and sea state were horrible, and the ocean was foam-filled, making it nearly impossible to spot a white sailboat. If not for the flickering mast light, it is doubtful the sailboat would have been spotted.

—*Aviation Survival Technician Scott Adlon*
U.S. Coast Guard Helicopter Rescue Swimmer

THE NEED FOR A SIGNAL

During an average year, the U.S. Coast Guard performs thousands of search-and-rescue missions. Some are successful, while others end without ever finding the lost vessel or passengers. Many factors contribute to a successful search. Leaving a float plan will help give rescuers an idea of where to look. Having signals and knowing how to use them will aid in the process. Although filing a float plan is optional (do it!), carrying visual distress signals is not. Coast guard regulations require visual distress signals (VDSs) on all boats that operate on the high seas, coastal waters (including the Great Lakes), territorial seas, and all waters directly connected to the Great Lakes or the territorial seas up to a point where the waters are less than two miles wide. For boats less than 16 feet, the USCG requires one electric distress light or three combination (day/night) red flares, which are only required to be carried on board when operating between sunset and sunrise. For boats between 16 and 65 feet, the USCG requires one orange distress flag and one electric distress light *or* three handheld or floating orange smoke signals and one electric distress light *or* three combination (day/night) red flares, whether handheld, meteor, or parachute-type. All signals, except for the distress flag and light, must show the words "Coast

Guard Approved" and be marked with the service life of the signal. The distress flag and light must carry the manufacturer's certification that they meet coast guard requirements. I strongly suggest carrying additional signaling devices! You can never have too many.

Although you should always carry a VDS, the USCG does allow exceptions for certain vessels during day operations. (Night signals are required for all vessels from sunset to sunrise.) These vessels include recreational boats less than 16 feet in length, boats participating in organized events, open sailboats less than 26 feet in length not equipped with propulsion machinery, and manually propelled boats.

RULES OF SIGNALING

Correctly using a signal increases a survivor's chances of being rescued. A signal has two purposes: to alert rescuers to your whereabouts, and to help them hone in on your exact location. The most effective electronic distress signals are your VHF handheld radio and the 406-MHz Emergency Position Indicating Radio Beacon. Aerial flares and parachute flares are the most effective nonelectronic signals because they move, are spectacular, and cover a large sighting area. Once help is on the way, signal mirrors, handheld signal flares, smoke signals, sea/rescue signal streamers, kites, sea marker dye, strobe lights, whistles, and ground-to-air signals serve as beacons to help rescuers pinpoint your position and keep them on course. When preparing a signal, use the following rules.

STAY PUT

Once lost, stay put. Only leave if the area you are in doesn't meet your needs, rescue is not imminent, and you know how to navigate (know where you are and have the skills to get to where you want to go). If you are lost or stranded in a car, plane, or ATV, stay with it. If your distressed vessel doesn't present a hazard, stay close to it. The vessel or vehicle will serve as a ground-to-air signal, and when a search is activated, rescuers will begin looking for you in your last known location. If you are on land and for some reason you need to move, be sure to leave a ground-to-air signal pointing in your direction of travel along with a note telling rescuers of your plans. If you do move, go to high ground and find a large clearing to signal from.

SIGNAL SITE

At sea, your signal site is not often something you can control. On land, however, your signal site should be close to your camp or shelter, located in a large clearing with 360-degree visibility, and be free of shadows.

ONE-TIME-USE SIGNALS

Many signals may be used just one time and thus should only be ignited when you see or hear a potential rescuer headed in your direction.

KNOW AND PREPARE YOUR SIGNAL IN ADVANCE

Since seconds can make the difference between life and death, don't delay in preparing or establishing a signal.

BE SAFE

Read the instructions for your flare in advance so you will know how to use it when a ship or aircraft is seen. Always fire the signal on the downwind side of your vessel while holding it slightly down and over the water. Never fire it above or inside the raft since burning particles might fall and burn you or damage your raft.

SIGNALS THAT ATTRACT RESCUE

The most effective distress signals for attracting attention are electronic devices. Other options include parachute and aerial flares, both of which cover a large area and attract rescuers with spectacular visual effects and movement.

VHF RADIO

The VHF radio is a quick and easy way to make a distress call. Because it does not use satellites, it has limits to how far away it can be picked up. Its normal range varies greatly but is estimated to average between 20 and 60 miles. If a repeater is within that 20- to 60-mile range, however, the signal range can increase significantly. Channel 16 is the recognized emergency channel.

Protect your VHF radio from moisture and wind, and consider having a radio that runs on alkaline or lithium batteries rather than rechargeable batteries. However, be sure you have packed multiple replacement batteries in the abandon-ship bag. There are three internationally recognized marine radio signals: Mayday, Pan-Pan, and Security. Mayday, which is used when there is an immediate threat to the loss of your vessel or someone's life, takes priority over all other calls.

A Mayday call should follow this basic design: Call MAYDAY, MAYDAY, MAYDAY. Repeat your vessel name and call sign three times. State your present location (give latitude and longitude if you can along with a distance and direction from a known point), the nature of the distress, and the number of people on board three times. Repeat this process until you either get a response or are forced to leave your vessel.

A Pan-Pan call is used when a potential threat exists, but at that moment there is no immediate danger to persons or vessel. Security calls are low priority and usually alert vessels to monitor another station for a safety message.

SATELLITE EPIRBS

Emergency Position Indicating Radio Beacons (EPIRBs) are well worth the cost, and every vessel should carry one. When activated, these beacons quickly and with great accuracy alert rescuers to your location. The 406-MHz EPIRB is the gold standard and by far outperforms the older rescue beacons, which, if you have them, should be replaced. Once activated,

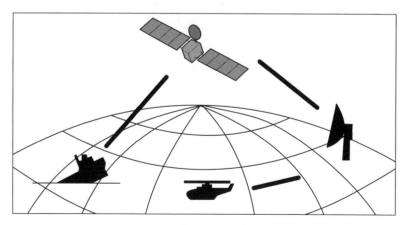

EPIRB transmission

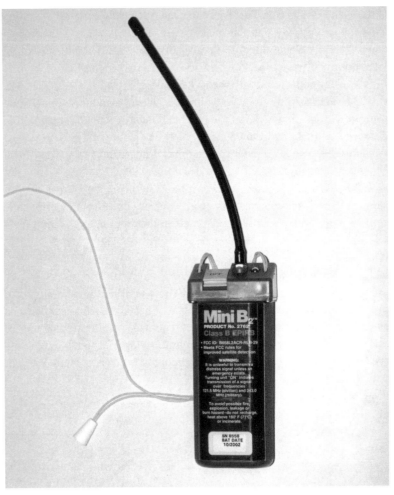

An Emergency Position Indicating Radio Beacon (EPIRB)

they automatically transmit a signal on two international distress frequencies that will be picked up by military and civilian aircraft. Most of these devices float, but make sure you have a good strong lanyard attached to your EPIRB before you even contemplate putting it in the water. Be sure to register the EPIRB according to the beacon manufacturer's instructions.

CELLULAR PHONES

Although a cellular phone is a great thing to have, it's not without limitations and often doesn't work in remote areas. Do not rely on one as your sole signaling and rescue device. Not only are cell phones limited by their service area, they are also vulnerable to cold, moisture, sand, and heat. You will need to protect the phone from these hazards by any means available. Cellular phones should not be considered a replacement for your VHF transceiver.

AERIAL FLARES

Because aerial flares can be used only once, they should only be fired when an aircraft or a vessel is sighted on the horizon. As with all pyrotechnic devices, they are flammable and should be handled with caution. Most aerial flares fire by pulling a chain. In general, you hold the launcher so that the firing end (where the flare comes out) is pointed overhead and skyward and the chain is dropped straight down. While the flare is pointed skyward, use your free hand to grasp and pull the chain sharply downward. Make sure the hand holding the launcher is located within the safe area as detailed on the device you are using. Hold the flare away from your body, outside the raft, and perpendicular to the water. The average aerial flares will have a 500-foot launch altitude, six-second burn time, and a 12,000 candlepower. Under optimal conditions, these flares have been sighted up to 30 miles away. Many aerial flares float and are waterproof, and most average in size at 1 inch in diameter and 4 inches long when collapsed. Depending on your needs, you can purchase disposable flares or flares with replacement cartridges. The Orion Star-Tracer and the SkyBlazer XLT aerial flares are two good examples that can be found in most sporting or marine stores. Read the instructions for your flare in advance so you will know how to use it when a ship or aircraft is seen. Never fire a flare above or inside the raft since burning particles might fall and burn you or damage your raft.

PARACHUTE FLARES

A parachute flare is simply an aerial flare attached to a parachute. The parachute allows for a longer burn time while the flare floats down to earth. Because these signals can only be used once, they should be fired only when an aircraft or a vessel is sighted on the horizon. As with all pyrotechnic devices, they are flammable and should be handled with caution. The Pains Wessex SOLAS Mark 3 parachute flare can reach a height of 1,000 feet and produce a brilliant 30,000 candlepower. The flare's red light, which drifts down to earth under a parachute, has a burn time of about forty seconds. Read the instructions for your flare in advance so you will know how to use it when a ship or aircraft is seen. Never fire the flare above or inside the raft since burning particles might fall and burn you or damage your raft.

When using an aerial or parachute flare, you need to adjust for any drift that will be created from the wind. Since you want the flare to ignite directly overhead, point the flare slightly into the wind. Exactly how much is hard to say, but usually 5 to 10 degrees will suffice.

SIGNALS THAT PINPOINT YOUR LOCATION

Once help is on the way, handheld red signal flares, orange smoke signals, signal mirrors, kites, strobe lights, whistles, and ground-to-air signals serve as beacons to help rescuers pinpoint your position and keep them on course.

SIGNAL MIRRORS (WITH SIGHTING HOLE)

On clear, sunny days, signal mirrors have been seen as far away as 70 to 100 miles, but on average they have about a 20-mile range. Although a mirror is a great signaling device, it requires practice to become proficient

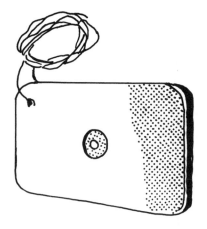

Commercial signal mirror

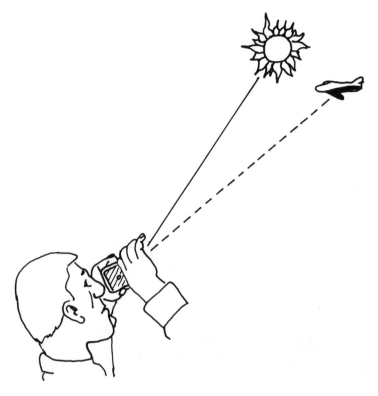

Using a signal mirror

in its use. Most signal mirrors have directions on the back, but the following steps are a general guideline on how they should be used. Holding the signal mirror between the index finger and thumb of one hand, reflect the sunlight from the mirror on to your other hand. While maintaining the sun's reflection on your free hand, bring the mirror up to eye level and look through the sighting hole. You should see a bright white or orange spot of light in the sighting hole. This is commonly called the aim indicator or fireball. Holding the mirror close to your eye, slowly turn it until the aim indicator is on your intended target. If you lose sight of the aim indicator, start over. Since the mirror can be seen from great distances, sweep the horizon periodically throughout the day even if no rescue vessel is in sight. If signaling an aircraft, stop flashing the pilot after you are certain he's spotted you, as the flash may impede his vision. On land, slightly wiggle the mirror to add movement to the signal. At sea, hold the mirror steady to contrast the sparkles created by the natural movement of the water. Since an aircraft can spot a flash long before you see the aircraft, scan the horizon on a regular basis when the sun is out.

IMPROVISED SIGNAL MIRRORS

A signal mirror can be created from anything shiny, such as a metal container, coin, credit card, watch, jewelry, or belt buckle. Although any of these make a great signaling device, you will need to practice to become proficient in using them as a signal mirror. To use an improvised signal mirror, follow these steps. While holding the device between the index finger and thumb of one hand, reflect the sunlight from the mirror onto the palm of your other hand. While keeping the reflection on that hand, create a V between your thumb and index finger. Move the light reflection and your hand until the rescuer is in the V. At this point, move the reflected light into the V and onto your intended target. If signaling an aircraft, stop

The flash of a signal mirror is an extremely effective signal.

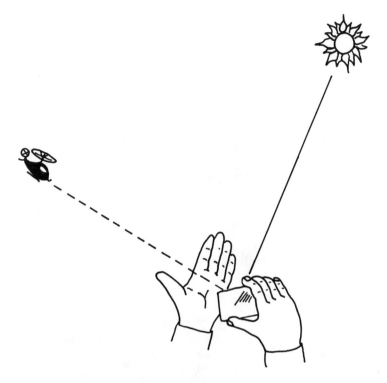

Improvised signal mirror

flashing the pilot after you are certain he's spotted you, as the flash may impede his vision. On land, slightly wiggle the mirror to add movement to the signal. At sea, hold the mirror steady to contrast the sparkles created by the natural movement of the water. Since the mirror can be seen from great distances, sweep the horizon periodically throughout the day even if no rescue vehicles are in sight.

HANDHELD RED SIGNAL FLARES

Because these signals may be used just once, they should only be lit when an aircraft or a vessel is sighted, close by, and headed in your direction. As with all pyrotechnic devices, they are flammable and should be handled with caution. To light them, stand with your back to the wind and point the device away from your face and body during and after it has been lit. Most

A smoke signal is a one-time-use item and should only be lit when rescue is sighted.

red signal flares are ignited by removing the cap and striking the ignition button with the cap's abrasive side. To avoid burns, be sure to hold the flare in its safe area and never overhead. Most devices will burn for two minutes, have a candlepower of 700, and are about the size of a road flare. On average, these signals can be seen from a range of 3 to 5 miles. Read the instructions for your flare in advance so you will know how to use it once a ship or aircraft is spotted. Always light the signal on the downwind side of your vessel while holding it slightly down and over the water. Never light it above or inside the raft since burning particles might fall and burn you or damage your raft.

ORANGE SMOKE SIGNALS

Because these signals may be used just once, they should only be lit during daylight when an aircraft or a vessel is sighted, close by, and headed in your direction. As with all pyrotechnic devices, they are flammable and should be handled with caution. The marine signal is about the size of a road flare and comes with easy-to-read directions right on the signal. To light one, stand with your back to the wind and point the device away from your face and body during and after it has been lit. Simply remove the cap and strike the ignition button with the abrasive part of the cap. To avoid burns, hold the signal in its safe area and never overhead. Most of these signals put out a lot of smoke and last between one and three minutes. Orion carries an orange floating smoke signal that floats and lasts for four minutes. Besides wind, snow, and rain, the biggest problem associated with a smoke signal is the cold air that keeps the smoke close to the ground or sometimes dissipates it before it reaches the heights needed to be seen. On average, these signals can be seen from a range of 3 to 5 miles at sea height and even farther from the air. Read the instructions in advance so you will know how to use the signal once a ship or aircraft is spotted. Always light the signal on the down-wind side of your vessel while holding it slightly down and over the water. Never light it above or inside the raft since burning particles might fall and burn you or damage your raft.

SEA MARKER DYE

These signals, which may be used just once, should only be used during daylight when an aircraft or a vessel is sighted, close by, and headed in your direction. The sea marker's yellow/green fluorescent dye comes in various sizes and works by making you appear larger in contrast to the water's natural color. The dye will last about twenty to thirty minutes in calm seas and less than that when seas are rough. From the air, the dye can be seen from as far as 10 miles away. To use, simply add the powder to the surrounding water. Avoid skin contact with the powder as it is caustic and can burn your skin. On land, the sea marker dye provides excellent contrast to snow, which makes it a great ground-to-air signal.

SEA RESCUE SIGNAL STREAMER

An option to the sea marker dye is a sea rescue signal streamer. Unlike the dye, it never runs out and can provide a constant ongoing signal that is easily seen from the air. The orange plastic floating streamer is 40 feet long and comes in various widths.

KITES

The highly visible kite not only attracts attention to your location, but it also helps rescuers pinpoint exactly where you are. David Instrument's Sky-Alert Parafoil Rescue Kite is a good example of this. The 28-inch by 38-inch kite flies in wind of 5 to 25 knots and only requires about 8 to 10 knots of wind to lift another signaling device, such as a strobe or handheld flare. A benefit of this signal is that it can be working for you while you attend to other needs.

STROBE LIGHTS

A strobe light fits in the palm of your hand and provides an ongoing intermittent flash. The Acr Electronics Personal Rescue Strobe, for example, delivers a bright flash (250,000 peak lumens) at one-second intervals and can run up to eight hours on AA batteries. The strobe is visible for up to one nautical mile on a clear night. As with all battery-operated devices, strobe lights are vulnerable to cold, moisture, sand, and heat, so you will need to protect the light from these hazards.

WHISTLES OR HORNS

A whistle will never wear out, and its sound travels farther than the screams of the most desperate survivor. In calm conditions, a whistle can be heard up to four miles away and is effective when trying to attract the attention of nearby rescuers. Storm's Whistle Storm Safety Whistle is the loudest whistle, even when soaking wet, that you can buy. It is made from plastic and has easy-to-grip ridges. You should always carry a whistle on your person. An alternative would be to carry a horn. A horn, however, uses a gas canister, and once the gas is gone, the horn is no longer useful.

IMPROVISED SIGNALS ON LAND

The same signals you can use at sea can also be used on shore. Since a lot of manufactured signals may only be used once or are limited by their battery life, you will want to augment your signals on shore with any available natural resources. A ground-to-air signal can be made from natural materials; a fire can be as effective as a red flare; and a smoke generator works better and lasts longer than an orange smoke signal.

GROUND-TO-AIR PATTERN SIGNAL

A ground-to-air signal is an extremely effective device that allows you to attend to your other needs, while continuing to alert potential rescuers of your location. Although you can use a sea rescue streamer, I suggest purchasing a 3-foot-wide by 18-foot-long piece of lightweight nylon—orange for winter and white for summer. Three basic signal designs can be made using the nylon:

V = Need assistance

X = Need medical assistance

→ = Proceed this way

Once the appropriate signal has been constructed, stake it out so that it holds its form and doesn't blow away. For optimal effect, focus on the following guidelines:

Size: The ideal signal will have a 6:1 ratio with its overall size at least 18 feet long by 3 feet wide.

Contrast: The signal should contrast with the surrounding ground cover. Orange on snow and white on brown or green are examples of how this can be accomplished.

Angularity: Because nature has no perfect lines, a signal with sharp angles will be more effective.

Shadow: In summer, elevate the signal. In winter, stomp or dig an area around the signal that is approximately 3 feet wide. If the sun is shining, both of these methods will create a shadow, which ultimately increases the signal's size.

Movement: Setting up a flag next to your signal may create enough movement to catch the attention of a rescue party. You should also suspend a flag high above your shelter so that it can be seen from all directions by potential rescuers.

If you don't have a signal panel, you can improvise a ground-to-air signal from available contrasting natural materials. In the snow, you might consider using sea marker dye to create a brilliant contrasting ground-to-air signal.

A ground-to-air signal as seen from the cockpit of a rescue helicopter

A large fire is an effective night signal.

FIRE AS A SIGNAL

During the night, fire is probably the most effective means of signaling. One large fire will suffice to alert rescue to your location. Don't waste your time, energy, and wood by building three fires in a distress triangle, unless rescue is uncertain. If the ground is covered with snow, build the fire on a snow platform to prevent the snow's moisture from putting out the fire. As with all signals, prepare the wood or other fuel for ignition prior to use.

SMOKE GENERATOR

Smoke is an effective signal if used on a clear, calm day. If the weather is bad, chances are the smoke will dissipate too quickly to be seen. The rules for a smoke signal are the same as those for a fire signal: You need only one; use a platform in snow environments; and prepare the materials for the signal in advance. To make the smoke contrast against its surroundings, add any of the following materials to your fire:

A smoke signal as seen from the cockpit of a rescue helicopter

To contrast snow: Use tires, oil, or fuel to create black smoke.

To contrast darker backgrounds: Use boughs, grass, green leaves, moss, ferns, or even a small amount of water to create white smoke.

In heavy snow or rain, you will need to set up your smoke generator in advance and protect it from the moisture. To accomplish this, I build an elevated platform by driving two 6-foot-long wrist-diameter branches 3 feet into the snow at a 10- to 20-degree angle to the ground. For best results, insert the branches in a location where the ground has a 10- to 20-degree slope, creating a level foundation for the smoke generator. Next, I place multiple wrist-diameter branches (each touching the other) on top of and perpendicular to the first two branches. In the center of my newly created surface, I build but don't light a tepee fire lay by using a lot of tinder and kindling. A log-cabin-style fire lay is then built around the tepee fire using fuel that is thumb size and larger. Be sure to leave a small quick-access opening that will allow you to reach the tinder when it comes time to light it. Finally, place a heavy bough covering over the top of the whole thing. The bough covering should be thick enough to protect the underlying structure from the snow and rain. When done, the generator should look like a haystack of boughs. Once you have been spotted and rescuers appear to be headed in your direction, light the smoke generator by gently picking up one side of the boughs. If you should have trouble getting the fire lit, use one of your red smoke flares as a heat source.

9

Drinking Water

While at sea, without the proper gear or ingenuity you'll be surrounded by water without a drop to drink.

—Aviation Survival Technician Timothy Fortney
U.S. Coast Guard Helicopter Rescue Swimmer

Water is far more important than food. You can live anywhere from three weeks to two months without food, but only days without water. Therefore, make sure you carry plenty of water and the necessary equipment to procure more.

Our bodies are composed of approximately 60 percent water, and water plays a vital role in our ability to get through a day. About 70 percent of our brains, 82 percent of our blood, and 90 percent of our lungs are composed of water. In our bloodstream, water helps to metabolize and transport vital elements, carbohydrates, and proteins that are necessary to fuel our bodies. Water also helps us dispose of our bodily waste.

During a normal nonstrenuous day, a healthy individual will need 2 to 3 quarts of water. When physically active or in an extremely hot or cold environment, that same person would need at least 4 to 6 quarts of water a day. In a cold climate, a person normally doesn't sweat or feel the need to drink until it is almost too late. When cold, the body loses fluids through the process of warming itself. Following the general rule of 4 to 6 quarts of water a day will keep the body hydrated and help to ward off hypothermia and dehydration. A person who is mildly dehydrated will develop excessive thirst and become irritable, weak, and nauseated. As the dehydration worsens, an individual will show a decrease in his or her mental capacity and coordination. At this point, it will become difficult to accomplish even the simplest of tasks. The ideal situation would dictate that you don't ration your water. Instead, you should ration sweat. However, since survival at sea requires a minimal amount of energy output, if water is scarce it may be best to decrease your intake to one quart a day. If water is not available, don't eat!

DISPELLING MYTHS ABOUT WATER

Never drink urine!

By the time you even think about drinking your urine, you are very dehydrated, and your urine would be full of salts and other waste products. For a hydrated person, urine is 95 percent water and 5 percent waste products such as urea, uric acid, and salts. As you become dehydrated, the concentration of water decreases while the concentration of salts increases substantially. When you drink these salts, the body will draw upon its water reserves to help eliminate them, and you will actually lose more water than you might gain from your urine.

Never drink salt water!

The concentration of salts in salt water is often higher than that found in urine. When you drink these salts, the body will draw upon its water reserves to help eliminate them, and you will actually lose more water than you might gain from salt water.

Never drink blood!

Blood is composed of plasma, red blood cells, white blood cells, and platelets. Plasma, which composes about 55 percent of blood's volume, is predominately water and salts, but it also carries a large number of important proteins (albumin, gamma globulin, and clotting factors) and small molecules (vitamins, minerals, nutrients, and waste products). Waste products produced during metabolism, such as urea and uric acid, are carried by the blood to the kidneys, where they are transferred from the blood into urine and eliminated from the body. The kidneys carefully maintain the salt concentration in plasma. When you drink blood, you are basically ingesting salts and proteins, and the body will draw upon its water reserves to help eliminate them. You will actually lose more water than you might gain from drinking blood.

WATER AT SEA

PACKED WATER

Packed water, which comes inside a pouch or a box, holds between ⅛ to 1 quart of water. USCG-approved packed water has a five-year shelf life. While emergency water is a great item to carry on your trip, you should also carry something that allows you to procure additional water once your emergency supply is gone. Be sure to protect the pouches and boxes of packed water so they aren't accidentally punctured. Storing them inside a hard plastic 1-quart water bottle (big-mouthed screw top) will not only protect them but will provide a container that will come in handy for storing other water that you procure. An option to the packed water would be to bring along tap water inside the hard plastic 1-quart container. The shelf life for tap water is approximately six months.

DESALTING TABLETS

One desalting tablet will desalt 1 pint of water. Salt water treated this way tastes like water obtained from a water hose that has set out in the sun all day. Desalting tablets come alone or in a kit. Kits have a plastic bag that holds about 1 pint of water and has a filter that will keep the sludge by-product from being drunk. To use, place seawater in the bag with the tablet, and wait one hour—agitating the water periodically—before drinking the water through the valve attached to the bag. If you don't have a kit, follow the same process using an available container, and be sure not to drink the sludge left at the bottom.

SOLAR STILLS

A solar still uses seawater and the sun to create drinkable water through a condensation process. Most stills are inflatable balls that allow you to pour seawater into a cup on top of the balloon. The balloon has a donut-shaped ballast ring that keeps it afloat and upright. It takes about a ½ gallon of seawater to fill the ballast. Note that the ballast ring has a fabric-covered center that must be wet before the balloon can be inflated. Additional seawater is required to fill the cup on top of the balloon, and this water provides a constant drip onto multiple cloth wicks located inside the balloon. As the outside air warms, condensation forms on the inner wall and runs down

Solar still

into a plastic container. The use of a solar still is limited to calm seas, and results will depend on temperatures. When seas are calm, stills should be put out as soon as possible even if clouds obscure the sun. For complete details on how to use these devices, read the manufacturers' directions.

REVERSE OSMOSIS WATER MAKER
Standard freshwater filters and purifiers will not desalt seawater and should not be used for this process. Instead, a reverse osmosis water maker that turns seawater into drinkable water should be part of your survival gear.

These hand-powered devices range in weight from 2 to 7 pounds and can roughly produce 6 gallons of water a day, depending on the model you have. To use, simply place the hose of the device into seawater and pull the handle. To achieve the maximum amount of water output requires a pump rate of thirty to forty times a minute. Be sure to follow the manufacturer's maintenance and use instructions, and have the system serviced accordingly.

COLLECTING PRECIPITATION

Most life rafts have canopies designed to catch rainwater. This catchment system uses gutters to funnel rainwater into a storage container inside the raft. Since salt spray has probably dried on top of the canopy, the initial water collected will probably be too contaminated to drink. Lining the gutters, when it starts to rain, with a space blanket or similar material can alleviate this problem. Contamination can also be an issue in rough seas where the wind and waves constantly splash seawater onto the canopy and raft. You can also procure rainwater by tying a piece of plastic (a space blanket or similar item) to two paddles and holding it out the raft's door in such a way as to funnel the rain into an awaiting container. Try to fill all available containers with rainwater, and drink this water before packaged water.

WATER FROM DEW

Although dew does not provide a large amount of water, it should not be overlooked as a source of water. Dew accumulates on the raft and canopy (on land, it can be found on grass, leaves, rocks, and equipment) at dawn and dusk and should be collected at those times before it freezes or evaporates. Any porous material will absorb the dew, and the moisture can be consumed by wringing the water out of the cloth and into your mouth.

ICE

As with snow, ice should be melted prior to consumption. To melt ice, add it to a partially full container of water and either shake the container or place it between layers of your clothing and allow your body's radiant heat to melt the snow. On land, you can melt ice with a fire. If using sea ice, you will want to make sure the ice is virtually free of any salts in the seawater. Sea ice that has rounded corners, shatters easily, and is bluish or black in color is usually safe to use. When in doubt, however, do a taste test. If it tastes salty, don't use it.

PROCURING WATER ON LAND

WATER INDICATORS
Once you have reached shore, water shouldn't be hard to find. Understanding water indicators created by birds, mammals, and the terrain will be helpful when trying to find water.

Birds
Birds frequently fly toward water at dawn and dusk in a direct, low flight path. This is especially true of birds, such as pigeons and finches, that feed on grain. Flesh-eating birds also exhibit this flight pattern, but their need for water isn't as great, and they don't require as many trips to the water source. Birds circling high in the air during the day are often over water.

Mammals
Like birds, mammals will frequently visit watering holes at dawn and dusk. This is especially true of mammals that eat a grain or grassy-type diet. Watching mammals' travel patterns or evaluating mammal trails may help you find a water source. Trails that merge into one usually lead to water.

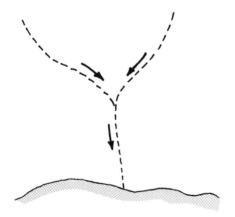

Two trails merging together often point toward water.

Land features that indicate water

Drainages, valleys, and winding trails of deciduous trees are good indicators of water. Green plush vegetation found at the base of a cliff or mountain may indicate a natural spring or underground source of water.

WATER SOURCES AND PROCUREMENT

Since your body needs a constant supply of water, you will eventually need to procure water from Mother Nature. The shore you reach may dictate your water options. Various sources include surface water, groundwater, precipitation, condensation, and plant sources.

Surface water

Surface water may be obtained from rivers, ponds, lakes, or streams. It is usually easy to find and access, but because it is prone to contamination from protozoan and bacteria, it should always be treated. If the water is difficult to access or has an unappealing flavor, consider using a seepage basin to filter the water. This filtering process is similar to what happens as groundwater moves toward an aquifer. To create a seepage basin well, dig a 3-foot-wide hole about 10 feet from your water source. Dig down until water begins to seep in the hole, and then go about another foot. Line the sides of your hole with wood or rocks so that no more mud will fall in, and let it sit overnight.

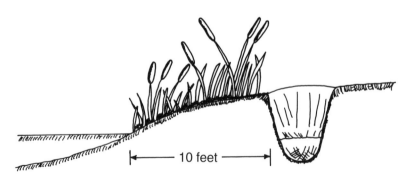

Seepage basin well

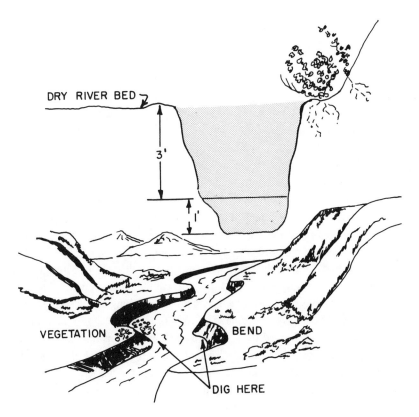

Dry riverbed water source

Groundwater

Groundwater is found under the earth's surface. This water is naturally filtered as it moves through the ground and into underground reservoirs called aquifers. Although treating this water may not be necessary, you should always err on the side of caution. Groundwater refers to water that is directly under the surface of the earth and the natural springs that push the water up to the surface. Locating groundwater is probably the most difficult part of accessing it. Look for things that seem out of place, such as a small area of green plush vegetation at the base of a hill or a bend in a dry riverbed that is surrounded by brown vegetation. A marshy area with a fair amount of cattail or hemlock growth may provide a clue that groundwater is available. Using these very clues, I have found natural springs in desert areas and running water less than 6 feet below the earth's surface. To easily access the water, I like to dig a small well at the source (see directions for seepage basin above), line the well with wood or rocks, and let it sit overnight before I begin to use the water. When close to shore, you can procure freshwater by digging a similar well one dune inland beyond the beach.

Precipitation

The three forms of precipitation are rain, snow, and dew. When it rains, you should set out containers or dig a small hole and line it with plastic or any other nonporous material to catch the rainwater. After the rain has stopped, you may find water in crevasses, fissures, or low-lying areas. Snow provides an excellent source of water but should not be eaten. The energy lost eating snow outweighs the benefit. Instead, melt snow by suspending it over a fire or adding it to a partially full canteen and then shaking the container or placing it between the layers of your clothing and allowing your body's radiant heat to melt the snow. If you are with a large group, a water generator can be fashioned from a tripod and some porous material. Create a large pouch by attaching the porous material to the tripod. Fill the pouch with snow and place the tripod just close enough to the fire to start melting the snow. Use a container to collect the melted snow. Although the water will taste a little like smoke, this method provides an ongoing large and quick supply of water. If the sun is out, try melting the snow by digging a cone-shaped hole, lining it with a tarp or similar nonporous material, and placing snow inside. As the snow melts, water will collect at the bottom of the cone. For details on sea ice and dew, see the water at sea section.

Condensation

Solar stills are a great way to procure water in hot climates. The vegetation bag and transpiration bag are two options. You could also use your seawater solar still to obtain water from the condensation process.

Vegetation bag

To construct a vegetation bag, you will need a clear plastic bag and an ample supply of healthy, nonpoisonous vegetation. A 4- to 6-foot section

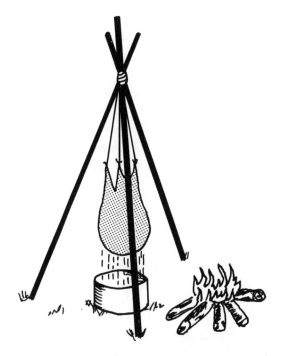

Snow water generators produce large volumes of water from snow.

of surgical tubing is also helpful. To use, open the plastic bag and fill it with air to make it easier to place the vegetation inside. Next fill the bag one-half to three-quarters full with lush green vegetation. Be careful not to puncture the bag. Place a small rock or similar item into the bag, and if you have surgical tubing, slide one end inside toward the bottom of the bag. Tie the other end in an overhand knot. Close the bag and tie it off as close to the opening as possible. Place the bag on a sunny slope so that the opening is on the downhill side slightly higher than the bag's lowest point. Position the rock and surgical tubing at the lowest point in the bag. For best results, change the vegetation every two to three days. If using surgical tubing, simply untie the knot and drink the water that has condensed in the bag. If no tubing is used, loosen the tie and drain off the available liquid. Be sure to drain off all liquid prior to sunset each day, or it will be reabsorbed into the vegetation.

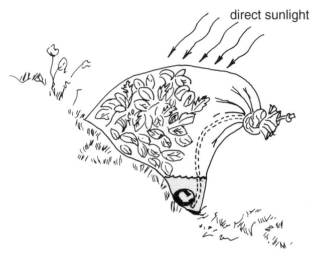

Vegetation bag

Transpiration bag

Because the same vegetation can be reused, after allowing enough time for it to rejuvenate, a transpiration bag is advantageous to a vegetation bag. To construct a transpiration bag, you will need a clear plastic bag and an accessible, nonpoisonous brush or tree. A 4- to 6-foot section of surgical tubing is also helpful. Open the plastic bag and fill it with air to make it easier to place the bag over the brush or tree. Next place the bag over the lush leafy vegetation of a tree or brush, being careful not to puncture the bag. Be sure the bag is on the side of the tree or bush with the greatest exposure to the sun. Place a small rock or similar item in the bag at its lowest point, and if you have surgical tubing, place one end at the bottom of the bag next to the rock. Tie the other end in an overhand knot. Close the bag and tie it off as close to the opening as possible. Change the bag's location every two to three days to ensure optimal outcome and to allow the previous site to rejuvenate so it might be used again later. If using surgical tubing, simply untie the knot and drink the water that has condensed in the bag. If no tubing is used, loosen the tie and drain off the available liquid. Be sure to drain off all liquid prior to sunset each day, or it will be reabsorbed into the tree or bush.

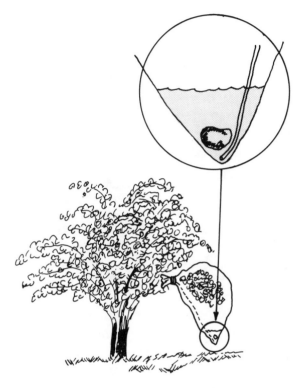

Transpiration bag

Vegetation

Depending on the type of jungle and time of year, tropical coastlines provide an abundant source of water from vegetation. Plants and trees with hollow portions or leaves that overlap, such as air plants and bamboo, often collect rainwater in these natural receptacles. Other options include water vines, banana trees, and coconuts.

Water vines

Water vines range from 1 to 6 inches in diameter, are relatively long, and usually grow along the ground and up the sides of trees. Not all water vines provide drinkable water. Avoid water vines that have a white sap when nicked, provide a cloudy milk-like liquid when cut, or produce liquids that

The initial water from a banana tree will be very bitter and should be avoided.

taste sour or bitter. Nonpoisonous vines will provide a clear fluid that often has a woody or sweet taste. To collect the water, cut the top of the vine first and then cut the bottom, letting the liquid drain into a container. If you plan to drink the water directly from the vine, avoid direct contact between your lips and the outer vine as an irritation sometimes results.

Banana trees

Banana trees, which are common in tropical rain forests, can be made into an almost unending water source by cutting them in half with a knife or machete, about 3 inches from the ground. Next, carve a bowl into the top surface of the trunk. Water will almost immediately fill the bowl, but don't drink it. This initial water will be bitter and upsetting to your stomach. Scoop the water completely out of the bowl three times before consuming.

Coconuts

Green unripe coconuts about the size of grapefruits provide an excellent source of water. Once coconuts mature, however, they contain an oil, which, if consumed in large quantities, can cause upset stomach and diarrhea. If you do not have a knife, accessing the liquid in coconuts presents the greatest challenge.

NATURAL WATER FILTRATION

Filtration systems do not purify water! At best, they remove unwanted particles and make the water more palatable. A seepage basin is one method of filtering water, but it may not always take away the awful taste of the water. You also could try a layered filtering device that uses grass, sand, and charcoal. Not only does running water through grass, sand, and black charcoal remove unwanted particles, but it also makes the water taste better. To create this system, either use a three-tiered tripod design or layer the materials inside a container that allows the water to pass through. I have seen large coffee cans used in this design. For a three-tiered tripod, tie three sections of porous material about 1 foot apart and fill each with grass, sand, and charcoal from top to bottom, respectively. Then simply pour water into the top, and catch it after it filters through and departs at the bottom.

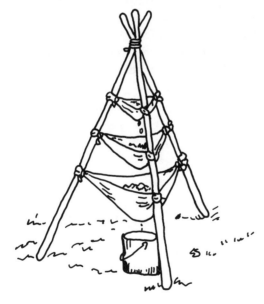

Three-tiered tripod

PURIFYING WATER

According to the Centers for Disease Control (CDC), water contaminated with microorganisms will cause over 1 million illnesses and 1,000 deaths in the United States each year. The primary pathogens (disease-causing organisms) fall into three categories: protozoans (including cysts), bacteria, and viruses.

Protozoans

A protozoan is a one-celled organism that varies in size from 2 to 100 microns, lives in many insects and animals, and survives in cysts (protective shells) when outside of an organism. *Giardia* and *Cryptosporidium* are included in the family. It only takes a few organisms to infect someone, and once inside a host, protozoans will rapidly reproduce and cause severe diarrhea, abdominal cramps, bloating, fatigue, and weight loss. *Giardia* is the main culprit here. *Cryptosporidium* rarely cause symptoms in a healthy individual.

Bacteria

Much smaller than protozoans, bacteria can be as tiny as 0.2 microns. Some examples include typhoid, paratyphoid, dysentery, and cholera. Bacteria are often present in both wild and domestic animals, and once in water, bacteria can survive for weeks or even longer if frozen in ice.

Viruses

A virus can be as small as 0.004 microns, which makes it easy for a virus to pass through a filter. Viruses found in water include hepatitis A and E, Norwalk virus, rotavirus, echovirus, and poliovirus. Unlike protozoans and bacteria, there is no treatment for a waterborne viral infection, which makes viruses a significant health risk, especially for people who have a compromised immune system.

Other potential risks found in water include disinfectants and its byproducts, inorganic chemicals, organic chemicals, and radionuclides. The three basic methods for treating your water are boiling, chemical treatments, and commercial filtration systems.

Boiling

To kill any disease-causing microorganisms that might be in your water, the Environmental Protection Agency's (EPA) Office of Water advocates vigorously boiling water for one minute. After seeing a friend lose about 40 pounds from a severe case of giardiasis, however, I almost always boil my water longer. Boiling water is far superior to chemically treating your water and should be done whenever possible.

Chemical treatment

When unable to boil your water, you may elect to use chlorine or iodine. These chemicals are effective against bacteria, viruses, and *Giardia,* although the EPA questions their ability to protect you against *Cryptosporidium.* In fact, the EPA advises against using chemicals to purify surface water, but you decide. Chlorine is preferred over iodine since it seems to offer better protection against *Giardia.* Both chlorine and iodine tend to be less effective in cold water.

Chlorine

The amount of chlorine you should use to purify water will depend upon the amount of available chlorine in the solution. This usually can be found on the label.

Available Chlorine	Drops per Quart of Clear Water
1%	10 drops
4–6%	2 drops
7–10%	1 drop
Unknown	10 drops

If the water is cloudy or colored, double the normal amount of chlorine required for the percentage used. Once the chlorine is added, wait three minutes and then vigorously shake the water with the cap slightly loose, allowing some water to weep out through the seams. Seal the cap on the container, and wait another twenty-five to thirty minutes before loosening the cap and shaking it again. At this point, consider the water safe to consume as long as the water does not contain *Cryptosporidium.*

Iodine

The two types of iodine commonly used to treat water are tincture and tablets. Tincture is nothing more than common household iodine that you may have in your medical kit. This product is usually a 2 percent iodine solution, and you will need to add five drops to each quart of water. For cloudy water, double the amount. The treated water should be mixed and allowed to stand for thirty minutes before used. If using iodine tablets, you should place one tablet per quart when the water is warm and two tablets per quart when the water is cold or cloudy. Each bottle of iodine tablets should include instructions for how to mix the tablets with the water and how long you should wait before drinking the water. If no directions are available, wait three minutes and then vigorously shake the water with the cap slightly loose, allowing some water to seep out through the seams. Seal the cap on the container, and wait another twenty-five to thirty minutes before loosening the cap and shaking it again. At this point, consider the water safe to consume as long as the water does not contain *Cryptosporidium.*

Commercial purifying systems

A filter is not a purifying system. In general, filters remove protozoans; microfilters remove protozoans and bacteria; and purifiers remove protozoans, bacteria, and viruses. Purifiers are simply a microfilter with iodine and a carbon element added. The iodine kills viruses, and the carbon element removes the iodine taste and reduces organic chemical contaminants, such as pesticides, herbicides, and chlorine, and heavy metals. Unlike filters, purifiers must be registered with the U.S. Environmental Protection Agency to demonstrate effectiveness against waterborne pathogens, protozoans, bacteria, and viruses. A purifier costs more than a filter. You must decide what level of risk you are willing to take as waterborne viruses are becoming more prominent. On the downside, a purifier tends to clog more quickly than most filters. Also, a purifying system can freeze, expand, and crack in subfreezing temperatures, so make sure you protect it as much as possible. To increase the longevity of your system, you should observe the following guidelines. Keep in mind that these guidelines should in no way supersede the recommendations of the manufacturer.

Cleaning

Clean, scrub, and disinfect the filter, according to the manufacturer's guidelines, after each use. Note that some filters should not be scrubbed and some are self-cleaning.

Use clean water

Obtain your water from a clean source, such as a creek's pool or similar area. To avoid sand, mud, and debris, keep the suction hose away from the bottom of the water. You may want to use a foam float for this.

If muddy water is your only choice

Fill a clean container with the muddy water, and let it sit for several hours (overnight if time permits) or until the sediment has settled to the bottom of the container. You could also run the water through an improvised filter (covered earlier in this chapter).

Backwash the filter

Backwash the filter according to the manufacturer's recommended schedule to remove any accumulated debris from the system.

Purifiers come in a pump or a ready-to-drink bottle design.

Pump purifiers

Probably the best-known pump purifiers are made by PUR Explorer. An ideal system for the wilderness traveler, this purifying system protects against protozoans, bacteria, and viruses. The Explorer is an easy-to-use, high-output, self-cleaning system that weighs 20 ounces. Its 0.3-micron filtering cartridge can produce up to 1.5 liters of water per minute and under normal conditions will not have to be replaced until after providing around 100 gallons (400 liters) of drinkable water. Follow the manufacturer's guidelines for maintaining your pump filter.

Bottle Purifiers

Probably the best-known bottle filter is the 34-ounce Exstream Mackenzie, an ideal system for the wilderness traveler. It protects against protozoans, bacteria, and viruses. The benefit of a bottle purifier is its ease of use:

Simply fill the bottle with water according to the manufacturer's directions and start drinking. The filter requires no assembly or extra space in your pack. However, it only filters about 26 gallons (100 liters) before the cartridge must be replaced. Unless you carry several bottle filters, you will need to be in an area with multiple water sources throughout your travel. Maintenance of these systems is simple. When not in use, allow the cartridge to completely dry before storing. Before resuming use, flush the system several times with tap water.

10

Food

Whether in the ocean or on an outdoor adventure, you should always carry an ample supply of food. Although not a high survival priority, it provides valuable energy that's needed in a survival setting.

—Aviation Survival Technician Ty K Aweau
U.S. Coast Guard Helicopter Rescue Swimmer

A BODY NEEDS FOOD

Although your need for food isn't high while you are in a survival craft, having food helps to decrease your stress. Initial food sources will probably come from rations in your survival kit, but these won't last long, and although you can live a long time without food—perhaps a month or more—you'll eventually want some. Finding food will be easier than you thought, but don't eat it unless you have at least one pint (½ quart) of water a day. Obviously, a varied diet that supplies you with a sampling from the various food groups is best but not always practical. The ideal diet has foods from the five basic food groups:

1. Carbohydrates. This easily digested food provides rapid energy and is most often found in fruits, vegetables, and whole grains.
2. Protein. This helps with the building of body cells and is most often found in fish, meat, poultry, and blood.
3. Fats. This slowly digested food provides long-lasting energy that your body usually uses once carbohydrates in the diet are gone. Fats are most often found in butter, cheese, oils, nuts, eggs, and animal fats. Natives in cold environments often eat fats before going to bed because they believe it will help keep them warm throughout the night.

4. Vitamins. Vitamins provide no calories but aid in the body's daily function and growth. Vitamins are found in most foods, and when you maintain a well-balanced diet, you will rarely become depleted. It's a good idea to include vitamins in your survival kit and to take them daily since food procured at sea will not meet your vitamin needs.

5. Minerals. Minerals provide no calories but aid with building and repairing the skeletal system and regulating the body's normal growth. Just as with vitamins, the need for minerals is met when a well-balanced diet is eaten. Minerals also are often present in water.

FOOD AT SEA

You should be able to procure enough food while at sea to sustain your life for an extended period of time. As long as water is available, chow down.

PLANTS

Seaweed, which is easily found in all oceans, is a good source of protein, fiber, vitamins, and minerals. Although a small percentage of the slender-branching seaweeds can cause an upset stomach, most are edible. The broad-leaved seaweed, which looks like lettuce leaf, is not known to cause

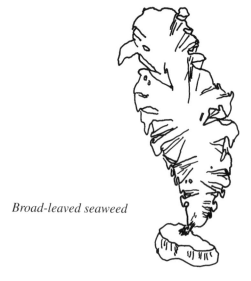

Broad-leaved seaweed

irritation and can often be found floating in the ocean. These floating islands of seaweed also provide a haven for small fish and crabs, which can be easily dislodged with a good shake. Seaweed should be rinsed, as long as you have enough freshwater, and may be eaten raw or dried until crisp.

PLANKTON

Plankton is a term used for an assortment of marine and freshwater organisms that drift on or near the surface of the water. Since these organisms are too small to swim, their movement depends largely on tides, currents, and winds. Although plankton is more common near land, it can be found anywhere. There are three types of plankton:

- Phytoplankton—microscopic plants and bacteria
- Zooplankton—microscopic animals
- Macrozooplankton—larger fish eggs and larvae and pelagic invertebrates

All types of plankton are high in protein, carbohydrates, and fats and should not be overlooked as a food source. Since they are located close to the water's surface, catching plankton is as simple as towing a net behind the raft. For best results, the net should be moving faster than the current. Plankton has a grayish paste-like appearance and, depending on the source, can take on a multitude of flavors. It can be eaten fresh or dried and crushed. Crushing is a good option if a lot of spines are noted in the fresh plankton.

During warm seasons, various forms of phytoplankton produce toxins (secondary to their rapid reproduction and large numbers) that lead to a change in water color called "red tide." The toxins are harmful to both marine and human life, and many are quite potent and can be potentially fatal. In most instances, it is safe to eat fish, crabs, and shrimp during a red tide as long as you didn't find the fish sick or dead and you only eat the meat (fillet or muscle). Shellfish (oysters, clams, mussels, whelks, scallops, etc.) accumulate red tide toxins in their tissues. Do not eat these during or within a month of red tide. Ingesting these toxins can lead to paralytic shellfish poisoning, which can be a life-threatening illness. Better safe than sorry: Avoid eating fish or shellfish during red tide.

BARNACLES

Given enough time, barnacles will appear on the bottom of your raft. Although they have a shell-like covering and look like mollusks, barnacles are crustaceans (related to lobsters, crabs, and shrimp). Newborn barnacles feed on plankton and in their larval stage look like tiny shrimp. As they grow, they let the currents carry them while they look for a place to build their shell-like home. If the life raft seems suitable, and it will, the barnacle secures itself to the surface using a self-made glue-like substance and then builds its home. Since they attach to the bottom of the raft, they are difficult to harvest and could actually result in raft damage. The best way to avoid this is to float sheet plastic around the raft. Barnacles will attach to the plastic, which makes them much easier to access. The plastic will also serve as a shark rub, reducing any potential problems related to sharks rubbing up against the side of the raft.

TURTLES

Turtles are found in water throughout the temperate and tropic regions of the world. Of the more than 250 species of marine turtles, only about 5 are considered poisonous. Although the cause of their potentially fatal poison is unknown, many believe it is related to their ingestion of poisonous marine algae. Poisonous turtles are primarily found in the tropical and subtropical seas, especially in the warmer months. Almost 50 percent of those who eat this poison will die, and there is no way to tell if a turtle is poisonous or not. If you decide to throw caution to the wind and eat a turtle, never eat the liver since it has a high concentration of vitamin A, which poses a risk to you. The smaller turtles can be clubbed or perhaps caught with fishing line. To eat the turtle, you must remove the shell, which can be done from its belly side. Don't discard the shell as it will provide for many improvising needs.

FISH

Because fish are commonly found in almost all sources of water, you should put out lines to catch them. Be sure you have an assortment of fishing tackle in your survival kit.

Edibility of fish

Most fish are edible, but not all are! As a general rule, deep-water fish are usually not poisonous. However, you can catch toxic fish in deep water, so you have no guarantee. To help decrease your chances of ingesting a poisonous fish, know these basic rules:

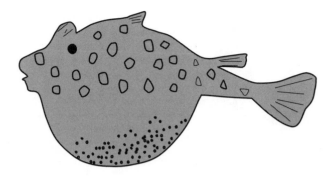

Puffer fish are poisonous.

1. Fish with poisonous flesh commonly have bodies with a boxed or round appearance, hard shell-like skin, and bony plates or spines. They also often have small parrot-like mouths, small gills, and small or absent belly fins. (See illustration.)
2. Barracuda and red snapper have been known to carry ciguatera, which although poisonous to humans is usually not fatal. It is caused by eating fish that have accumulated these toxins through their diet. Fish that live around shallow waters or lagoons pose the greatest risk. The toxins originate from several dinoflagellate (algae) species, which are known to cause red tides.
3. Avoid fish that have slimy bodies, bad odor, suspicious color (gills should be pink and scales pronounced), and flesh that remains indented after being pressed on.
4. Do not eat fish organs as many are poisonous.
5. Avoid fish during or around red tide!

Catching fish

The world is covered with water, and fish as a food source should not be overlooked. If you have fishing tackle, use it. You should pack a tackle kit. The ideal kit should include the following:

- Hooks varying in size from 1/0 to 8. The more the better! Also, buy several large barbed hooks to use with an improvised gaff.
- Line varying in size from 20 to 100. Again, the more the better! Carry at least 200 yards.

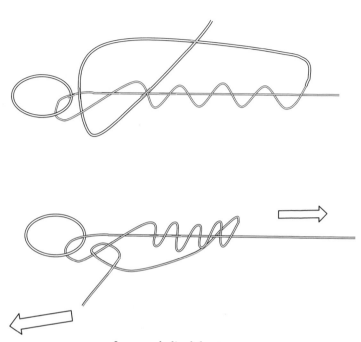

Improved clinch knot

- Sinkers and swivels in various sizes.
- Spinners, spoons, and lures in various sizes and designs.
- Lucky Luras, which are premade systems consisting of line with several small hooks and yarn (or plastic) that can be used to catch several small fish at the same time.
- Wire, which can be used for various improvised tasks and should be included in any fishing kit.
- A 1-inch-diameter dowel 3 to 4 feet long that can be used to improvise a gaff or spear.

An improved clinch knot can be used to attach line to a standard hook, safety pin, or fixed loop, using the following instructions:

1. Run the free end of the line through the hook's eye and fold it back onto itself.
2. Wrap the free end of the line up and around the line six or seven times.
3. Run the line's free end down and through the newly formed loop that is just above the hook's eye.

4. Finally, run the line through the loop formed between the two lines that are twisted together and the free end that just went though the loop next to the hook's eye.
5. Moisten the knot and pull it tight. Cut the excess line.

If you have line but no hooks, you might improvise a hook from plastic or wood. The three most commonly used improvised hooks are the skewer, cross hook, and safety pin.

Skewer hook

A skewer hood is a sliver of wood or plastic that is notched and tied at the middle. When baited, this hook is turned parallel to the line, making it easier for the fish to swallow. Once the fish takes the bait, a simple tug on the line will turn the skewer sideways, lodging it in the fish's mouth.

Shank hook

A shank hook is made by carving a piece of wood or plastic until it takes on the shape of a hook that is notched and tied at the top. When the fish swallows the hook, a gentle tug on the line will set it by causing the hook end to lodge in the throat of the fish.

Safety pin hook

A safety pin can be manipulated to create a hook, as shown in the following diagram. Depending on the size of the safety pin, this system can catch fish of various sizes and is a good improvised hook option.

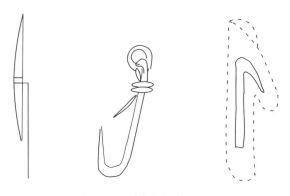

Improvised fish hooks

Fishing tips

Never wrap the fishing line to your hands or the raft. Ideally, you should wrap the line around a round container or piece of wood, which will protect your hands from cuts and also keep the line organized and untangled. Use small spinners, spoons, lures, and hooks to catch bait (or perhaps a small meal) and your bigger devices for the larger fish in the area. I advise against trying to catch a shark. Protect the floor of the raft from your gear and fish with sharp fins. Be cautious when using sharp items. As long as sharks aren't around, fish day and night.

Eating fish

Don't eat fish unless you have at least 1 pint (½ quart) of water available. To prevent spoilage, prepare the fish as soon as possible. Gut the fish by cutting up its abdomen and then removing the intestines and large blood vessels (kidney) that lie next to the backbone. Remove the gills and, when applicable, scale or skin the fish. For bigger fish, you may want to fillet the meat off of the bone. To do this, cut behind the fish's gill plates on each side of its

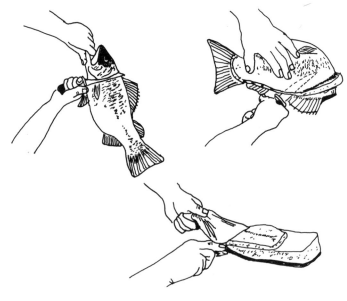

Filleting a fish

head, and slide the knife under the meat next to the backbone. Keeping the knife firmly placed against the backbone, begin slicing toward the tail. Next, hold the tail's skin and slide the knife between the skin and meat, cutting forward using a slight sawing motion. If you cannot eat all the fish at once and the weather is warm, cut the fish meat into thin, narrow strips and hang them to dry. Drying the meat should keep it edible for a couple of days. Dark meat, however, is prone to rapid spoilage, and leftover dark fish meat should be used only for bait. Don't throw spoiled meat or guts overboard when sharks are near your raft as this may encourage them to stay. If you have no other options, then do it at night.

BIRDS

Almost all birds are edible. It is not uncommon for seabirds to land on your vessel, and if you act quickly enough, you should be able to club or catch them. You may also want to try using a baited hook that trolls on top of the water. A caught bird will thrash around and thus should be killed as soon as possible. Wringing its neck will do the trick. Then cut the head off close to the body. Although plucking birds is usually preferred to skinning them, seabirds should be skinned. To gut the bird, cut open the chest and abdominal cavity and remove the insides. Don't eat the intestines of seabirds. Instead, save them for bait. Seabirds can be eaten raw.

FOOD ON SHORE

PLANTS

More than 300,000 species of plants can be found on the earth's surface. With this in mind, it seems logical that plants can provide a major source of your diet while on shore. If food is scarce and you don't have any plant references, you can perform the universal edibility test, but only use this under the most extreme conditions when survival doesn't seem imminent.

Universal edibility test

General rules of the edibility test
1. Ensure there's an abundant supply of the plant.
2. Use only fresh vegetation.

3. Always wash your plants with treated water.
4. Only perform the test on one plant or plant part at a time.
5. During the test, don't consume anything else other than purified water.
6. Don't eat for eight hours prior to starting the test.

Identifying characteristics of plants to avoid
These are general guidelines only; there are always exceptions.
1. Mushrooms or mushroom-like appearance.
2. Umbrella-shaped flower clusters that resemble parsley, parsnip, or dill.
3. Plants with milky sap or sap that turns black when exposed to the air.
4. Bulbs that resemble onion or garlic.
5. Carrot-like leaves, roots, or tubers.

Six characteristics of plants to avoid

6. Plants that are bean and pea-like in appearance.
7. Plants with fungal infection, which is common in spoiled plants procured off the ground.
8. Plants with shiny leaves or fine hairs.

To test a plant

1. Break the plant into its basic components: leaves, stems, roots, buds, and flowers.
2. Test only one part of the potential food source at a time.
3. Smell the plant for strong or acid-like odors. If present, it may be best to select another plant.
4. Prepare the plant part in the fashion (raw, boiled, baked) in which you intend to consume it.
5. Place a piece of the plant part being tested on the inside of your wrist for fifteen minutes. Monitor for burning, stinging, or irritation. If any of these occur, discontinue the test, select another plant or another component of the plant, and start over.
6. Hold a small portion (about a teaspoon) of the plant to your lips, and monitor for five minutes. If any burning or irritation occurs, discontinue the test, select another plant or another component of the plant, and start over.
7. Place the plant on your tongue and hold it there for fifteen minutes. Do not swallow any of the plant juices. If any burning or irritation occurs, discontinue the test, select another plant or another component of the plant, and start over.
8. Thoroughly chew the teaspoon portion of the plant part for fifteen minutes. Do not swallow any of the plant or its juices. If you experience a reaction, discontinue the test, select another plant or another component of the plant, and start over.
9. If you experienced no burning, stinging, or irritation, swallow the plant. Wait eight hours while you monitor for cramps, nausea, vomiting, or other abdominal irritations. If any occur, induce vomiting and drink plenty of water. If you do experience a reaction, discontinue the test, select another plant or another component of the plant, and start over.
10. If you experience no problems, eat 1 cup of the plant, prepared in the same fashion as before. Wait another eight hours. If no ill effects

occur, the plant part is edible when prepared in the same fashion as tested.

11. Test all parts of the plant you intend to use. Some plants have both edible and poisonous sections. Do not assume that a plant part that is edible when cooked is edible when raw or vice versa. Always eat the plant in the same fashion in which the edibility test was performed on it.

12. If a plant is determined to be edible, eat it in moderation. Although considered safe, large amounts of one plant may cause cramps and diarrhea.

The berry rule

In general, the edibility of berries can be classified according to their color and composition. The following is a guideline to help you determine if a berry is poisonous, but in no way should the berry rule replace the edibility test. Use the berry rule as a general guide first to determine whether to perform the edibility test. The only berries that should be eaten without testing are those that you can positively identify as nonpoisonous.

1. Green, yellow, and white berries are 10 percent edible.
2. Red berries are 50 percent edible.
3. Purple, blue, and black berries are 90 percent edible.
4. Aggregate berries, such as thimbleberries, raspberries, and blackberries, are considered 99 percent edible.

Edible parts of a plant

Some plants are completely edible, whereas others have both edible and poisonous parts. Unless you have performed the edibility test on the entire plant, only eat the parts that you know are edible. A plant can be broken down into several distinct components: underground, stems and leaves, flowers, fruits, nuts, and seeds and grains. Some plants also provide gums, resins, and saps that are edible.

Underground (tubers, roots and rootstalks, and bulbs)

Found underground, these plant parts have a high degree of starch and are best served baked or boiled. Some examples include potatoes (tuber), cattail (root and rootstalk), and wild onion (bulbs).

Aggregate berries are 99 percent edible.

Stems and leaves (shoots/stems, leaves, pith, and cambium)
Plants that produce stems and leaves are probably the most abundant source
of edible vegetation in the world. Their high-vitamin content makes them a
valuable component to our daily diet.

Shoots grow like asparagus and taste best when parboiled (boiled five
minutes, drained, and boiled again until done). Some examples of these
would be bracken fern, which should only be eaten in moderation, young
bamboo, and cattail. Leaves may be eaten raw or cooked but have the highest nutritional value when eaten raw. Dock, plantain, amarath, and sorrel
are a few examples of edible leaves. Pith, which is found inside the stem of
some plants, is often very high in its food value. Some examples are sago,
rattan, coconut, and sugar. Cambium is the inner bark found between the
bark and the wood of a tree. It can be eaten raw, cooked, or dried and then
pulverized into flour.

Flowers (flowers, buds, and pollens)
Flowers, buds, and pollens are high in food value and taste best when eaten
raw or in a salad. Some examples include hibiscus (flower), rosehips (buds),
and cattail (pollen).

Fruits (sweet and nonsweet)

Fruits are the seed bearing part of a plant and can be found in all areas of the world. Fruits retain all of their nutritional value when eaten raw, but may also be cooked. Examples of sweet fruits are apples, prickly pear, huckleberries, and wild strawberries. Examples of nonsweet fruits include tomatoes, cucumber, and plantain.

Nuts

Nuts, which are high in fat and protein, can be found around the entire world. Most can be eaten raw, but some, such as acorns, require leaching with several changes of water to remove their tannic acid content.

Seeds and grains

The seeds and grains of many fruits are a valuable food resource and should not be overlooked. Grasses and millet are best eaten when grounded into flour or roasted. Purple or black grass seeds should not be eaten as they often contain a fungal contamination that can make you very sick.

Gums and resins

Gums and resins are sap that collects on the outside of trees and plants. Their high nutritional value makes them a great addition to any meal. Examples can be found on pine and maple trees.

Plants are an abundant food source that should be a major part of your daily diet. However, if you do not know if a plant is edible, don't eat it until you either positively identify it or perform an edibility test on one or all of its various parts. Become familiar with plants indigenous to your area.

BUGS

In many cultures around the world, people eat bugs as part of their routine diet. Our phobia about eating bugs is unfortunate since they provide ample amounts of protein, fats, carbohydrates, calcium, and iron. A study done by Jared Ostrem and John VanDyk for the Entomology Department of Iowa State University compared lean ground beef and fish to certain bugs and found the following results:

	Protein (g)	Fats (g)	Carbohydrates (g)	Calcium (mg)	Iron (mg)
Crickets	12.9	5.5	5.1	75.8	9.5
Small grasshoppers	20.6	6.1	3.9	35.2	5
Giant water beetles	19.8	8.3	2.1	43.5	13.6
Red ants	13.9	3.5	2.9	47.8	5.7
Silk worm pupae	9.6	5.6	2.3	41.7	1.8
Termites	14.2	N/A	N/A	0.050	35.5
Weevils	6.7	N/A	N/A	0.186	13.1
For Comparison					
Lean ground beef (baked)	24.0	18.0	0	9.0	2.09
Fish (broiled cod)	22.95	0.8	0	0.031	1.0

Bugs are found throughout the world and are easy to catch. In addition, the larvae and grubs of many bugs are edible and easily found in rotten logs, under the ground, or under the bark of dead trees. Although a fair number of bugs can be eaten raw, it is best to cook them to avoid the ingestion of unwanted parasites. As a general rule, avoid bugs that may carry disease (flies, mosquitoes, and ticks), poisonous insects (centipedes and spiders), and bugs that have fine hair, bright colors, and eight or more legs.

Bugs are a great source of food.

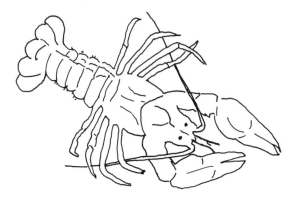

Crustaceans are a great source of food but in some instances can be poisonous.

CRUSTACEANS
Freshwater and saltwater crabs, crayfish, lobster, shrimp, and prawns are all forms of crustaceans. Although all crustaceans are edible, many freshwater crustaceans carry parasites and should be cooked first.

Freshwater shrimp
Freshwater shrimp are abundant in most tropical streams, especially where the water is sluggish. They can be seen swimming or clinging to branches and are easily caught with a scoop net or your hand.

Saltwater shrimp
Saltwater shrimp live on or near the sea bottom. Since these shrimp are attracted to light, hunt them during a full moon or lure them to the water's surface with a flashlight. Once you spot the shrimp, simply scoop them up with a net or pluck them from the water with your hand.

Freshwater crabs and crayfish
Freshwater crabs and crayfish are found on moss beds and under rocks and brush at the bottom of streams or swimming in a stream's shallow water. Since they are nocturnal, they are easier to spot at night and can be caught by hand or with a scoop net. To catch during the day, use a lobster trap

or baited hook. To improvise a lobster trap, securely place bait to the inside bottom of a container the size of a large coffee can. If using a can, puncture small holes in its bottom so that water can pass through it. Punch the holes from outside to inside to decrease the chance of cutting yourself on the sharp points. Attach enough line to the trap's sides to lower and raise it from the stream's bottom. Once the trap is placed, it won't be long before the crab or crayfish crawls inside to eat the bait. Therefore, you should check the trap often. When pulling the container from the water, do it swiftly but with enough control to avoid pouring out your dinner.

Saltwater crayfish and lobster
Saltwater crayfish and lobster are found on the bottom of the ocean in 10 to 30 feet of water. These crustaceans behave similar to freshwater crabs and crayfish and can be caught using the same techniques. If you find yourself on land next to a tropical reef, avoid saltwater crabs as many are poisonous.

MOLLUSKS
Mollusks provide an almost never-ending food source. However, they should be avoided during the warm months of April to October, when they accumulate certain poisons that can be harmful to humans. You should also avoid marine shellfish that is not covered by water at high tide. The most common types of mollusks are freshwater and saltwater shellfish: bivalves—those with two shells, such as clams, oysters, scallops, and mussels—and river and sea snails, freshwater periwinkles, limpets, and chitons. All can be boiled, steamed, or baked.

Mollusks are easy to catch during low tide.

Freshwater mollusks

Freshwater mollusks, which include some bivalves, river snails, and periwinkles, are easily caught. Bivalves are found worldwide under all water conditions, while river snails and freshwater periwinkles are most plentiful in the rivers, streams, and lakes of the northern coniferous forests.

Saltwater mollusks

Mussels, chitons, sea snails, and limpets are seawater mollusks that are easily caught at low tide. They can be found in dense colonies on rocks and logs above the surf line.

FISH

Fish are found in almost all sources of water.

When and where to fish

The best time to fish is just before dawn or just after dusk, at night when the moon is full, and when bad weather is imminent. Fish tend to be close to banks and shallow water in the morning and evening hours. They also can be found in calm deep pools, especially where it transitions from ripples to calm or calm to ripples; under outcroppings and overhanging undercuts, brush, or logs; in eddies below rocks or logs; and at the mouth of an intersection with another stream. To decrease your odds of catching a poisonous fish when fishing in salt water, avoid shallow lagoons with sandy or broken coral bottoms and the leeward side of an area (sheltered from the wind). These locations tend to house reef-feeding fish, and some may be poisonous. You should also avoid fishing in areas where the water is an unnatural color, indicating a red tide. Fish or shellfish in red tides contain a poison that is harmful to humans. If you have the option, fish on the lee (windward) side of your location and try to find a place with deep open water (usually found where the open sea enters a lagoon). Fish in deep water are often considered safe, but those in the lagoon are not. If you catch a fish and are not sure of whether it came from the reef or the deep open water, don't eat it. Also avoid fish with slimy bodies, bad odor, suspicious color (gills should be pink and scales pronounced), or flesh that remains indented after being pressed on. Various methods of catching fish are covered below.

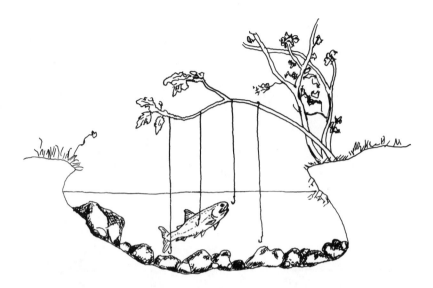

Fishing with multiple lines increases your chances of success.

Fishing tackle

The world is covered with water, and fish as a food source should not be overlooked. If you have fishing tackle, use it. If you don't, you will have to improvise. See the open-water section above for more information on fishing tackle and its use. If you can, set out multiple lines and tend to other duties while checking the lines from time to time.

Gill net

The gill net is a very effective way to catch fish. Because it will work for you while you tend to other needs, a gill net is an excellent thing to pack for your trip. If you have parachute cord or a similar material, its inner core provides an ideal material for making a net. Other options are braided stinging nettle, milkweed, and dogbane line. To keep the net clear of debris, place it at a slight angle to the current, using stones to anchor the bottom and wood to help the top float. Use the following steps to make a gill net:

1. Tie a piece of line between two trees at eye height. The bigger the net you want, the farther apart the trees should be.

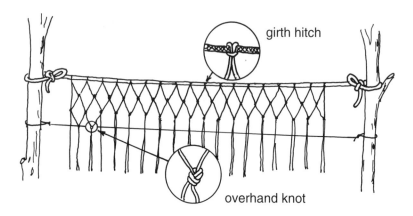

girth hitch

overhand knot

Constructing a gill net

Gill net placement

2. Using a girth hitch, tie the center of your inner core line or other material to the upper cord. Use an even number of lines. Be sure to space each line at a distance equal to the width you want for your net's mesh. For creeks and small rivers, 1 inch is about right.

3. No matter which side you start on, skip the line closest to the tree. Tie the second and third lines together with an overhand knot, and continue on down the line, tying together the fourth and fifth, sixth and seventh, etc. When you reach the end, there should be one line left.

4. Moving in the opposite direction, tie the first line to the second, the third to the fourth, etc. When you reach the end, there shouldn't be any lines left.

5. Repeat the last two steps until done.

6. If you are concerned about the mesh size, tie a guideline between the two trees. For a 1-inch mesh, tie the line 1 inch below the top and use it to determine where the overhand knots should be placed. Once a line is completed, it is moved down another inch and so on.

7. When done, run the parachute line or other material along the net's sides and bottom to help stabilize it.

Scoop net

To make a scoop net, find a 6-foot sapling and bend the two ends together to form a circle. You can also use a forked branch and form a circle with the forked ends. Allow some extra length for a handle, and lash the ends together. The net's mesh can be made in the same method as described for building a gill net by tying the initial girth hitch to the sapling. Once you have the appropriate size, tie all the lines together using an overhand knot and trim off any excess line. A net should be used in shallow water or a similar area where fish are visible. Because of the difference in light refraction above and below the water, be sure to place the net into the water to obtain proper alignment. Next, slowly move the net as close to the fish as possible, and allow them to become accustomed to it. When ready, scoop the fish up and out of the water.

Spears

To make a straight spear, find a long, straight sapling and sharpen one end to a barbed point. If you can, fire-harden the tip to make it more durable by

Wooden forked spear

holding it a few inches above a hot bed of coals until it is brown. To make a forked spear, find a long straight sapling and fire-harden the tip. Snuggly lash a line around the stick 6 to 8 inches down from one end. To keep the two halves apart, lash a small wedge between them. (For best results, secure the wedge as far down the shaft as possible.) Sharpen the two prongs into inward pointing barbs. A throwing spear should be between 5 and 6 feet long.

To throw a spear, hold it in your hand, and raise it above your shoulder so that the spear is parallel to the ground. Be sure to position your hand at the spear's center point of balance. Place your body so that the foot opposite your throwing hand is forward and your trunk is perpendicular to the target. Point your other arm and hand toward the fish or animal to help guide you when throwing the spear. Once positioned, thrust your arm forward, releasing the spear at the moment that will best enable you to strike the animal in the chest or heart.

Using a spear to catch fish is time-consuming and challenging but, under the right circumstances, can yield a tasty supper. When using a spear, compensate for the difference in light refraction above and below the water's surface. To obtain proper alignment, you will need to place the spear tip into the water before aiming. Moving the spear tip slowly will allow the fish to become accustomed to it until you are ready to release the spear. Once the fish has been speared, hold it down against the bottom of the stream until you can get your hand between it and the tip of the spear.

Fish traps

A better name for fish traps would be corrals since you try to herd the fish into the trap's fenced enclosure. The opening is designed like a funnel with the narrow end emptying into a cage. When building these traps in ocean water, select your location during high tide and construct the trap during low tide. On rocky shores, use natural rock pools; on coral islands, use the natural pools that form on reefs; and on sandy shores, create a dam on the lee side of the offshore sandbar. If you can, block all the openings before

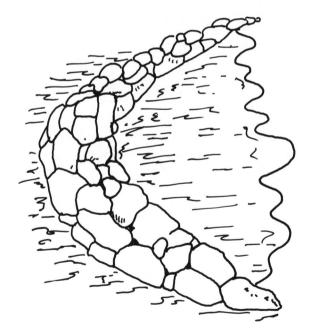

Offshore fish trap

Fish trap in a creek

the tide recedes. Once the tide goes back out, you can use either a scoop net or spear to bring your dinner ashore. As always, you must consider the potential for poisonous fish. When building a trap in creeks and small rivers, use saplings to create the trap and its funnel. The opening should be on the upstream side so the current will aid in the funneling process. To herd the fish into your trap, start upstream and wade down toward your corral. Once there, close its opening and scoop net or spear the fish out.

Preparing fish to eat

To prevent spoilage, prepare the fish as soon as possible. Gut the fish by cutting up its abdomen and then removing the intestines and large blood vessels (kidney) that lie next to the backbone. Remove the gills and, when applicable, scale or skin the fish. On bigger fish, you may want to fillet the meat off of the bone. For details on filleting, see the section on fishing in open water. Be sure to prepare the fish well away from your shelter. If you do not plan to eat the fish immediately, see the section on preserving meat.

BIRDS

Almost all birds are edible. If nests are nearby, you can also eat the birds' eggs. Birds are commonly found at the edge of the woods where clearings end and forests begin, on the banks of rivers and streams, and on lakeshores and seashores. Eggs are available for the taking, and young birds are easy to catch with snares or baited hooks or by clubbing. Pluck all birds unless they are scavengers or seabirds, both of which should be skinned. Leaving the skin on other kinds of birds will retain more of their nutrients when cooked. Cut off the neck of the bird close to the body. Cut open the chest and abdominal cavity, and remove the insides. Save the neck, liver, heart, and gizzard, which are all edible when cooked. Before eating the gizzard, split it open and remove the stones and partially digested food. Cook the bird anyway you desire. Be sure to cook scavenger birds a minimum of twenty minutes to kill parasites.

MAMMALS

Mammals provide a great source of meat and should not be overlooked as a viable food source. To find mammals, look for well-traveled trails, which usually lead to feeding, watering, and bedding areas; fresh tracks and droppings; and fresh bedding, such as nests, burrows, and trampled-down field grass. Trying to catch a big-game animal without a rifle is dangerous and not likely to succeed. If you are out of food and looking to catch a mammal, seek out small game. Look for their superhighway trail in heavy cover or undergrowth or parallel to roads and open areas. Most critters use the same pathway during summer and winter. A simple loop snare is the best way to catch animals in all climates. More details on primitive snares and triggers can be found in my book *Wilderness Living*.

Simple loop snare

An animal caught in a simple loop snare will either strangle itself or be held securely until you arrive. To construct a simple loop snare, use either snare wire or improvised line that is strong enough to hold the mammal you intend to catch. If using snare wire, start by making a fixed loop at one end. To do this, bend the wire 2 inches from the end, fold it back on itself, and twist or wrap the end of the wire and its body together, being sure to leave a small loop. Twist the fixed loop at its midpoint until it forms a

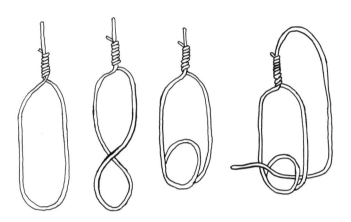

Four steps of constructing a simple loop snare

figure eight. Fold the top half of the figure eight down onto the lower half, and run the free end of the wire through the fixed loop. The size of the snare will determine the diameter of the resulting circle. The circle should be slightly larger than the head size of the animal you intend to catch. In extremely cold weather, you should double the wire to prevent the snare from breaking.

If using an improvised line, make a slipknot that tightens down when the animal puts its head through the snare and lunges forward.

Avoid removing the bark from any natural material used in constructing the snare. If the bark is removed, camouflage the exposed wood by rubbing

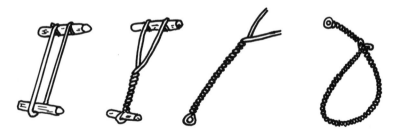

Doubling snare wire

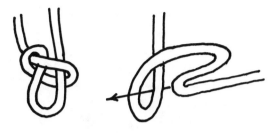

Slipknot

dirt on it. Since animals avoid humans, it's important to remove your scent from the snare. To mask your scent, hold the snaring material over smoke or underwater for several minutes prior to its final placement. Place multiple simple loop snares—at least fifteen for every one animal you want to catch—at den openings or well-traveled trails. Make sure the snare is placed so that the loop is equal in height to the animal's head. When placing a snare, avoid disturbing the area as much as possible. If laying a snare on a well-traveled trail, try to use the natural funneling of any surrounding vegetation. If natural funneling isn't available, create your own with strate-

Simple loop snare

Funneling

gically placed sticks. (Again, hide your scent.) Attach the free end of the snare to a branch, rock, or drag stick. A drag stick is a big stick that either is too heavy for the animal to drag or gets stuck in surrounding debris when the animal tries moving. Be sure to check your snares at dawn and dusk, and always make sure any caught game is dead before getting too close.

Twitch-up strangle snare
An animal caught in this type of snare will either strangle itself or be held securely until you arrive. The advantage of the twitch-up snare over the simple loop snare is that it will hold your catch beyond the reach of other predatory animals that might wander by. To construct a twitch-up strangle snare, make a simple loop snare out of either snare wire or strong improvised line. Then find a sapling that you can bend down 90 degrees directly over the snare site you have selected. Use a two-pin toggle trigger to attach the sapling to the snare.

Two-pin toggle trigger

To construct a two-pin toggle, find two small forked or hooked branches that fit together when the hooks are placed in opposing positions. If unable to find appropriate forked or hooked branches, construct them by carving notches into two small pieces of wood until they fit together.

To complete the twitch-up snare, firmly secure one branch of the trigger into the ground so that the fork is pointing down. Attach the snare to the second forked branch, which is also tied to the sapling (or rubber tubing under tension) at the location that places the sapling, when bent 90 degrees, directly over the snare. To arm the snare, simply bend the twig and attach the two-pin toggle together. The resulting tension will hold the snare in place. Adjust the snare height to the approximate position of the animal's head. When an animal places its head through the snare and trips the trigger, it will be snapped upward and strangled by the snare. If using improvised snare line, you may have to place two small sticks into the ground to hold the snare open and in its proper place on the trail.

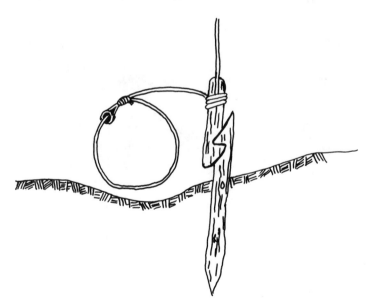

Two-pin toggle trigger

Twitch-up strangle snare using a two-pin toggle trigger

Squirrel pole

Squirrel pole

With a squirrel pole, you will be able to catch a number of squirrels with minimal time, effort, or materials. Attach several simple loop snares to a pole approximately 6 feet long, then lean the pole onto an area with visible signs of multiple squirrels feeding—look for mounds of pinecone scales, usually on a stump or a fallen tree. The squirrel will inevitably use the pole to try get to his favorite feeding site and will be trapped in a snare.

Figure-four mangle snare

The figure-four mangle snare is often used to catch small rodents, such as mice, squirrels, and marmots. An animal caught in this snare will be mangled and killed. To construct a figure four, find two sticks that are 12 to 18 inches long and approximately ¾ to 1 inch in diameter (upright and diagonal pieces) and one stick that is the same diameter but 3 to 6 inches longer (trigger).

Upright piece

To prepare the upright stick, cut a 45-degree angle at its top end and create a squared notch 3 to 4 inches up from the bottom. For best results, cut a diagonal taper from the bottom of the squared notch to the stick's bottom,

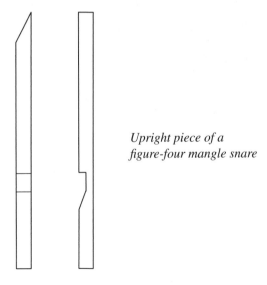

*Upright piece of a
figure-four mangle snare*

which will aid in the trigger's release from the upright. In addition to being at opposite ends, the squared notch at the bottom and the 45-degree angle at the top must also be perpendicular to one another.

Diagonal piece
To create the diagonal piece, cut a diagonal notch 2 inches from one end and a 45-degree angle on the opposite end. While at opposite ends, the diagonal notch and the 45-degree angle must also be on the same sides of the stick.

Trigger
The trigger piece must have a diagonal notch cut 1 to 2 inches from one end and a squared notch created at the spot where this piece crosses the upright when the three sticks are put together. To determine this location, place the upright perpendicular to the ground and insert its diagonal cut into the notch of the diagonal piece. Put the angled cut of the diagonal stick into the trigger's notch, and hold it so that the three sticks create the number four when the trigger passes the upright's square notch. Mark the trigger stick, and make a squared notch that has a slight diagonal taper from its bottom toward

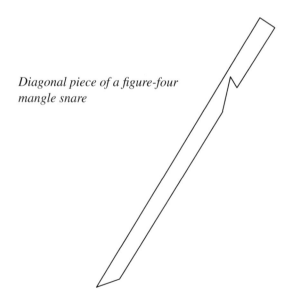

Diagonal piece of a figure-four mangle snare

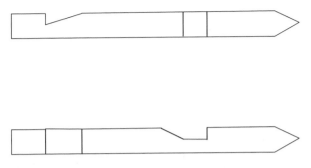

Trigger piece of the figure-four mangle snare

its other notched end. If you intend to bait the trigger, then sharpen its free end to a point.

To use a figure four, put the three pieces together and lean a large rock or other weight against the diagonal at approximately 45 degrees to the upright. The entire structure is held in place by the tension that occurs between the weight and the stick's design. When an animal trips the trigger, this object will fall and mangle the animal.

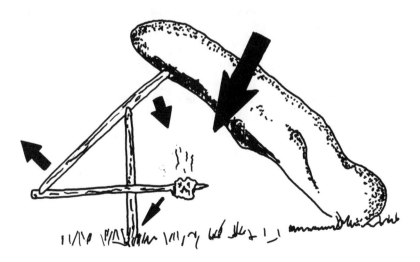

The force created by the rock's weight holds the trigger of the figure-four mangle snare together.

Rodent skewer

Rodent skewer

A forked spear made from a long sapling can be used as a rodent skewer. To use it, thrust the pointed end into an animal hole until you feel the animal. Twist the stick so that it gets tightly snagged in the animal's fur and pull the animal out of the hole. The rodent will try to bite and scratch you, so keep it at a distance. Use a club or rock to kill it.

To eat your catch, you must skin, gut, and butcher the game. Do this well away from your camp and your food cache. Before skinning an animal, be sure it is dead. Then, cut the animal's throat and collect the blood in a container to use later in a stew. If time is not an issue, wait thirty minutes before starting to skin the animal. This allows the body to cool, which in turn makes it easier to skin and provides enough time for most parasites to leave the animal's hide.

Glove skinning is the method most often used for skinning small game. Hang the animal from its hind legs, and make a circular cut just above the legs' joints, being careful not to cut through the tendon. To avoid dulling your knife, which occurs when cutting from the fur side, slide a finger between the hide and muscle, and place your knife next to the muscle so that you cut the hide from the nonfur side. Cut down the inside of each leg, ending close to the genital area, and peel the skin off of the legs until you reach the animal's tail. Firmly slide a finger under the hide between the tail and spine until you have a space that allows you to cut the tail free. Do the same on the front side. At this point, the hide can be pulled down and freed from the animal's membrane with little effort. Avoid squeezing the belly since this may cause urine to spill onto the meat. Pull the front feet inside out through the hide by sliding a finger between the elbow and the membrane and pulling the leg up and free from the rest of the hide. Cut off the feet. The head can be either severed or skinned, depending on your talents.

A larger animal can be hung from a tree by its hind legs or skinned while lying on the ground. To hang it by its hind legs, find the tendon that connects the upper and lower leg and poke a hole between it and the bone. If musk glands are present, remove them. (Musk glands are usually found at the bend between the upper and lower parts of the hind legs.) Free the hide from the animal's genitals by cutting a circular area around them, and then make an incision that runs just under its hide and all the way up to the neck. To avoid cutting the entrails, slide your index and middle fingers between the hide and the thin membrane enclosing the entrails. Use the V between your fingers to guide the cut and push the entrails down and away from the knife. The knife should be held with its backside next to the membrane and the sharp side facing out so that it cuts the hide from the nonhair side. Next, cut around the joint of each extremity. From there, extend the cut down the insides of each leg until it reaches the midline incision.

Try to pull the hide off using the same method explained for small game. If you end up needing to use your knife, be sure to cut toward the meat so as to not damage the hide. Avoid cutting through the entrails or the hide. If skinning on the ground, use the hide to protect the meat and don't remove it until after you gut and butcher the animal. Once the hide has been removed, it can be tanned and used for many different needs, such as clothing, shelter cover, or containers (covered in my book, *Wilderness Living*).

To gut an animal, place the carcass, belly up, on a slope or hang it from a tree by its hind legs. Make a small incision just in front of the anus, and insert your index and middle fingers into the cut, spreading them apart to form a V. Slide the knife into the incision between the V formed by your two fingers. Use your fingers to push the internal organs down away from the knife and as a guide for the knife as you cut up the abdominal cavity to the breastbone. Avoid cutting the bladder and internal organs. Cut around the anus and sex organs so that they will be easily removed with the entrails. If the bladder or internal organs are punctured, wash the meat as soon as possible.

Remove the intact bladder by pinching it off close to the opening and cutting it free. Remove the entrails, pulling them down and away from the carcass. To do this, you will need to sever the intestines at the anus. Save the liver and kidneys for later consumption. (A spotted liver signals disease. Discard all internal organs and thoroughly cook the meat.) Cut through the diaphragm, and reach inside the chest cavity until you can touch the windpipe. Cut or pull the windpipe free, and remove the chest cavity contents. Save the lungs and heart for later consumption. (Although internal organs can be cooked in any fashion, they are best when used in a stew.)

Small game such as rabbits can be dressed without a knife. First, singe off the hair in a fire. Then firmly grasp the rabbit between both hands at its rib cage and squeeze toward the stomach. Using a firm grip, raise the rabbit over your head and fling it down hard, allowing your arms to go between your legs, which will cause the rabbit's entrails to be expelled.

If you intend to eat the liver, you must remove the inedible small black sack (gallbladder). If it breaks, wash the liver immediately to avoid tainting the meat. Since fat spoils quickly, it should be cut away from the meat and promptly used. It is best in soups.

To butcher an animal, cut the legs, back, and breast sections free of one another. When you are butchering large game, cut it into meal-sized roasts and steaks, which can be stored for later use. Cut the rest of the meat along the grain into long, thin strips about ⅛ inch thick to be preserved by smoking or sun drying. (Both are covered later in this chapter.) Don't forget the head: the meat, tongue, eyes, brain, and the marrow inside the bones are all edible. Keep the bones, brain, sinew, hoofs, and other parts, as each will serve many different survival needs.

COOKING METHODS

In addition to killing parasites and bacteria, cooking your food can make it more palatable. There are many different ways to prepare game, and from a nutritional standpoint, some are better than others. Boiling is best but only if you drink the broth that contains much of the nutrients lost in the cooking process. Frying tastes great but is probably the worst way to cook since a lot of nutrients are lost during the process.

Boiling

Boiling is the best cooking method since all of the food's nutrients are retained in the broth. If no container is available, you may have to improvise one. Try a rock with a bowl-shaped center (avoid rocks with high-moisture content, as they may explode), green bamboo, or a thick, hollowed-out piece of wood that can be suspended over the fire. If your container cannot be suspended over the fire, stone boiling is another option. Use a hot bed of coals to heat up numerous stones. Then set your container of food and water close to your bed of hot stones, and add rocks to it until the water begins to boil. To keep the water boiling, cover the top with bark or another improvised lid, and keep it covered except when removing or adding stones. Instead of a rolling rapid boil, a steady, slow bubbling will occur with this process.

Frying
Place a flat rock on or next to the fire (avoid rocks with high-moisture content, as they may explode). Let it get hot, and use it in the same fashion as you would a frying pan.

Broiling
Broiling is ideal for cooking small game over hot coals. Before cooking the animal, sear its flesh with the flames from the fire. This will help keep the juices, which contain vital nutrients, inside the animal. Next, run a nonpoisonous skewer, such as a small, straight, strong branch, along the underside of the animal's backbone. Finally, using any means available, suspend the animal over the coals.

METHODS OF STORING FOOD

Keep it alive
If you are able, keep all animals alive until you are ready to consume them. This ensures that the meat stays fresh. If you are keeping a small rodent or rabbit alive to eat, and not for bait, be sure to protect it from becoming a coyote's meal instead of yours.

Winter storage
In winter, freeze the meat into meal-sized portions. You may also want to bury the food in a snow refrigerator.

Summer storage
During nonwinter months, create a refrigerator by digging a 2-foot hole in a moist, shady location, and place your food, wrapped in a waterproof container, inside the pit. Surround it with vegetation. Cover the food with sticks and dirt until the hole is filled.

METHODS OF PRESERVING MEAT

Sun drying

Use the long, thin strips of meat you cut when butchering the animal, and hang them in the sun out of any animal's reach. To do this, run snare wire or line between two trees. If using snare wire, be sure to skewer the line through the top of each piece of meat before attaching it to the second tree. If using other line, hang it first and then drape the slices of meat over it. Make sure the meat does not touch itself or another piece.

Smoking

For smoked meat, use the long, thin strips of meat you cut when butchering the animal. Here are instructions for constructing and using a smoker:

1. Build a 6-foot-tall tripod that is lashed together.
2. Attach snare wire or line around the three poles, in a tiered fashion, so that the lowest point is at least 2 feet above the ground.
3. If using snare wire, skewer the line through the top of each slice of meat before extending it around the inside of the next pole. If using other line, hang it first and then drape the strips of meat over it, making sure the meat does not touch itself or another piece.
4. Cover the outer aspect of the tripod with any available material, such as a poncho. Avoid contact between the outer covering and the meat. For proper ventilation, leave a small opening at the top of the tripod.
5. Gather an armload of green deciduous wood, such as willow or aspen, and either break the branches into smaller pieces or cut the bigger pieces into chips.
6. Build a fire next to the tripod, and once a good bed of coals develops, transfer the coals to the ground in the center of the smoker. Continue transferring coals as needed.
7. To smoke the meat, place small pieces or chips of green wood on the hot coals. Once the green wood begins to heat up, smoke should occur. Keep adding chips until the meat is dark and brittle—about twenty-four to forty-eight hours.
8. Since an actual fire will destroy the smoking process, monitor the wood to make sure it doesn't flame up. If it does, put out the flame, but try to avoid disrupting the bed of coals too much.

11

Navigation

*Just as drivers are required to get a driver's license,
boaters should be required to take a basic boating safety
and navigation course. In addition, they should be
required to carry a compass, chart, GPS, and EPIRB or
radio as a minimum. The ability to provide rescue with a
simple latitude and longitude can mean the difference
between immediate rescue and hours or days of survival.*
—*Aviation Survival Technician Brian Matos*
U.S. Coast Guard Helicopter Rescue Swimmer

Navigation is the ability to get from point A to point B, using landmarks and references to identify your position and plan a route of travel. Whether you are stranded at sea or on land, rescue attempts are far more successful when rescuers search for someone who is at their last known location. At sea, you're better off staying close to your distressed vessel. On land, as long as you are able to meet your survival needs, stay put. When on land, only consider traveling from your present location to another in three situations:

1. Your present location doesn't have adequate resources to meet such needs as personal protection, sustenance, and signaling.
2. Rescue doesn't appear to be imminent.
3. You know your location and have the navigational skills to travel to safety.

At sea, stay put unless your vessel is burning or sinking and poses a threat. In that case, cut free of the boat and move away from it as soon as possible. Since resources will be limited, you should travel toward shipping lanes, land, or rain.

1. Shipping lanes. These lanes run from continent to continent and tend to have an east-west pattern.
2. Land. Most large land masses are oriented north and south.
3. Rain. Since rain forms from accumulated vapor and wind picks up vapors when traveling over water, following the winds is perhaps the best way to find rain.

Hopefully, you will have an idea of your general location. Knowing how to identify your location to determine a direction of travel and to avoid obstacles requires a good understanding of a compass and map or nautical chart's nomenclature.

MAPS AND CHARTS

To understand a map's nomenclature, look within its main body and the surrounding margins. For a map to be an effective tool, however, you must become familiar with it before you depart. Maps and charts are two-dimensional representations of the earth's surface and use symbols to depict the various features. Topographic maps are used for land navigation, and charts are used for navigation at sea.

COLORS AND SYMBOLS OF MAPS AND CHARTS

To make it easier to understand a map or chart, colors and symbols are used.

Topographical map features

Most maps are published by the United States Geological Survey. The following colors are standard representations:

    Green—woodland
    White—nonforested areas, such as rocks and meadows
    Blue—water
    Black—man-made structures, such as buildings and trails
    Red—prominent man-made items, such as major roads
    Brown—contour lines, which are usually not shown on charts

Chart features

Most nautical charts are published by the National Ocean Service (NOS) and use the following standard features.

Chart colors

Land areas on charts often have a yellowish or gray tint.

Shallow or shoal waters are often shown in blue, and deep-water areas are shown in white.

Shoal areas are often circled or shaded to give them greater visibility.

Areas that may be submerged at high tide, such as sandbars, mud flats, and marshes, are often shown in green.

Magenta is used for a lot of chart information because it is easier to read under a boat's red night-lights.

Letters and numbers

Bottom soundings (depth), which are marked in feet, fathoms, or meters throughout the chart, relate to depths at mean low water.

Slanting or italic lettering identifies submerged or floating features with their height at mean high tide.

Upright or Roman lettering is used to identify features that are dry at high water.

Lines to show channel limits

The shoreline is represented as a solid line with the land portions shaded.

Land features on charts are often limited to major landmarks that help you with navigation. These include peaks, buildings, radio towers, and other prominent man-made and natural features.

The location of man-made safety markers are labeled with a symbol and brief description. Lighthouses, buoys, and markers help you to avoid shallow water and other dangerous areas (covered below).

Charts have a multitude of symbols that help you navigate the waterways. An inexpensive booklet called *Chart No. 1,* published by the National Oceanic and Atmospheric Administration (NOAA) and National Image and Mapping Agency (NIMA), provides the most comprehensive review of chart symbols and is well worth the purchase. Take the time to review these symbols in advance of your trip, and learn to recognize their meaning. Knowledge is power.

SCALE AND SERIES
Exactly how much surface area (water or land) a map represents can be found within its margins and will be shown as either a scale or series relationship.

Scale

A scaled map or chart represents the ratio of the map to real life. Here are some common examples of a scale. (An inch is used in this example, but any unit of measurement can be done using the same process.)

1:10,000 to 1:50,000: Extremely detailed maps covering small areas, these charts are often used by backpackers and kayakers who travel in harbors, anchorage areas, and smaller inland waterways.

1:50,000 to 1:150,000: These charts are used by vessels that navigate large bays and harbors and navigate large inland waterways.

1:150,000 to 1:600,000: These charts are used by vessels that navigate beyond the reefs yet within sight of land or navigational aids.

1:600,000 and up: Often called a sailing chart and used by vessels covering large areas of water, these charts cover large surface areas, and their details are limited to larger features.

Series

A series map represents the relationship of the map to the amount of latitude and longitude that is displayed. Here are some common examples:

15-minute series: This map covers 15 minutes of latitude and 15 minutes of longitude.

7.5-minute series: This map covers 7.5 minutes of latitude and 7.5 minutes of longitude. It would take four of these maps to cover the same surface area as one 15-minute series map.

MAGNETIC VARIATION
Maps are drawn to true north. The north-seeking arrow on a compass points toward magnetic north. The variation between true north and magnetic north must be accounted for and is usually listed within the margins of a map or chart. On a topographical map, it is often shown by two arrows whose bases meet. The magnetic north arrow has an "MN" at its point and the true north arrow has a star.

MN

Magnetic variation allows you to adjust the difference between true north and magnetic north.

On charts, the magnetic variation is normally shown using a compass rose. The compass rose has an outer ring that provides a true north heading without compensating for magnetic variation. The zero on the outer ring should be directly perpendicular to the chart. The middle ring, which provides the magnetic heading as it relates to your location on the map, compensates for the variation between magnetic north and true north. It allows you to determine a heading, provided you know where you are and where you are going, without orienting the chart or using a protractor. The amount of declination (variance) between true north and magnetic north is listed in the center of the compass rose. Charts covering a large surface area will have more than one compass rose located within its borders.

LATITUDE AND LONGITUDE LINES
Latitude and longitude are imaginary lines that encircle the globe and create a crisscross grid system. These lines help you identify your location on a map or chart.

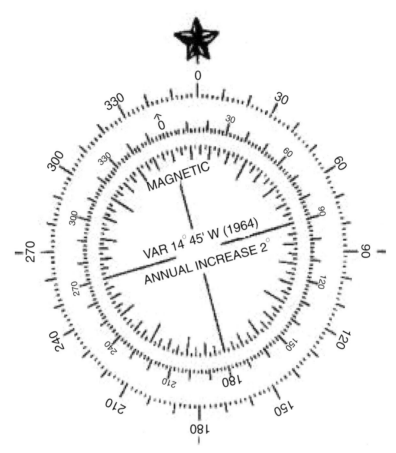

A chart shows magnetic variation using a compass rose.

Latitude lines

Latitude lines run east to west and are numbered from 0 to 90 degrees north and south of the equator. The 0 degrees latitude runs around the globe at the equator, and from there the numbers rise north 90 degrees and south 90 degrees. Thus, the equator is 0 degrees latitude, the North Pole is 90 degrees north latitude, and the South Pole is 90 degrees south latitude. Latitude is often noted at the extreme ends of the horizontal map edges.

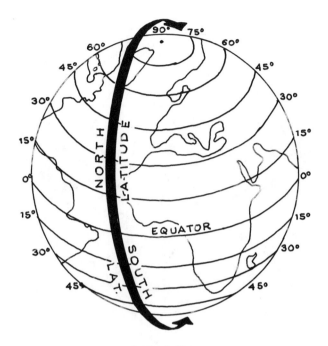

Latitude lines

Longitude lines

Longitude lines run north to south and are numbered from 0 to 180 degrees east and west of Greenwich, England, at the line commonly referred to as the prime meridian. Longitude lines begin at 0 at Greenwich, England, and travel east and west until they meet at the 180th meridian, which is often referred to as the international dateline. The 0 meridian becomes the 180th meridian once it intersects the extreme north and south sections of the globe. Longitude is often noted at the extreme ends of the vertical map edges.

Both latitude and longitude lines are measured in degrees (°), minutes ('), and seconds ("). Each degree of latitude and longitude is divided into 60 minutes, and each minute is further divided into 60 seconds. One minute of one degree of latitude is equal to one nautical mile or 1,852 meters. However, since longitude lines converge at the North and South Poles, the

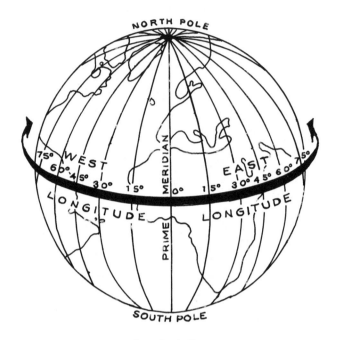

Longitude lines

distance between one minute of one degree of longitude decreases as you move up or down the longitude line. You must remember to distinguish north from south when defining your latitude, and east from west for longitude. Whenever you give latitude and longitude coordinates, always read the latitude first.

Rules for reading latitude lines
Latitude, for example, might read 45° 30' and 30". If north of the equator, your latitude would read 45 degrees, 30 minutes, and 30 seconds north latitude; if south of the equator, your latitude would read 45 degrees, 30 minutes, and 30 seconds south latitude. A latitude line will never be more than 90 degrees north or south.

Rules for reading longitude lines
Longitude, for example, might read 120° 30' 30". If east of the prime meridian, your longitude would be 120 degrees, 30 minutes, and 30 sec-

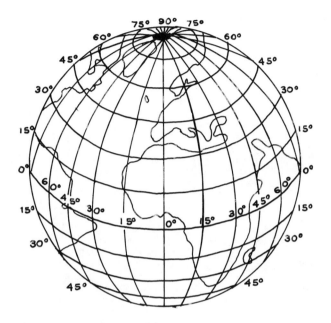

Latitude and longitude intersecting

onds east longitude; if west of the prime meridian, your longitude would be 120 degrees, 30 minutes, and 30 seconds west longitude. A longitude line will never be more than 180 degrees east or west.

CONTOUR LINES

Contour lines are not shown on charts, which list water depths as numbers and provide information regarding passageways and shallow areas to help you avoid these obstacles. Topographical maps use contour lines to help you understand the elevation changes of the land. Contour lines are imaginary lines, superimposed on a topographic map, that connect points of equal elevation. The contour line interval, usually found in the margins of a map, is the distance between two contour lines. The actual distance will vary from one map to the next. The following is a basic guide on how to interpret the lay of the land when looking at a map's contour lines:

- Steep terrain—lines will be close together.
- Gradual elevation gains and losses—lines are relatively far apart.

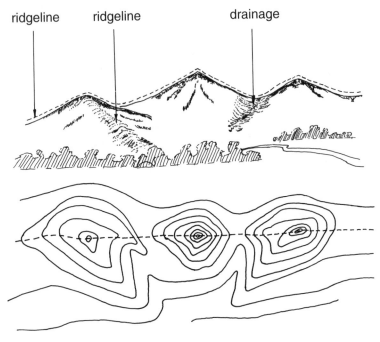

Contour lines

- Drainage—lines will form a V pointing toward a higher elevation.
- Ridgelines—lines will form a V pointing away from a higher elevation.

MAN-MADE SAFETY MARKERS

Charts provide several navigational aids that help mariners avoid hazards and identify their position. These aids consist of lighthouses, buoys, and markers.

Lighthouses

Since the visibility of light increases with height, lighthouses provide an exceptional marker that can be seen from a great distance. They help mariners with navigation and to avoid dangerous areas. In addition to light, lighthouses often have fog-signaling and radio-beacon equipment.

Buoys

Buoys are anchored floating markers that help vessels avoid dangers and navigate in and out of channels. Buoys come in several shapes and colors, which help identify their purpose.

Right-sided buoys

Buoys located on the right side of a channel—leading in from seaward—will be painted red and support even numbers that decrease as you move seaward. If a light is used, it will be red. Nun-shaped buoys (buoys with a cone-shaped top) are used when the buoys aren't lit.

Left-sided buoys

Buoys located on the left side of a channel—leading in from seaward—will be painted green and support odd numbers that decrease as you move

A lighthouse helps mariners avoid obstacles.

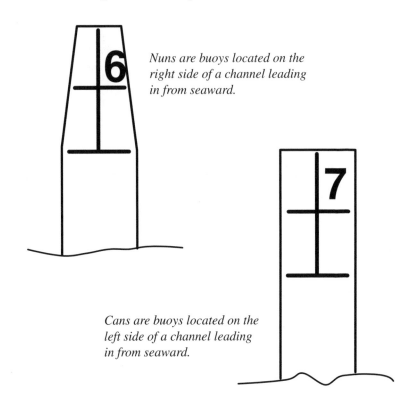

Nuns are buoys located on the right side of a channel leading in from seaward.

Cans are buoys located on the left side of a channel leading in from seaward.

seaward. If a light is used, it will be green. Can-shaped buoys (buoys with a cylinder shape) are used when the buoys aren't lit.

Channel junction and safe approach buoys

Buoys located at a junction or midchannel can be either nuns or cans and may or may not have numbers on them. Junction buoys are painted with horizontal red and green stripes, and midchannel buoys are painted with horizontal red and white strips. If a light is used, it will be white.

Day markers

Day markers are small signs held in place by poles. During daylight hours, these markers help vessels avoid dangers and navigate in and out of channels. Markers come in several shapes and colors, which help identify their purpose.

Right-sided day markers
Markers located on the right side of a channel—leading in from seaward—will be triangular-shaped, painted red, and support even numbers that decrease as you move seaward.

Left-sided day markers
Markers located on the left side of a channel—leading in from seaward—will be square-shaped, painted green, and support odd numbers that decrease as you move seaward.

Midchannel markers
Markers located midchannel will be in the shape of an octagon.

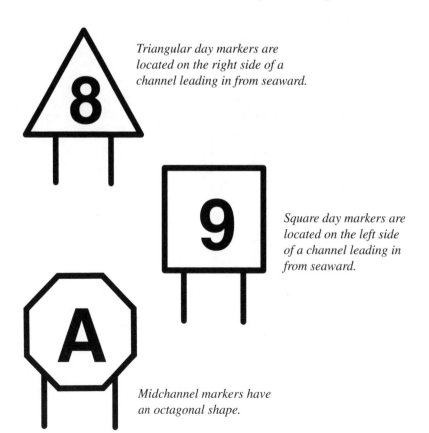

Triangular day markers are located on the right side of a channel leading in from seaward.

Square day markers are located on the left side of a channel leading in from seaward.

Midchannel markers have an octagonal shape.

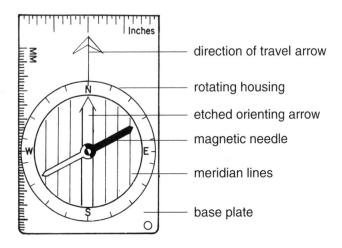

Orienteering compass

COMPASSES

For purposes of this book, the nomenclature for orienteering and marine compasses will be explained. Both compasses, however, can perform any of the various tasks outlined later in this chapter.

ORIENTEERING COMPASS

An orienteering compass has a circular housing mounted on a rectangular base.

Rectangular base plate

The sides of the base plate have millimeter and inch markings that are used to relate a map measurement to that of a relative field distance. The front of the plate has a direction-of-travel arrow that is parallel to the long edge and perpendicular to the short edge. Compass headings are read from the point where the bottom of the direction of travel arrow touches the numbers on the edge of the circular compass housing. If the direction of travel arrow is not present or centered on the circular housing, your compass will probably have a stationary index line (sometimes called an index pointer). This non-moving short white line is located either on the base plate next to the circular housing or inside the circular housing just beneath the moving numbers. It will be centered on the short wall of the base plate and on the same side of the compass as the direction of travel arrow(s). Headings are read where the numbers touch or pass over this line. The direction of travel arrow must always point toward the intended destination when a heading is taken.

Circular housing
A circular rotating housing sits on the base plate. Its outer ring has the four cardinal points (N, S, E, W) and degree lines starting at north with 0 and numbered clockwise to 360 degrees. The bottom of the housing has an etched orienting arrow that points toward the north marking on the outer ring.

Magnetic needle
The compass needle, which sits beneath the glass of the circular housing, floats freely, and one end, usually marked in red, points toward magnetic north (not true north). Magnetic north lies near Prince of Wales Island in northern Canada. In the illustration below, see how the magnetic variance affects readings in the United States. Notice the line that passes through the Great Lakes and along the coast of Florida. This is an agonic line, which

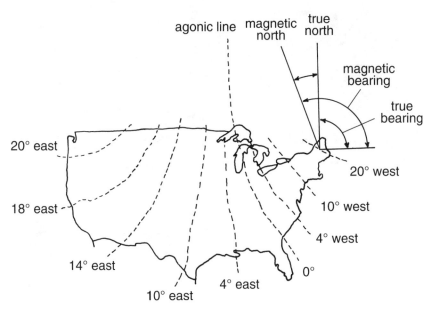

Agonic and isogonic lines depict the variation between magnetic and true north.

has no variation. Here, a compass heading of 0 or 360 degrees would point toward both magnetic north and true north. The other lines, which are isogonic lines, have variations from true north. The line that extends through Oregon has a variation of 20 degrees east. Note that when this line is extended the compass bearing of 360 is 20 degrees to the east of true north. The opposite would be true for the line extending through Maine. In this case, a compass bearing of 360 would be 20 degrees west of true north. Because of these variations, adjustments must be made when using a map and compass together (see below). Note that if you hold the compass close to metal objects, the needle will be drawn toward them.

MARINE COMPASS

Marine compasses are designed especially for vessels in rough seas. Unlike an orienteering compass, a marine compass has numbers on a card that rotates around a fixed needle. The compass card is mounted on a float that sits on a pivot directly above the magnetic needle mechanism. The card is

A marine compass mounted on a kayak.

finely balanced, allowing it to float and move constantly as it aligns with magnetic north. Headings are taken from the fixed lubber line located on the body of the compass. If attached to the vessel, the lubber line is aligned with the front of the vessel so that all headings represent the direction of travel. The top of these compasses typically have a hemispherical shape, and the compasses are usually mounted close to the steering apparatus but away from metals that may interfere with their heading. When mounted, compass bowls are kept horizontal by the use of gimbals, which allow the compass to compensate for sea roll.

While an orienteering compass has its scale (0 to 360 degrees) located on the circular housing, which rotates around the arrow seeking magnetic north, a marine compass uses a circular scale located on the compass card. With an orienteering compass, a heading is only established when the circular housing is turned and the north-seeking arrow is boxed (see below). With a marine compass, the numbers are simply read below the lubber line (stationary index line).

FINDING YOUR POSITION WITH A MAP OR CHART AND COMPASS

If you stay constantly aware, you should be able to determine your general and specific location at all times.

DETERMINING GENERAL LOCATION

Anytime you're traveling in the wilderness or at sea, you should maintain a constant awareness of your general location. This awareness keeps you focused on the surrounding terrain and how it relates to the map you are carrying. If you have done this throughout your trip, you will never have to use any other means of establishing where you are. One way to keep a constant awareness is with dead reckoning. Dead reckoning uses a simple math formula to help you find your present location:

$$\text{Rate} \times \text{Time} = \text{Distance}$$

Rate

The rate of speed you have been traveling is usually measured in knots per hour at sea and miles per hour (kilometers per hour) on land. One knot equals a traveling speed that covers one nautical mile per hour. A nautical mile is equal to one minute of latitude—1.852 kilometers or 1.1508 miles or 6,076 feet—and is used as the distance reference in most charts. Note that a nautical mile is not equal to a statute mile, which is used for measurement on land. If your vessel is propelled in a direction by paddling or motor, then you must consider the impact of the current and wind on your rate and adjust the formula accordingly. For our scenario, however, we are using the current and the wind as a means of moving our vessel.

The best way to determine your vessel's rate of speed is with a chip log, which consists of a heaving line and a heavy object that floats. This object could be improvised from something as simple as a container filled with seawater. Make sure the container weighs enough to prevent the wind from affecting its movement in the water. To build a chip log, attach a line to the container and tie two knots in the line. The first knot should be positioned far enough away from the container so that it meets the water after the container has settled. The second knot should be placed at a premeasured distance from the first. To use, place the container in the water and allow the line to pass through your hands. As the line advances, calculate the time that passes between hand contact with the first knot and second knot. Using this time along with the distance between the two knots, you can calculate your speed with the following formula:

$$\text{Speed in knots} = \frac{0.6 \times \text{feet between marks}}{\text{Seconds of time between knots}} = \text{feet/second}$$

Measurements (speed, heading, etc.) should be taken every hour to ensure accuracy and constant awareness. Applying the result to your dead-reckoning formula helps you determine how far you have traveled. Note that one nautical mile per hour equals $1\frac{2}{3}$ feet per second.

Time
If you have kept track of your location throughout the day, time will be related to the amount of time that has passed since leaving the last known location.

Distance

For this formula to work, you will need to know your starting point and the heading you took. Apply the answer (distance) to your line of travel (heading) to give you an approximate location. Direction of travel can be calculated by shooting an azimuth off your chip line (once extended and straight) and adding or subtracting 180 degrees.

Adjusting your location (latitude and longitude) can be done based on your direction of travel and the distance traveled. There are several other methods you might use to determine your location and direction of travel.

DETERMINING SPECIFIC LOCATION

When using a topographical map and orienteering compass, you have to first orient the map to find your specific location. This step is not always necessary when using a chart.

Orienting a map

To orient the map, you must align its features to those of the surrounding terrain. On land, this process is extremely helpful in determining your specific location. At sea, it will help you orient land features to their location on the map.

1. If on land, go to high ground to evaluate the terrain once the map is oriented. If you're on the water, your ability to see landmarks might be limited by the earth's curvature and its impact on your line of sight.
2. If you can, open the map and place it on a flat, level surface. Be sure it is protected from dirt and moisture.
3. When using an orienteering compass, rotate the circular housing on the compass until the bottom of the direction-of-travel arrow is touching the true north heading. When doing this, you must account for the area's given declination, as outlined above. Declination is the difference between magnetic north (MN) and true north (★). True north is represented on a map, and magnetic north is a compass heading. In other words, a 360-degree map heading—true north—is not necessarily a 360-degree compass heading. This variation is usually depicted on the bottom of most topographic maps. If magnetic north is located west of true north, which is the case for most of the eastern United States, you

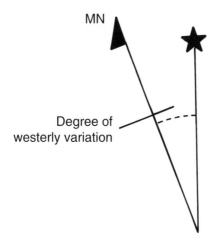

Westerly magnetic variation

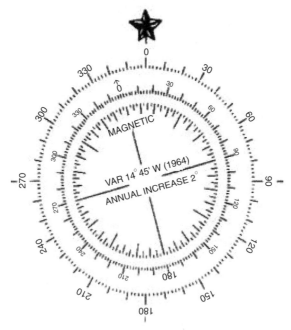

Compass rose showing a westerly magnetic variation

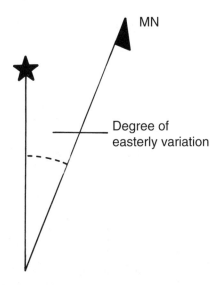

MN

Degree of
easterly variation

Easterly magnetic variation

would add your declination to 360 degrees. The resultant bearing would be the compass heading equivalent to true north at that location. If magnetic north is located east of true north, which is the case for most of the western United States, you would subtract your declination from 360 degrees. The resultant bearing would be the compass heading equivalent to true north at that location. *Note:* When using a marine compass and chart with a compass rose, you can skip step 3 as long as the map is oriented using the compass rose's middle ring, which reflects the magnetic variation.

4. Set the compass on the map with the edge of the long side resting next to and parallel to the left north–south margins (longitude line). Be sure that the direction of travel arrow is pointing toward the north end of the map.

5. Holding the compass in place on the map, rotate the map and compass until the floating magnetic needle is inside the etched orienting arrow of the base plate (red portion of the needle forward). This is called boxing the needle. *Note:* When using a marine compass and chart with a compass rose, steps 4 and 5 can be accomplished two ways:

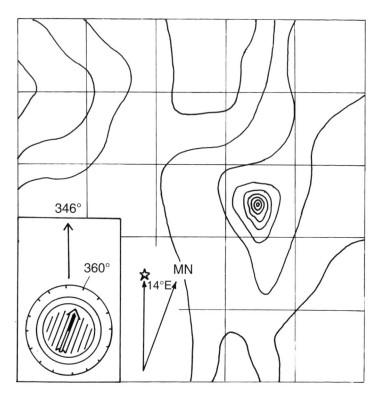

Using the magnetic variation to orient the map with a compass

- For a handheld marine compass, hold your compass so that it reflects a magnetic north heading (as displayed on the middle ring of the compass rose) and then rotate your map until the compass rose's magnetic line is oriented with the compass heading.
- For a deck-mounted marine compass, turn your vessel until your compass reflects a magnetic north heading (as displayed on the middle ring of the compass rose). Then rotate your map until the compass rose's magnetic line is oriented with the compass heading.

6. Double-check to make sure that the compass is still set for the variation adjustment, and if correct, weigh down the map edges to keep it in place.

7. At this point, the map is oriented to the lay of the land, and the map features should reflect those of the surrounding terrain.

Line of position to determine your location

A line of position is used when either land features can provide an optimal fix or no other features are available. Optimal land features include a road that runs east to west or north to south or two land features that can be visualized in a straight line. For best results on land, go to high ground with 360 degrees of visibility. At sea, try to shoot your headings on features during the height of a wave.

1. Orient the map as outlined above. Note that charts with a compass rose do not need to be oriented; however, all headings must be used with the middle ring of the compass rose in order to skip this step. It is a major error to use the outer ring of the compass rose without orienting the chart.

2. Positively identify the prominent land feature, buoy, or light used to aid with sea navigation. On land, the following gross guidelines can help in the identification process.

   - Contour: Evaluate the landmark's contour, translating it into a two-dimensional appearance, and search for a matching contour outline on your map. (See the map nomenclature section above.)

   - Distance: Determine the distance from your present position to the landmark to be identified. This may be calculated as follows:

        From 1 to 3 kilometers, you should be able to see the individual branches of each tree.

        From 3 to 5 kilometers, you should be able to see each individual tree.

        From 5 to 8 kilometers, trees will look like a green plush carpet.

        At greater then 8 kilometers, trees appear like a green plush carpet and there is a bluish tint to the horizon.

   - Elevation: Determine your landmark's height as compared with that of your location.

   On charts, land features, buoys, or lights may be shown as symbols, making it relatively easy to identify them.

   Lights are described on charts by their behavior, height (at mean high-water tide level), and projected visible range. For example, a chart that lists a light as Fl 4sec 20ft 10M is telling you that the light flashes every four seconds, is 20 feet above mean high-water tide level, and has a predicted range of ten nautical miles.

LIGHT BEHAVIOR CHART SYMBOLS

Symbol	Meaning
F	Fixed light; a continuous steady light.
Fl	Flashing lights; a single flash at regular intervals where the duration of the flash is always less than the duration of darkness.
F Fl	Fixed light varied by bright flashes at regular intervals.
F Gp Fl	Fixed light varied by two or more bright flashes at regular intervals.
Gp Fl	Two or more bright flashes shown at regular intervals.
Gp Fl (1 + 2)	Bright flashes are shown in an alternating sequence of numbers.
E Int	Flashing lights; a single flash at regular intervals where the duration of the flash is equal to the duration of darkness.
Occ	Flashing lights; a single flash at regular intervals where the duration of the flash is always longer than the duration of darkness.
Gp Occ	Two or more bright flashes shown at regular intervals (flash longer than darkness).
Gp Occ	Bright flashes shown in an alternating sequence of numbers (flash longer than darkness).

When floating at sea level, the height of the light is probably the single most important factor at how well and far away it can be seen. Charts that list a light's projected visibility do so based on the brightness of the light. This *normal range* is calculated using a direct line of sight and doesn't account for the earth's curvature. If sitting on the floor of a life raft or deck of a sea kayak, the earth's curvature will reduce the light's visible distance.

3. Using your orienteering compass, point the direction-of-travel arrow at one of the identified landmarks, and then turn the compass's housing until the etched orienting arrow boxes the magnetic needle (red end

forward). At the point where the direction-of-travel arrow intersects the compass housing, read and record the magnetic bearing. When using a handheld marine compass, point the front of the compass at the landmark and read the heading under the fixed lubber line; when using a deck-mounted marine compass, point the front of the vessel at the landmark.

4. Before working further with a topographic map, be sure it's still oriented.

5. For topographical maps, place the front left tip of the long edge of the compass on the identified map landmark, and while keeping the tip in place, rotate the compass until the magnetic needle is boxed (red end forward). For a chart, position your compass so that the desired heading (to the landmark) is under the lubber line, and while holding this position, rotate the chart until an imaginary line (from the left side of the compass's long edge) crosses the identical heading on the inner circle of the compass rose (magnetic heading). Be sure the imaginary line is drawn backwards and crosses the closest compass rose to your general location. In both instances, double-check that your compass heading is correct for the landmark being used (see step 3).

6. Using a pencil, lightly draw a line from the landmark down, following the left edge of the compass base plate or straightedge. You may need to extend the line. If you have a protective plastic cover, grease pencils are an ideal way to avoid exposing the map or chart to moisture and dirt.

7. Your position should be located on or close to the line.

8. For final position determination, evaluate the surrounding terrain and how it relates to your line along with believed distances to land or light features.

Triangulating to determine your position

Triangulating is a process of identifying your specific location by doing three lines of position. The ideal scenario allows you to positively identify three landmarks that are 120 degrees apart, forming a triangle where the three lines cross. Your position should be located within or around the triangle. For final position determination, evaluate the surrounding terrain, light features, and distances along with how they relate to the triangle displayed on the map.

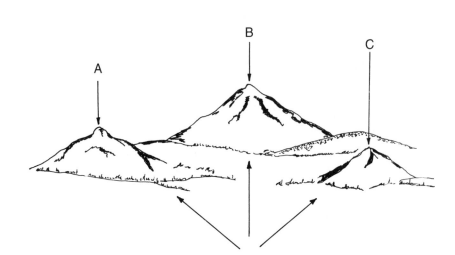

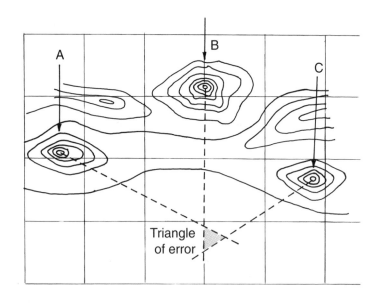

Triangulation of error

ESTABLISHING A BEARING

Never travel unless you know your present position and where you intend to go.

ESTABLISHING A FIELD BEARING
WITH A TOPOGRAPHIC MAP AND COMPASS

1. Orient your map to the lay of the land.
2. Lightly draw a pencil line from your present location to your intended destination.
3. Place the top left edge of the compass on your intended destination.
4. Rotate the compass until the left edge is directly on and parallel to the line you drew.
5. Next, rotate the compass housing—keeping the base of the compass stationary—until the floating magnetic needle is boxed inside the orienting arrow (red portion of the needle forward).
6. Read the compass heading at the point where the bottom of the direction-of-travel arrow touches the numbers of the circular compass housing. This heading is the field bearing to your intended destination.

ESTABLISHING A MAGNETIC BEARING
USING A CHART AND COMPASS ROSE

Determining a bearing with a chart's compass rose is a fairly simple process. Draw a line from your present position to your desired destination. Find your heading by identifying where the line crosses or runs parallel to the middle circle on the compass rose. Make sure you read the heading on the side closest to your destination.

ESTABLISHING A FIELD BEARING
WITH AN ORIENTEERING COMPASS

1. Hold the compass level, and point the direction-of-travel arrow directly at the intended destination site.
2. Holding the compass in place, turn its housing until the magnetic needle is boxed directly over and inside the orienting arrow (red portion of the needle forward).
3. Read the heading at the point where the bottom of the direction-of-travel arrow touches the numbers of the circular housing. This heading is the field bearing to your intended destination.

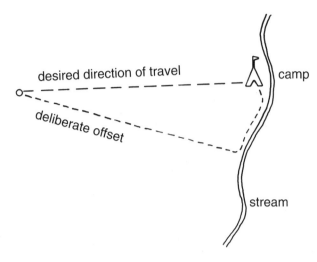

Deliberate offset

ESTABLISHING A MAGNETIC BEARING
WITH A MARINE COMPASS

For a handheld marine compass, hold your compass so that the lubber line is pointing toward your destination and read the heading beneath it. For deck-mounted marine compasses, simply turn your vessel toward your intended target and read the heading.

DELIBERATE OFFSET

If your destination is a road or shore structure, consider a heading with a deliberate offset. In other words, use a heading several degrees to one side of your final location. Since it is very difficult to be precise in wilderness travel, this offset will help you in deciding to turn left or right once you intersect the road.

MAINTAINING A FIELD BEARING

Point to point

Pick objects in line with your field bearing. Once one point is reached, recheck your bearing and pick another point. This method allows the traveler to steer clear of obstacles. Because winds and currents will throw you

Use the compass to recheck your bearing and pick your next point.

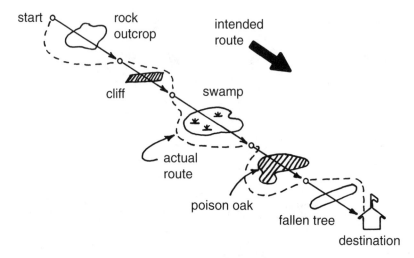

Point-to-point navigation and avoiding obstacles

off your heading, you should know the wind velocity and current's force and factor them into your heading, especially when you are in a vessel propelled by motor, sail, or paddle.

Following the compass

To follow a heading with an orienteering compass, walk forward (in line with the direction-of-travel arrow), while holding the compass level and keeping the magnetic needle boxed. To follow a heading with a marine compass, maneuver your vessel so that the heading is always in line with the lubber line.

SIX-POINT CHECKLIST FOR TRAVEL

Before you depart any location or begin a new heading, write down a travel checklist. This list will help you maintain your course and determine your exact location throughout your route.

1. Heading. Establish the compass heading (azimuth) to your desired location. Once confident of your azimuth, trust your compass and stay on your heading.

2. Distance. Determine the total number of kilometers or nautical miles your route will cover.

3. Pace count (used when on land). Estimate the number of paces it will take to reach your final destination. A pace is measured each time the same foot hits the ground. For fairly level terrain, estimate 650 paces to one kilometer. For steep terrains, paces will nearly double for each kilometer.

4. Terrain evaluation. Evaluate your route's major terrain features (roads, clearings, buoys, lights, etc.) and determine the distance or paces it takes to each. By doing this, you will maintain a constant awareness of your location within your route of travel.

5. Point description. Take the time to evaluate the appearance of your final location. This will help you when the time comes to evaluate if you have had a successful trip.

6. Estimated arrival time. Calculating your estimated arrival time will help you with setting realistic goals on the distance to travel each day.

DIRECTION FROM THE STARS

NORTHERN HEMISPHERE
In the Northern Hemisphere, Cassiopeia and the Big Dipper are very useful tools for helping you find Polaris, the North Star. The Big Dipper looks like a cup with a long handle. Cassiopeia is made up of five stars that form a large W with its opening facing the Big Dipper. The Big Dipper and Cassiopeia rotate around Polaris, and halfway between these constellations, Polaris (the North Star) can be found at the very end of the Little Dipper's handle. Contrary to popular belief, the North Star is not the brightest star in the sky, but instead is dull and uninviting. Between 5 and 50 degrees north latitude, Polaris is within 1 degree of true north, and at latitudes between 50 and 60 degrees north, it may be off as much as 2 degrees. Cassiopeia provides the key to this variance.

- Polaris is due north when Cassiopeia is directly above or below its location.
- Polaris is at a 001° heading when Cassiopeia is to its right (002° above 50° north).
- Polaris is at a 359° heading when Cassiopeia is to its left (358° above 50° north).

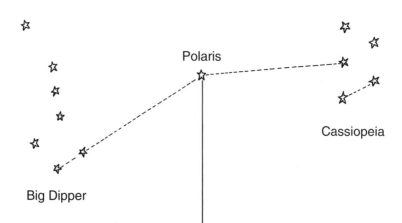

The Big Dipper and Cassiopeia

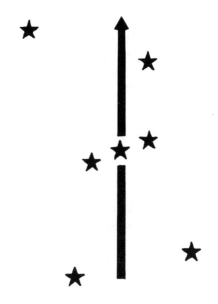

Orion's Belt

Even when both constellations cannot be seen, you can still find Polaris or determine your cardinal directions by doing the following:

- At the forward tip of the Big Dipper, there are two stars. Extend a line approximately four to five times the distance between the two stars beyond the second star to find Polaris.
- From the center of Cassiopeia, extend a line out approximately four to five times the distance between any two of its stars to find Polaris.
- Orion the hunter circles the earth directly above the equator. The leading star of Orion's Belt (called Mintaka) rises exactly due east and sets exactly due west. The belt is formed by three close stars in line at the center of the figure. When Orion is not directly on the horizon, its east–west path makes it ideal for use with a night stick and shadow.

SOUTHERN HEMISPHERE

To find the cardinal directions in the Southern Hemisphere, use the Southern Cross (four stars forming a cross) and the Pointer Stars. Because the False Cross looks similar to the Southern Cross, it may present a problem. Keep in mind that the False Cross is less bright than the Southern Cross,

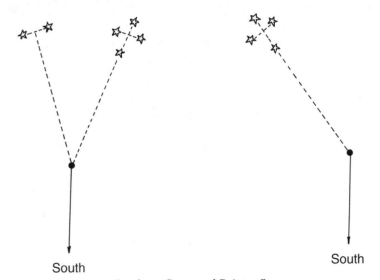

Southern Cross and Pointer Stars

and its stars are more widely spaced. In fact, the southern and eastern arms of the actual Southern Cross are two of the brightest stars in the sky. The Pointer Stars are simply two stars—side by side—and in close proximity to the Southern Cross.

To establish a southern heading, extend an imaginary line, from the top toward the bottom, out of the bottom of the cross. Draw another imaginary line perpendicular to the center of the Pointer Stars. At the point where the lines intersect, draw a third line straight down toward the ground, and this line would represent a southern direction.

STAR VERSION OF THE STICK AND SHADOW
At night, most travelers will use Polaris (the North Star) or the Southern Cross and Pointer Stars to determine their cardinal directions. When these constellations cannot be found, however, you may opt to use stars—located on the horizon away from the celestial poles—to create cardinal directions. Since these stars generally move from east to west, they can provide an east–west line when created with a stick and shadow. Find a straight 5-foot stick, and push it into the ground at a slight angle. Next, tie a piece of line—long enough to reach the ground with lots to spare—to the top of the stick. Lying on your back, position yourself so that you can pull the cord tautly and hold it next to your temple. Move your body around until the taut line is pointing directly at the selected, noncircumpolar star or planet. At this point, the line represents the star's shadow. Place a rock at the place where the line touches the ground and repeat the process again in ten minutes. The first mark is west, and the second one is east. Draw a perpendicular line between the two marks to determine north and south.

If you travel at night, you should find and use a sturdy 7-foot-long walking stick. When walking, keep the stick in front of you to feel the ground and to protect your face from branches.

DIRECTION FROM THE SUN

USING A STICK AND SHADOW
On a flat, level area, clear away all debris until a 3-foot circle of dirt is all that remains. Sharpen both ends of a long straight stick, and push one end into the ground until the stick's shadow falls onto the center of the cleared

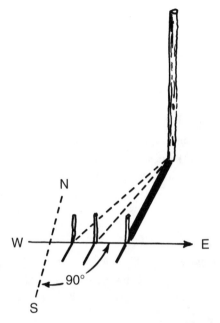

Stick and shadow in the Southern Hemisphere

area. Mark the shadow tip with a twig or other appropriate material. Wait approximately ten minutes and place another twig at the new location of the shadow's tip. Draw a straight line between the two markers and then another line perpendicular to it. Since the sun rises in the east and sets in the west, the first marking on the shadow line is west and the second one is east.

In the Northern Hemisphere, the sun will be south of your location, and in the Southern Hemisphere, the sun will be north of you. This is not always true, however, and, depending on where you are, the stick and shadow may not even be an option to use. For a stick and shadow method to be reliable, it cannot be used at locations greater than 66.6 degrees north and south latitude. Between 23.4 and 66.6 degrees north and south latitude, the sun's shadow will be pointing directly north or south at local apparent noon when the sun has reached its highest point and creates the shortest shadow of the day. If you are between 0 and 23.4 degrees north and south latitude, the sun can be north or south of your location, depending on the time of year. This should pose no problem if you realize that the first shadow is west and that the subsequent shadows move toward the east. A perpendicular line to the east–west line allows you to find which way is north–south.

NAVIGATING WITH A WATCH

Northern Hemisphere
Point the watch's hour hand toward the sun, and while holding it in this position, draw an imaginary line between the hour hand and twelve o'clock (one o'clock if daylight savings time). This imaginary line represents a southern heading. Draw another line perpendicular to this one to determine east and west.

Southern Hemisphere
In the Southern Hemisphere, point the watch's twelve o'clock hour symbol (one o'clock if daylight savings time) toward the sun, and holding the watch in this position, draw an imaginary line midway between the twelve o'clock

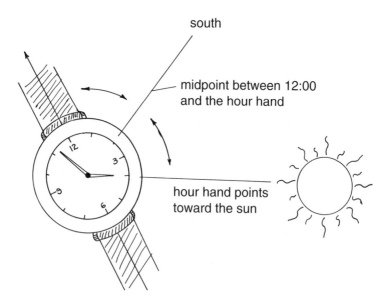

south

midpoint between 12:00 and the hour hand

hour hand points toward the sun

Using a watch to determine a southern heading in the Northern Hemisphere

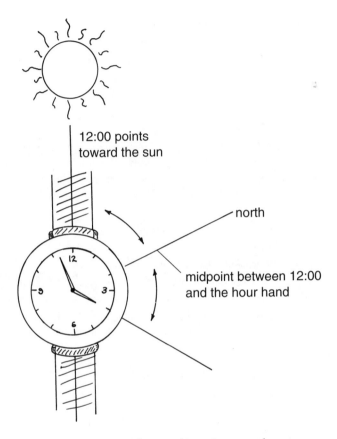

12:00 points
toward the sun

north

midpoint between 12:00
and the hour hand

*Using a watch in the Southern Hemisphere to determine a northern
heading*

hour symbol and the hour hand. This imaginary line provides an approximate northern heading. Another line drawn perpendicular to this one makes
it possible to determine east and west.

LOCAL APPARENT NOON

At local apparent noon, the sun has reached its highest point and will be
due south of you in the Northern Hemisphere and due north of you in the
Southern Hemisphere. Don't confuse local apparent noon with a twelve

o'clock reading on your watch; it is unlikely that the sun will always be at its highest or even close to it at this time. There are several methods of determining local apparent noon. For these methods to work, the horizon height used must be the same for the first recording (sometimes called sunrise) as for the second (sometimes called sunset).

Using the horizon
Record the exact times of sunrise and sunset (based on a twenty-four-hour clock), add them together, and divide the total by two. Based on a nonobscured view of the horizon, sunrise is when the top of the sun first appears on the horizon; sunset is when the top of the sun disappears on the horizon. The resultant figure is your local apparent noon, when the sun is directly north or south depending on your hemisphere.

$$\frac{\text{time of sunrise} + \text{time of sunset}}{2} = \text{local apparent noon}$$

For example, let's say sunrise occurred at 0720 hour and sunset at 1930 hour.

$$\frac{0720 + 1930}{2} = \frac{2650}{2} = 1325 \text{ hour}$$

In this example 1325 hour (1:25 P.M.) is local apparent noon, and this figure can be used to help you navigate using your established cardinal directions. Since the sun moves 15 degrees an hour, you can maintain a course by simply watching the sun and adjusting your heading appropriately throughout the day.

The kamal
If the horizon is obscured by shadows, use a kamal device to determine local apparent noon. This device allows you to create a new horizon above any cloud or haze that obscures your view. You can create a kamal by attaching a string to something flat, such as a credit card, and tying a knot in the free end of the string. Place the knot on the line so that it is tight when you hold out the flat plate with an extended arm. To use, place the knot between your

teeth, hold the flat plate out so that its bottom touches the horizon, and record the exact times of sunrise and sunset. Sunrise is when the top of the sun first appears at the top of the card; sunset is when the top of the sun disappears below the top of the card. If more height is needed, simply increase the size of the card.

HOW TO USE GPS

A Global Positioning System (GPS), an electronic device that works by capturing a satellite's signal, can augment solid navigation skills, but it should NEVER replace them. Learn how to use a map and compass before ever laying hands on a GPS! A GPS identifies your location (in latitude and longitude coordinates) by locking on to three or more satellites. To identify your altitude, it must lock on to at least four satellites. As with all electronic devices, a GPS is vulnerable to cold, moisture, sand, and heat, and even though satellite signals are now easier than ever to capture, there are still times when a signal cannot be obtained. In such instances, the GPS is nothing more than added weight to the pack. It's a great tool, but don't rely on it for your sole source of navigation. Since GPS units are extremely reliable over the open water, the U.S. Coast Guard recommends them as part of your routine gear. The ability to give an exact position could save hours in a search.

LOOKING FOR NEARBY LAND WHILE AT SEA

When you are searching for land while stranded at sea, look for the following indicators.

- Cumulus clouds often hover over or slightly downwind from an island.
- The sky will often have a greenish tint close to shallow lagoons or shelves of coral reefs. Look for this tint on the bottoms of clouds.
- The sky will often show a reflection of light on the bottoms of clouds when close to snow or ice-covered land.
- Deep water is often dark, whereas shallow water close to land tends to be a lighter shade.
- You will probably hear the sounds of birds and surf long before seeing the shore.
- Likewise, you will probably smell wood smoke, fruits, and other shore scents long before seeing the shore.

- An increase in the bird population may indicate land, but don't count on it. But note that birds often fly toward land and their nesting areas at dusk. During day hours, the flight pattern of birds is not reliable since they tend to search for food during this time.
- Winds often blow toward land during the day and out to sea at night. However, unless land is close, the pattern of the wind is not a factor you can rely on.

12

Travel

When lost, deciding whether or not to travel boils down to one question: "Does anyone know where to look for me?" If the answer is no, your ability to use a compass and chart may make the difference between being rescued or not.

> —*Aviation Survival Technician Alan Auricchio*
> *U.S. Coast Guard Helicopter Rescue Swimmer*

Once you have identified your position and planned a route, you will want to use a few travel techniques to get from point A to point B. Remember, if you are at sea, you are better off staying close to your distressed vessel. If you are on land, you should stay put as long as you are able to meet your survival needs. If traveling on foot, head toward a well-traveled road or prominent man-made feature. If traveling on open water, head for shipping lanes, land, or rain. Your movement at sea will be influenced by paddles, wind, and current.

TRAVEL AT SEA

LIFE RAFT
Movement in a life raft is influenced by wind and currents, and to some extent you can influence this movement by using paddles, sails, and a sea anchor.

Paddles
Trying to move a life raft with a paddle is often futile and a waste of energy. Paddles should only be used for steering when approaching shore.

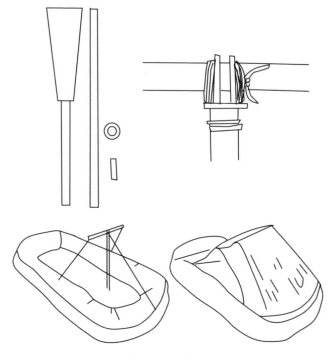

Improvised sail

Sailing

Some rafts come with sails, and for those that don't, you can improvise one, although a sail is not advisable for a bigger twenty- to twenty-five-man life raft. You cannot sail a raft into the wind, so you should sail about 10 degrees off from the wind's direction. Sailing a raft does have its risks and thus should not be done unless land is near and the direction of the wind will move you toward land. If these criteria are met, fully inflate the raft, take in the sea anchor, improvise a sail, and use the paddle as a rudder. Stow the sea anchor so that it will deploy in case the raft would capsize. To avoid falling out of the raft, don't make any sudden movements, stand up, or sit on the raft's sides. If seas are rough, don't use a sail, leave the sea anchor out (but keep it away from the bow), and sit low in the raft with everyone's weight toward the upwind side.

Improvised square sails can be made using paddles and any other solid panel of material, such as a tarp or blanket. Tie the paddles together using a square lash to form a T, and then secure the paddles upright to the raft with line. If the raft doesn't have a mast socket, pad the bottom to prevent damage to the raft. You could try using a shoe on top of a protective cloth and insert the mast into the shoe's heel. If you can, slip the toe of the shoe under the seat to hold it in place. Attach the top of your square sail to the mast, but hold the lower lines in your hand so that you can adjust tension or let go when winds gusts.

Sea anchor

A sea anchor, which will help you control the raft's movement, may automatically deploy with the raft, or you may need to deploy it once aboard. If you don't have a sea anchor, improvise one from a duffle bag or bucket.

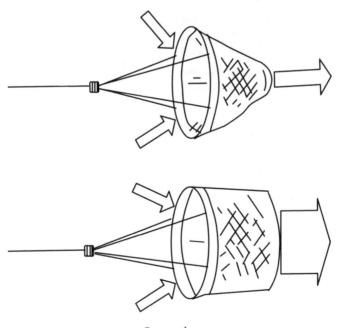

Sea anchor

Sea anchor deployed

Most sea anchors have an apex that opens and closes and allows you to adjust for the impact of the current on your movement. When the apex is open, the sea anchor acts like a drag and keeps your movement to a minimum. You may decide to do this when you want to stay close to your vessel or within a shipping lane. When the apex is closed, the sea anchor allows the current to push the raft in its direction of movement. Do this when you want to move faster to reach your destination. Some sea anchors come with a trip line that allows you to collapse the sea anchor and makes it easier to vary your speed or pull in the anchor. If your sea anchor does not have a trip line, you can improvise one by attaching a floating line to the outside edge of the sea anchor. The line will need to be long enough to allow the sea anchor to fully open. If you don't have any floating line, improvise a float and tie the line so that it runs from the sea anchor to the float and then the raft. Make sure that the improvised trip line is rigged in such a way that you avoid getting it tangled in the sea anchor or its line. For best performance, adjust the sea anchor so it is in the wave's trough when the raft is at the wave's crest. To prevent damage to the raft, wrap the line of the sea anchor with a cloth or similar material.

REACHING SHORE

Beaching a raft is perhaps the most dangerous part of your journey. Before attempting a surf landing, exhaust all other options first. If no other option is available and you have a chart of the area, take a look at the various shoreline options. What type of bottom contours and makeups (sand, rock, etc.) do you see? Are there any obstacles (man-made or natural) that should be avoided? Avoid coral reefs and rocky cliffs, and try to land on the lee side of the island or at the junction of a stream and the sea. Take time to evaluate the waves' patterns. Waves usually come in sets, and not all sets are the same. Pick the least threatening approach you can, and begin your approach with the start of a set of gentler waves. To keep control of your vessel, don't surf the waves.

Before starting your approach to shore, let the sea anchor out, remove the sail, and use your oar to paddle and steer toward the shore. If you are in a large raft with a group, disperse the weight equally on both sides of the raft. When contact is made with the first wave, paddle backward on both sides of the raft to maintain control and prevent the raft from taking off when its front is lifted by the wave. Begin a forward hard paddle as soon as you feel the front of the vessel dropping. This drop indicates that the wave has passed. As another wave overtakes you, repeat this process.

If the raft capsizes in the surf, grab hold of it and try to ride it in. If you lose the raft and have to swim ashore, use the side- or breaststroke. If you're in moderate surf, swim with the wave and dive just below the water before the wave breaks. In high surf, swim toward the shore in the wave's trough, and submerge just before the next wave starts to overtake you. If an undertow pulls you down, push off the bottom and swim to the surface. As you get closer to the shore, select a landing spot where the waves run up onto shore rather than violently crash upon the beach. Once you enter the breakers, move into a sitting position with your feet forward and about 2 to 3 feet lower than your head. You are better off absorbing the shock of an unexpected reef or rock with your feet than your head.

KAYAK

Before departing on any kayak adventure, carefully consider the difficulty of the trip, your skills, what gear to take, and how it should be packed. Do you have the skills necessary for the trip? As you inventory your gear, make sure it meets your daily and survival needs, is protected from moisture, and is packed to allow for vessel buoyancy. For proper balance, heavy items should be securely located close to the center and centerline of the vessel. As disposable items are used up, fill the empty space with air-filled dry bags. Filling the space helps to keep all items secure. Once the kayak is packed, you are ready to enter the water.

The following pages summarize basic kayaking use. To fully understand these skills, I encourage you to attend classes from a qualified kayaking instructor.

Getting in and out of the kayak

Getting in and out of your kayak will often leave you wet and frustrated. A balance or support is the key to staying dry when entering the vessel. Try entering from a dock or in shallow water using a paddle. Wet exit and reentry into a kayak are covered in chapter 4.

High-dock entry

A high-dock entry refers to docks that are above the kayak's coaming but not higher than 3 or 4 feet. To perform a high-dock entry, set the kayak in the water parallel to the dock, and lay the paddle parallel and close to the dock's edge. While facing the front of the kayak, place your feet in the vessel, bend at your waist, lift your buttocks, and roll onto your belly. This position should place you so that your buttocks is directly above the cockpit. From this position, slide your weight down into the cockpit, and extend your legs into the vessel while supporting yourself with your hands on the deck. To get out, reverse the steps.

Low-dock entry

A low-dock entry refers to docks that are at or below the kayak's coaming. To perform a low-dock entry, set the kayak in the water parallel to the dock, and lay the paddle perpendicular and behind the kayak's coaming to the rear. Extend the paddle so that approximately two-thirds of it is in contact with the dock and the blade is flat with its surface. With your hands opening toward the back of the vessel, use your hand over the cockpit to hold the paddle and coaming together while your other hand is placed on the dock. Avoid placing excessive weight on the paddle. While facing the front of the vessel, squat down and sit on the edge of the cockpit. Insert one foot at a time into the cockpit, and slide in while using the dock and kayak to maintain balance. To get out, reverse the process.

Shallow-water entry

To enter a kayak in shallow water, use a paddle to balance the vessel. Place the paddle perpendicular to the vessel and behind the cockpit coaming. Extend the blade so that the paddle on your side can rest on the water's bottom. With your hands opening toward the back of the vessel, use your hand over the cockpit to hold the paddle and coaming together while your other hand holds the paddle's shaft. Avoid placing excessive weight on the paddle. While facing the front of the vessel, squat down and sit on the edge of the cockpit. Insert one foot at a time into the cockpit, and slide in while using the paddle and kayak to maintain balance. To get out, reverse the process.

Launching a kayak through surf

Try to avoid launching your kayak through surf! If you can, plan your trips so that they begin and end in protected areas. If you have no choice, take the time to evaluate the waves and surrounding underwater structures. The two basic types of beach breakers (waves) are often referred to as "spilling" and "curling." Spilling breakers have foam that falls over the front of the wave as it breaks; curling breakers curl over the front and extend to the bottom of a breaking wave. Because spilling breakers are the calmer of the two, seek them out. Take the time to evaluate the timing and sequence of the waves, and plan your launch accordingly. Before launching your vessel, make sure everything is secured and that the vessel has adequate buoyancy. To launch, decrease the impact of the wave's force by attacking the surf straight on so that your vessel is perpendicular to the waves. Time your entry with the beginning of a wave, and paddle aggressively through a surf, making sure you're out of the wave before it begins to break. Waves greater than 6 feet should not be attempted. To know when a wave is reaching this height, stand on the shore and watch the horizon and the waves as they break. If the top of a breaking wave extends above the horizon, the wave is too high.

Kayak stability in the water

When the vessel is level, your body's center of gravity is directly above the kayak's center of buoyancy. Stability within a kayak, however, is a constantly changing process as the kayak's center of buoyancy constantly changes. Your body's center of gravity, however, should never change and should always be kept over your waist. To keep it that way, you must compensate for the kayak's changing center of buoyancy by bending your upper body—to the opposite side—just above your hips.

How to hold a paddle

The position of your hands on the paddle may change, depending on your activity. When you need a slow powerful stroke to overcome wind or other forces, hands are often extended out on the paddle. Determining how far to extend this grasp is personal, but as a general rule you will want to extend your hands equal to the distance created when your upper arms are perpendicular (90 degrees) to your body and your forearms are parallel to it.

For a cruising stroke, which expends less energy, place your hands closer together at a distance equal to your shoulder width. Regardless of the type of stroke you use, a nonfeathered paddle allows for two control hands, whereas a feathered paddle allows for only one control hand. A control hand is placed on the paddle (palm back) with your knuckles closest to the wrist in line with the top edge of the blade so that its working side is facing the back of the kayak. To maintain a proper blade angle, the handgrip should be firm and unchanging. Both hands are used this way for a nonfeathered paddle; only one hand is used for a feathered paddle. When the blade-to-water angles change, adjust the paddle angle using your wrists and forearms, but do not change your grip.

Maneuvering a kayak

Basic forward stroke

For a basic stroke, extend your forward hand and bend the other one close to the body. The forward hand, which is on the side with the paddle in the water, pulls its end of the paddle back and through the water while the other hand pushes its end forward and away. Adding a torso twist to the stroke makes it more powerful and less tiring. Good paddlers will use the torso and not their arms to drive the stroke. A torso twist starts with the upper body parallel to the paddle with the shoulder on the extended arm side forward, and as the stroke proceeds, the powerful torso rotates from the waist, augmenting the pushing and pulling movements of the arms. Developing a smooth cadence and keeping your upper arm below chin height, thus ensuring a low paddle angle, will produce the best results while expending the least amount of energy.

Turning the kayak

To turn a kayak, simply make strokes on one side of the vessel. For better results, use long sweeping strokes, which start similar to the basic stroke except the forward arm and shoulder are extended as far outward as they will go. Keep the paddle close and as near level as possible. Completely

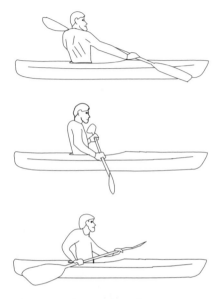

Forward stroke

Basic forward stroke

immerse the blade into the water, and using a torso twist, swing the blade through the water in a low, broad sweeping motion. A reverse sweep has the same effect, except the stroke begins at the rear of the vessel and the back side of the blade leads the stroke. In addition to turning the kayak, sweeping strokes can be used to stop the vessel.

Stopping and backing up

Stopping a kayak is an important skill to master, as the ability to stop allows you to plan a route of attack or avoid upcoming obstacles. To stop, keep the blade slightly behind your hips with its angle vertical or slightly forward. Without changing your handgrip, immerse the blade in the water and give a slight forward push to the back of the blade. The process should last one to two seconds and be repeated from side to side. To back up the

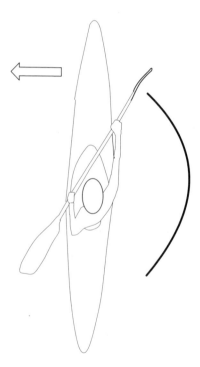

Turning the kayak

Backing up the kayak

kayak, extend the forward hand while the other hand is kept bent and close to the body. The back hand on the side with the paddle in the water pushes its end of the paddle forward and through the water while the forward hand pulls its end back. Adding a torso twist to the stroke makes it more powerful and less tiring. Good paddlers will use the torso rather than their arms to drive the stroke. A torso twist starts with the upper body parallel to the paddle, with the shoulder on the extended arm side forward, and as the stroke proceeds, the powerful torso rotates from the waist, augmenting the pushing and pulling movements of the arms. Developing a smooth cadence and keeping your upper arm below chin height, thus ensuring a low paddle angle, will produce the best results while expending the least amount of energy. To maintain paddle orientation, use the back of the paddle and do not move your hand placement with this stroke.

Moving sideways

A draw stroke is often used to move a kayak sideways. To perform, rotate your torso in the direction of the movement, insert the blade 2 to 3 feet into

Draw stroke

the water (keep the paddle perpendicular to the kayak with the blade parallel to it), and using the power surface of the blade, draw the blade toward the kayak. At the start of the stroke, the lower arm should be straight and the upper arm bent. The lower arm pulls the paddle as the upper arm pushes it away. The stroke's power comes from the pulling lower arm. Just before the paddle reaches the kayak, rotate the blade so it is perpendicular to the vessel and remove it from the water. Avoid letting the blade move under the kayak.

Crossing currents

Current and wind make it difficult to take a direct route from point A to point B. To compensate, point your vessel into the wind or current so that you compensate for the force of the current or wind while paddling from point A to point B.

Recovery skills

Even though a kayaker is often dressed for the conditions, he or she still faces the threats of hypothermia and drowning if he or she should capsize. The keys to surviving are knowledge, skill, and remaining calm, all of which came from practice. Take lessons and learn how to correct your kayak before, during, and after it capsizes. Bracing strokes can be broken down into two categories: support and recovery. A support stroke helps you maintain stability; a recovery stroke brings you upright if an unstable posture has occurred. For details on capsized recovery, refer to chapter 4. These strokes can be classified as either low or high brace, which best describes how the paddle is held when they are performed.

Low bracing strokes

With low bracing strokes, you must hold the paddle perpendicular to the boat's plane and at your side or slightly behind your hips. The paddle's shaft should be shifted to the bracing side and held in a low horizontal position with the back side of the blade down. All low brace strokes use the back side (nonpower surface) of the blade. Hands should be placed on the shaft with palms down, which allows for optimal control and force when performing the maneuver. The bracing arm should be out and away from the vessel, often almost straight, and the hand on the nonbracing arm should be held close to the stomach, where it provides a pivot point for the low bracing strokes. Low bracing strokes position you right over the paddle and allow you to push down with all your weight. Once the maneuver stops the capsizing process, the kayak can be flicked back into the upright position. (See chapter 4 on flicking.)

Standard low brace

If you're thrown off balance while your vessel is moving, the standard low brace stroke helps you regain stability. To perform this stroke, hold the paddle in the low brace position (see above) and bring the back side of the blade down until it skims the water's surface. For optimal lift, the leading edge of the blade should be tilted up. (The angle will vary.) Once a lift is felt, place your weight down and forward over the blade as much as is necessary to push you back up. If you need additional leverage, pull up with your nonbracing arm while you continue to push down with the bracing

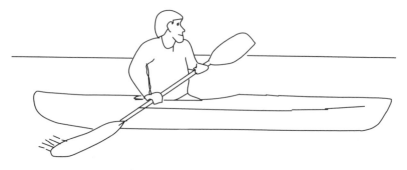

A standard low brace helps you quickly regain balance in a kayak.

arm. This stroke can also help when you are bracing against surf that is pushing you sideways. To be effective against a wave, you must get your vessel perpendicular to the force of the wave, place the back side of the paddle on top of the breaker, and lean on the paddle. Note that this maneuver is not effective in boats that are not moving.

Sweeping low brace

When the vessel is at a stop or just barely moving, you can use a sweeping low brace stroke in place of the standard low brace to help regain vessel stability. To perform this stroke, hold the paddle in the low brace position (see above) and twist your body—opening up on the bracing side—until the back side of the paddle can be placed in the water near the rear of the boat. Use the heel of the palm on your bracing hand to create a broad arched stroke that ends when your blade is perpendicular to the craft. Just before the stroke is to end, place your weight down and forward over the blade as much as is necessary to push you back up, although this may not be required. For optimal results, the leading edge of the blade should be tilted up (angles will vary) during the core of the stroke.

Slap brace (low brace maneuver)

A slap brace is a reflex stroke that you can use when rapid recovery is necessary. To perform this stroke, hold the paddle in the low brace position (see above) and strike the water on the bracing side with the back side of the blade. The movement should allow you enough momentary stability to quickly regain control of your vessel.

A sweeping low brace helps regain kayak stability.

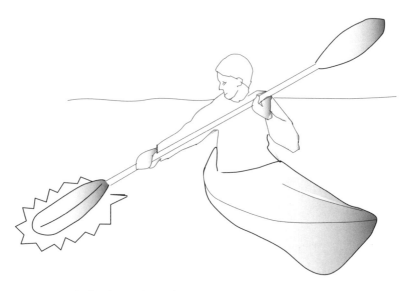

A slap brace is used when rapid recovery is needed.

High bracing strokes

High bracing strokes are helpful for stability and recovery when your paddle is located within the front half of your kayak. This technique requires you to shift the paddle's shaft to the bracing side and to place the blade's power surface down. All high brace strokes use the front side (power surface) of the blade. Place your hands on the shaft with your palms facing up and away from your body and your elbows pointing down close to your body. To use this technique, keep the paddle shaft as level as you can and never let your hands go above your head. The nonbracing hand provides a pivot point for the high bracing strokes. Recovery occurs when you pull down on the paddle's shaft. Once the maneuver stops the capsizing process, the kayak can be flicked back into the upright position.

Downward high brace

Use the downward high brace stroke when you are thrown off balance while your vessel is moving forward and the paddle is forward of your hips. To perform this stroke, hold your paddle in the high brace position (see above)

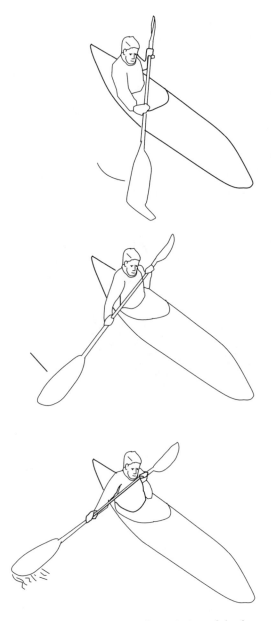

The sweeping high brace is a simple variation of the forward stroke.

and reach out approximately 3 feet to strike the water with the flat surface on the power side of the blade. Let your nonbracing arm act as a pivot, while your bracing arm is pulling the blade down and toward you. As the blade approaches your position, it will likely increase its water depth and blade steepness, which in turn will cause a decrease in the amount of support provided. To retrieve the blade, turn it until it is perpendicular to the water surface and bring it up and out of the water.

Sweeping high brace

The sweeping high brace is also used when you are thrown off balance while your vessel is moving forward and the paddle is forward of your hips. This maneuver is actually a simple variation of the forward stroke. By angling the back of the blade away from you, with the power face down and the leading edge angled up, you can transform the forward stroke into a supporting high brace.

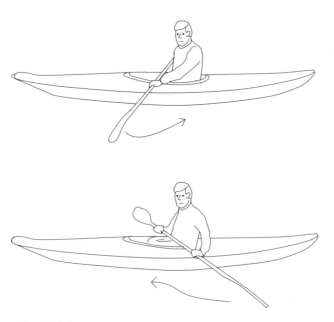

The sculling high brace helps you hold your position in winds and strong waves.

Sculling high brace

This technique is especially useful when you need to hold your position in winds and strong waves. The sculling stroke uses a never-ending forward and backward sweeping technique (see above) where the blade is rotated so the power surface is always leading the stroke and the leading edge is angled up. The ideal stroke will have a 45-degree arch and a 3-foot side-to-side sweep and follow a shallow and horizontal figure-eight pattern. To use this stroke to maintain your position in strong winds or surf, lean into the wind or wave and use the sculling stroke on the opposite windward side.

Landing a kayak through surf

Landing a kayak through surf presents a great problem: You will not be able to evaluate the type of wave you will be tackling since you'll be looking at the back side of the wave and will not be able to see it break. Before attempting a surf landing, be sure you have exhausted all other options. If no other option is available and you have a chart of the area, take a look at the various shoreline options. What type of bottom contours and makeups (sand, rock, etc.) do you see? Are there any obstacles (man-made or natural) that you should avoid? Take time to evaluate the waves' patterns. Waves usually come in sets, and not all sets are the same. Pick the least threatening approach you can, and begin your approach with the start of a set of gentler waves. To keep control of your vessel, don't surf the waves.

With your kayak facing 90 degrees to the waves, paddle backward when contact is made with the first wave. Doing this allows you to maintain control and prevent the vessel from taking off when its front is lifted by the wave. Begin a forward hard paddle as soon as you feel the front of the vessel dropping. This drop indicates that the wave has passed. As another wave overtakes you, repeat this process.

If the kayak capsizes in the surf, grab hold of it and try to ride it in. If you lose the kayak and have to swim ashore, use the side or breast stroke. If you're in moderate surf, swim with the wave and dive just below the water before the wave breaks. In high surf, swim toward the shore in the wave's trough, and submerge just before the next wave starts to overtake you. If an undertow pulls you down, push off the bottom and swim to the surface. As you get closer to the shore, select a landing spot where the waves run up on to shore rather than violently crash upon the beach. Once you enter the breakers, move into a sitting position with your feet forward and about 2 to 3 feet lower than your head. You are better off absorbing the shock of an unexpected reef or rock with your feet than your head.

ON LAND

HOW TO CARRY A PACK

When carrying an internal frame pack on the trail, organize your gear so that the heavier items are on top and close to your back. This technique focuses most of the pack's weight on your hips and makes it easier to carry. If off trail, organize the pack so that the heavy items are placed close to the back from top to bottom. The majority of the pack's weight will be carried by your shoulders and your back, which gives you better balance. If you don't have a pack and you have to travel, improvise one. (See chapter 3.)

BASIC TRAVEL TECHNIQUES

Breaking trail and setting the pace
The person breaking trail works harder than anyone else. Therefore, this job should be switched on regular intervals between the members of a team. If in a team, always set a comfortable pace for yourself and others who are traveling with you. Remember the COLDER acronym. If you have dropped layers of clothing and are still sweating, you are going too fast.

Kick step
When traveling uphill in snow or small rock (scree), a kick step will make the ascent easier for you and those who are following you. Using the weight of your leg, swing the toe of your foot into the snow or scree to create a step that supports at least the ball of your foot (if you are going straight up) or at least half of your foot (if traversing). If you're in a group and are leading an ascent using this technique, be sure to consider the stride of those who are following you. When going uphill, lean forward until your body is perpendicular to the earth's natural surface but not that of the hill.

Plunge stepping (down-climbing)
Plunge stepping is similar to a kick step except that you are going downhill and are kicking your heels, and not your toes, into the slope. Slightly bend

Kick stepping

the knees and keep your body perpendicular to the ground at the base of the hill. When going downhill, lean backward until your body is perpendicular to the earth's natural surface and not that of the hill.

Traversing
The traverse (diagonal climbing) is a quick and easy way to get up or down a hill. When traversing a hill, you may have to slightly shorten your strides as the grade changes. An adjustable pole, if you have one, would be nice.

Using a ridgeline to your advantage
When traveling through mountainous terrain, try to stay high on the ridgeline when moving from point A to point B. You are better off traveling a little farther than trying to deal with the constant up-and-down travel associated with elevation changes.

Rest step
When walking uphill, use a rest step by locking your knee with each step. This process takes the weight off the muscle, allowing it to rest, and places it on the skeletal system. For best results, take a short pause with each step.

Plunge stepping

Deep snow and desert

Traveling in deep snow and desert can be exhausting and should be avoided unless absolutely necessary.

Creeks

Crossing a creek can pose a problem, especially during the winter. If you have to cross a small creek, loosen your pack's shoulder straps and undo your waistband so you can quickly remove the pack if you fall in. In snow, try to cross in a shaded area where there is a large amount of snow and no water to be seen. Use a pole to evaluate the snow's depth and stability before taking each step. Have one person cross at a time. For larger creeks without a bridge or road crossing, try to find a narrow area where passage is possible. (You may have to travel upstream closer to the creek's origin to find this opportunity.)

Frozen bodies of water

Avoid crossing large bodies of ice since you do not want to risk breaking through the ice. Always go around a lake. If you have no other choice but to cross a river, cross on the outside of a riverbend or in a straight stretch where the river is more likely to be shallow. Avoid areas that have anything, such as logs, stumps, or rocks, sticking up out of the ice. The radiant heat from these objects will weaken the ice directly next to them.

Prepare for rescue

If rescue doesn't appear imminent, the area you are in doesn't meet your needs, and you have solid navigational skills, you may want to risk traveling to safety. If you do decide to depart, be sure you leave a note detailing your time of departure, intended route, and planned destination. In addition, mark your trail by tying flags to branches or breaking branches.

13

Health

*The will to survive is always superior to all the best
training and latest high-tech gadget or tool. It's this will
that often makes the difference between a happy life and
6 feet under.*

> —*Aviation Survival Technician Thomas Smylie*
> *U.S. Coast Guard Helicopter Rescue Swimmer*

The medicine you need to survive in the wilderness is simply first aid
and CPR with a twist. Ultimately, the environment you encounter and the
amount of time you must survive before you return to civilization will have
the biggest impact upon any health issues that arise. The weather may be
bad, and the nearest medical facility may be miles from your location.
Before you leave on a trip, you should receive adequate first aid and CPR
training. In no way should you consider this chapter a replacement for that
instruction.

GENERAL HEALTH ISSUES

Your ability to fend off an injury or infection will play a significant role in
how well you handle any given survival situation. Proper hydration, nutri-
tion, hygiene, and rest all affect our ability to ward off problems found in
the wilderness.

STAYING HYDRATED

Without water, you will die in approximately three to five days. Dehydration
will also directly affect your ability to make logical decisions about how
to handle any given problem. Fluids are lost when the body works to warm

itself, when you sweat or perform intense activity, and when you urinate or defecate. As dehydration starts to set in, you will begin to have excessive thirst and become irritable, weak, and nauseated. As your symptoms advance, you will have a headache and become dizzy, and eventually your tongue will swell and your vision will be affected. Prevention is the best way to avoid dehydration. You should drink at least 2 quarts of water during minimal activity and 4 to 6 during more intense activity. If you should become dehydrated, decrease your activity, get out of the sun, and drink enough potable water to get your urine output up to at least one quart in a twenty-four-hour period. Hopefully you will have the ability to obtain enough water.

NOURISHMENT
Nourishing foods increase morale, provide valuable energy, and replace lost nutrients, such as salt and vitamins. Although food has many benefits, it's not usually necessary and you may be able to go without food for several weeks.

CLEANLINESS
Staying clean helps to increase morale and prevent infection and disease. To stay clean in the wilderness, take a bath or sunbathe anywhere from thirty minutes to two hours a day. Keep your hair trimmed, brush your teeth and gums, monitor your feet, and clean your cooking utensils after each use to decrease the risk of illness or infestation.

REST
You must provide the body with proper rest to ensure you have adequate strength to deal with the stress trials associated with a survival situation.

TRAUMATIC INJURIES AND THEIR TREATMENT
Traumatic injuries are extremely taxing on a survivor, and whether you keep your composure during such an experience may mean the difference between survival and death. Follow a logical process when treating traumatic injuries. Treat the most life-threatening injuries first: breathing, bleeding, and shock. Use the following six-step approach to evaluate a victim.

SIX STEPS FOR A LIFE-THREATENING EMERGENCY

1. Take charge of the situation. When you are part of a survival group, the person who was in charge of the vessel and crew welfare may not be the best-qualified person to handle a medical emergency. In this case, the person with the most medical experience should take charge.
2. Determine if the scene is safe to enter. If risk to the victim or rescuer exists, don't enter the area until it is considered safe.
3. Treat life-threatening injuries. If an area is unsafe, move the victim to an area that is safe. Then perform a head-to-toe evaluation using the ABCD format in this order:

     A——Airway
     B——Breathing
     C——Circulation and C-spine
     D——Deadly bleeding

4. Treat for shock. Because shock can lead to death, early intervention is critical. Treating shock involves appropriate body positioning, dry clothing, insulation, pain control, and comforting words.
5. Secondary evaluation. Once life-threatening issues have been addressed, perform a secondary survey to evaluate all injuries. Treat each injury.
6. Treatment plan. Discuss how to prevent the victim's condition from worsening and implement an appropriate treatment plan.

AIRWAY, BREATHING, CIRCULATION (ABCs)

To successfully treat someone who has had his or her airway, breathing, or circulation compromised, you must know CPR. I advise you to learn CPR before you depart for the wilderness. In cold-water submersions or drownings, CPR can be successful even when the subject has been submerged for up to one hour.

BLEEDING (HEMORRHAGE)

There are three types of bleeding, and contrary to popular belief, color is not always the best indicator of the source of the bleeding. Arterial bleeding, the most serious of the three, normally involves bright-red spurting blood. Venous bleeding, which can also be very serious, is usually seen as a steady stream of dark red blood. Capillary bleeding is minor, and since the vessels are so close to the skin's surface, dark red blood typically oozes from the site. To treat a hemorrhage, try direct pressure, pressure points, and only in rare circumstances a tourniquet.

Direct pressure

Do not delay in applying pressure to a bleeding wound, even if you have to use your hand or finger. If materials are available, use a pressure dressing, which is applied by packing the wound with several sterile dressings and then wrapping it with a continuous bandage. Make sure the bandage is snug but not so snug as to cut off circulation to the rest of the extremity. To ensure this doesn't occur, regularly check for pulses and sensations on the extremity beyond the wound site. If the dressing soaks through, apply subsequent dressings directly over the first. Leave the dressing in place for two days; thereafter, change it daily. If the wound is on an extremity, elevate it above the heart level. In most cases, applying direct pressure for ten minutes will stop the bleeding.

Pressure points

Applying pressure to a blood vessel between the heart and the wound will decrease the amount of blood loss from the injury site. To be effective, you must apply pressure for about ten minutes. Refer to the diagram on the next page for examples of different pressure points.

Tourniquet

A tourniquet is rarely necessary and should only be used when direct pressure, elevation, and pressure points have failed and you deem a tourniquet necessary to save a life. Because a tourniquet increases the likelihood of losing an extremity, once a tourniquet has been applied, never loosen it. To use a tourniquet, apply a 3- to 4-inch band 2 inches above the wound in between the wound and the heart. After wrapping the band around the limb several times, tie it into a square knot with a sturdy stick placed in the knot's center. Tighten the tourniquet by turning the stick until the blood flow comes to a stop, and secure the stick in place. Finally, mark the victim's head with a big T, and note the time when the tourniquet was applied.

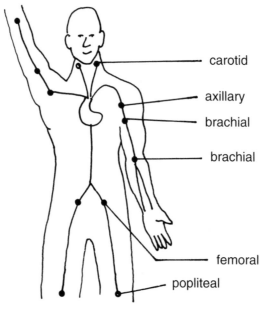

Pressure points

SHOCK

Shock is a direct result of the body's inability to provide a sufficient blood supply to its vital organs. If not corrected, shock could ultimately lead to death. Signs and symptoms of shock include pale, cold, and clammy skin, a weak rapid pulse, and feelings of restlessness, disorientation, and faintness. All injuries, no matter how small, can potentially lead to shock, and all victims should be treated as if shock were present. To treat shock, reduce the patient's heat loss by covering him or her with any form of dry insulating material and providing insulation from the ground. If hypothermia is present, treat it. If the victim is conscious, lay him or her on his or her back. If the victim is unconscious, lay him or her on his or her side, in case of vomiting. Elevate the victim's lower extremities 8 to 12 inches, unless there is a serious head, neck, chest, or abdomen injury. For a head or chest injury, raise the victim's upper torso about 15 degrees toward a sitting position.

INJURIES TO THE HEAD
Signs and symptoms of a head injury include bleeding, increasing head-ache, drowsiness, nausea, vomiting, unequal pupils, and unconsciousness. To treat a suspected head injury, first immobilize the neck if a neck injury is suspected. Then monitor the victim for any change in mental status, and if the victim is conscious, treat him or her for shock by slightly elevating the head and keeping him or her warm. If the victim is unconscious, treat him or her for shock by laying the victim on his or her side to avoid aspiration of vomit.

INJURIES TO THE SPINE
Signs and symptoms of a spinal injury include pain, numbness, tingling, decreased sensation or lack of feeling in extremities, and the inability to move the body below the injury site. Be sure to immobilize the neck and body on a firm flat surface, if a spinal injury is suspected, and treat for shock.

INJURIES TO THE ABDOMEN
Signs and symptoms of an abdominal injury include bleeding, abdomi-nal wall bruising, pain, drowsiness, nausea, and vomiting. An open wound where intestines are exposed should be covered, and care should be taken to prevent drying of the wound. To treat an open intestine wound, rinse away any dirt and debris with a mixture of sterile water and salt (1 quart of ster-ile water mixed with 1 teaspoon of salt). After cleaning the area, cover it with a clean dressing that is wetted with the above solution. It's extremely important to prevent the intestines from drying out. Both open and closed abdominal injury should be treated for shock.

INJURIES TO THE CHEST
Signs and symptoms of a chest injury can vary tremendously, depending on the cause or problem. As a general rule, subjects may have pain, coughing and shortness of breath, irregular breathing pattern (rapid or slow), anxiety, and cyanosis. An open chest wound should be covered with a piece of plas-tic or other airtight material. (While dressing may be used, it is not as effec-tive.) Tape the covering on three sides to allow air to escape but not enter the

opening. If the victim's breathing pattern worsens, remove the patch. Both open and closed chest injuries should be treated for shock.

FRACTURES

Closed fractures

Signs and symptoms of a closed fracture include site deformity, swelling, pain, and an inability to bear weight on the extremity. To treat a closed fracture, clean all open wounds, and apply a splint that immobilizes the extremity one joint above and below the fracture site. A splint can be improvised with strong branches that are held in place with 1-inch-wide bands of clothing or similar material. Once you have applied a splint, monitor the extremity for any changes in circulation or sensation. When in doubt about whether something is broken, treat it as if it were.

Open fracture

An open fracture has all the signs and symptoms of a closed fracture with the addition of bone protruding through the skin. Don't handle bones or push bone ends back in during the treatment process. To treat an open fracture, rinse away any dirt and debris with a mixture of sterile water and salt (1 quart of sterile water mixed with 1 teaspoon of salt). After cleaning the bone and the surrounding area, cover the end of the bone with a clean dressing that is wetted with the above solution. It's extremely important to prevent the bone ends from drying out. Secure the dressing in place, splint the fracture, and monitor the extremity for any changes in circulation or sensation.

INJURIES OF JOINTS AND MUSCLES

Sprains

A sprain, which is an area of pain over a joint, will present symptoms similar to those of a closed fracture. A sprain should be treated the same way as a fracture.

Strains

A strain, which is an area of pain over muscle, not bone, will present such symptoms as localized muscle tenderness. A strain is usually the result of overuse or trauma. To treat a strain, apply moist heat and discontinue the activity that appears to make it worse.

BURNS
Burns are rated by depth as first, second, or third degree. A first-degree burn causes superficial tissue damage and is similar in appearance to a sunburn. A second-degree burn causes damage into the upper portion of the skin, where it appears as blisters surrounded by first-degree burn damage. Third-degree burns cause complete destruction of the skin's full thickness and beyond. First- and second-degree burns are usually present with third-degree burns. To treat burns, cool the skin as rapidly as possible for at least forty-five minutes. Burns can continue to cause damage for up to forty-five minutes even after the heat source has been removed. As soon as possible, remove jewelry and clothing, except for clothing stuck in the burn. Never cover a burn with grease or fats, as they will only increase the risk for infection. Clean the burn with sterile water, if available, apply antibiotic ointment, and cover the burn with a clean, loose dressing. To avoid infections, leave the bandage in place for six to eight days. After that time, change the bandage as necessary. If the victim is conscious, have him or her drink plenty of fluids. Major burns cause a significant amount of fluid loss, which may cause the victim to go into shock. If pain medications are available, use them. Burns are extremely painful.

FOREIGN BODIES IN THE EYE
Most eye injuries occurring in the wilderness result from dust or dirt blown into the eye by the wind. Signs and symptoms include a red and irritated eye, light sensitivity, and pain in the eye. To treat, first look for any foreign bodies that might be causing the irritation. Since most dirt or dust can be found under the upper eyelid, invert the lid and try to isolate and remove the irritant. If unable to isolate the cause, rinse the eye with clean water for at least ten to fifteen minutes. When rinsing, be sure that the injured eye is lower than the other eye to avoid contamination during the rinsing process. If available, apply ophthalmic antibiotic ointment to the eye.

WOUNDS, LACERATIONS, AND INFECTIONS
Clean all wounds, lacerations, and infections, and apply antibiotic ointment, dressing, and bandage daily.

CORAL CUTS

Coral is very sharp and can cause severe cuts. These types of cuts heal slowly and often are accompanied by a poison contained in the coral. To treat, clean the wound as thoroughly as you can, and apply antibiotic ointment and a dressing. Change daily.

BLISTERS

Blisters result from the constant rubbing of your skin against a sock or boot. The best treatment for blisters is prevention. Monitor your feet for hot spots or areas that become red and inflamed. If you develop a hot spot, apply a wide band of adhesive tape across and well beyond the effected area. If you have tincture of benzoin, use it to make the tape adhere better and to help toughen the skin. To treat a blister, cut a blister-size hole in the center of a piece of moleskin, and place the moleskin with the hole directly over the blister. This takes the pressure off of the blister and places it on the surrounding moleskin. Try to avoid popping the blister. If it does break open, treat it as an open wound by applying antibiotic ointment and a bandage.

THORNS AND SPLINTERS

Thorns and splinters should be removed, and to prevent infection, antibiotic ointment, dressing, and a bandage should be applied.

FISH HOOK INJURIES

A fish hook can be left in place for short periods of time if rescue is imminent. If rescue is not expected within several hours, however, remove the fish hook. The easiest way to do this is to advance it forward until the barb clears the skin and then cut the barb off and reverse the hook back out.

ENVIRONMENTAL INJURIES AND ILLNESSES

The environment challenges us in many different ways and must be respected. It cannot be conquered. Adapting and being properly prepared will play a significant role in surviving nature's sometimes awesome power. Problems associated with dangerous marine life will be covered in chapter 14.

COLD INJURIES

Hypothermia

Hypothermia occurs if you have an abnormally low body temperature. Heat may be lost through radiation, conduction, evaporation, convection, and respiration. Signs and symptoms of hypothermia include uncontrollable shivering, slurred speech, abnormal behavior, fatigue and drowsiness, decreased hand and body coordination, and a weakened respiration and pulse. The best treatment is prevention by avoiding long exposures to cold and early recognition of the signs of hypothermia. Dressing appropriately for the environment and maintaining adequate hydration can help you avoid most problems with hypothermia. If hypothermia does occur, treat it without delay. First, try to stop the continued heat loss by getting out of the wind and moisture and putting on dry clothes, a hat, and gloves. If you have a sleeping bag, take off your clothes, fluff the bag, and climb inside. If you have an extreme case of hypothermia, someone else should disrobe and climb inside the bag with you. If conscious, the victim should drink warm fluids and eat carbohydrates.

Frostbite

The best treatment for frostbite, which commonly affects toes, fingers, and the face, is prevention. To ensure frostbite doesn't occur, use the COLDER acronym and understand how heat is lost. The two types of frostbite are superficial and deep. Superficial frostbite causes cold, numb, and painful extremities that appear white or grayish in color. To treat, rewarm the affected part with your own body heat. (Place your hands in your armpits; put your feet on another person's abdomen.) Cover other exposed areas with loose, layered material. Never blow on your hands since the resultant moisture will cause the skin to freeze or refreeze. Deep frostbite causes your skin to take on a white appearance, lose feeling, and become extremely hard. If you should sustain a deep frostbite injury, don't attempt to rewarm it as this will be extremely painful. If the frostbitten area is a limb, rewarming it will render it useless. (You can walk on a frostbitten limb.) Prevent any further freezing and injury by wearing proper clothing and avoiding further exposure to the elements.

Immersion injuries

Trench feet occur if your feet have had long-term exposure to cold, wet socks. It usually takes several days to weeks of this exposure before the damage occurs. Signs and symptoms include painful, swollen feet or hands that have a dishpan appearance. Since immersion injuries can be so debilitating, try to avoid them altogether. To do this, change wet socks quickly, don't wear tight clothing, and increase foot circulation with regular massages. Treat an immersion injury by keeping the feet dry and elevated. Pat wet areas, since rubbing may result in further tissue damage.

Snow and sun blindness

Snow and sun blindness, which results from exposing your eyes to the sun's ultraviolet rays, occurs most often in areas where the sun is reflected off the snow, water, or light-colored rocks. The resultant burn to the eyes' surfaces can be quite debilitating. Signs and symptoms include bloodshot and tearing eyes, a painful and gritty sensation in the eyes, light sensitivity, and headaches. Prevent this injury by wearing 100 percent UV sunglasses. If snow and sun blindness does occur, treat it by avoiding further exposure, applying a cool wet compress to the eyes, and treating the pain with aspirin as needed. If symptoms are severe, apply an eye patch for twenty-four to forty-eight hours.

HEAT INJURIES

Sunburn

Prevent sunburn by using a strong sunscreen, whenever necessary. If a burn should occur, apply cool compresses, avoid further exposure, and cover any areas that have or may become burned.

Muscle cramps

Muscle cramps result from excessive salt loss from the body, exposure to a hot climate, or excessive sweating. Painful muscle cramps may occur in the calf or abdomen while the victim's body temperature is normal. To treat, immediately stretch the affected muscle. Prevent reoccurrence by consuming 2 to 3 quarts of water during minimal activity and 4 to 6 quarts of water when in cold or hot environments or during heavy activity.

Heat exhaustion

Heat exhaustion can occur if you are physically active in a hot environment. It is usually accompanied by some component of dehydration. Signs and symptoms include feeling faint or weak, cold and clammy skin, headache, nausea, and confusion. To treat, rest in a cool, shady area and consume plenty of water. Since heat exhaustion is a form of shock, the victim should lie down and elevate his feet 8 to 12 inches.

Heatstroke

Heatstroke occurs when the body is exposed to prolonged high temperatures. As a result, the body temperature rises to such high levels that damage to the brain and vital organs occur. Signs and symptoms include flushed dry skin, headache, weakness, lightheadedness, rapid full pulse, confusion, and in severe cases unconsciousness and convulsions. Heatstroke is a true emergency and should be avoided at all costs. Immediate treatment is imperative. Immediately cool the victim by removing his clothing and covering him with wet towels or by submersion in cool but not icy water. Fanning is also helpful. Be careful not to cool to the point of hypothermia.

ALTITUDE ILLNESS

As your elevation increases, so does your risk of developing a form of altitude illness. As a general rule, most mountaineers use the following three levels of altitude to determine their potential for medical problems:

High altitude: 8,000 to 14,000 feet

Very high altitude: 14,000 to 18,000 feet

Extremely high altitude: 18,000 feet and above

Since most travelers seldom venture to heights greater than 14,000 feet, the majority of altitude illnesses are seen in the high-altitude range of 8,000 to 14,000 feet.

As the altitude increases, your body goes through a compensatory change marked by an increased respiratory and heart rate, increased red blood cell production and capillaries, and changes in the body's oxygen delivery capacity. Most of these changes occur within several days to weeks of exposure at high altitudes. To diminish the impact of altitude, do a gradual ascent, avoid heavy exertion for several days after rapidly ascending to high altitudes, ingest only small amounts of salt, and if you have a history of pulmonary edema or worse consider taking the prescription medication Diamox (Acetaxolamide), unless you have kidney, eye, or liver disease. The usual dose is 250 milligrams two to four times a day. Start the medication twenty-four to forty-eight hours prior to ascent and continue it, while at high altitude, for forty-eight hours or as long as needed.

High-altitude illnesses are a direct result of a reduction in the body's oxygen supply. This reduction occurs in response to the decreased atmospheric pressure associated with higher elevations. The three illnesses of high altitude are acute mountain sickness, high-altitude pulmonary edema, and high-altitude cerebral edema.

Acute mountain sickness

Acute mountain sickness is a group of unpleasant symptoms that usually occur from decreased oxygen supply to the brain at altitudes greater than 8,000 feet. Signs and symptoms include headache, fatigue, dizziness, shortness of breath, decreased appetite, nausea and vomiting, feeling of uneasiness, cyanosis (bluing around lips and fingers), and fluid retention of face and hands. In severe cases, there may be evidence of some impaired mental function, such as forgetfulness, loss of memory, decreased coordination, hallucinations, and psychotic behavior. To treat, allow time for your body to acclimate to the high altitude by keeping activity to a minimum for the first two to three days after arriving at elevations greater than 8,000 feet. Avoid alcohol and tobacco, eat a high-carbohydrate diet, and drink plenty of fluids. If symptoms are severe and oxygen is available, give 2 liters per minute through a face mask for a minimum of fifteen minutes. If symptoms persist or worsen, then descend at least 2,000 to 3,000 feet, which is usually enough to relieve symptoms.

High-altitude pulmonary edema (HAPE)

This extremely common and dangerous type of altitude illness results from abnormal accumulation of fluid in the lungs. It most often occurs when a climber rapidly ascends above 8,000 feet and, instead of resting for several days, immediately begins performing strenuous activities. Signs and symptoms are similar to those of acute mountain sickness. In addition, you may experience shortness of breath with exertion that may progress to shortness of breath at rest as time goes by, shortness of breath when lying down that usually causes great difficulty in sleeping, and a dry cough, which in time will progress to a wet, productive, and persistent cough. If symptoms progress, the climber may show signs and symptoms of impaired mental function similar to those seen in acute mountain sickness. If the climber becomes unconscious, death will occur within several hours unless quick descent and oxygen treatment is started. Early diagnosis is the key to successfully treating pulmonary edema. Once identified, immediately descend a minimum of 2,000 to 3,000 feet or until symptoms begin to improve. Once down, rest for two to three days and allow the fluid that has accumulated on the lung to be reabsorbed by the body. If oxygen is available, administer it through a tight-fitting face mask at 4 to 6 liters per minute for fifteen minutes and then decrease its flow rate to 2 liters per minute. Continue using the oxygen for an additional twelve hours if possible. If the victim has moderate to severe HAPE, he should be evacuated to the nearest hospital as soon as possible. If you are prone to HAPE, you may want to try Diamox prior to the climb. As this is a prescription drug, discuss its use with your primary care provider.

High-altitude cerebral edema (HACE)
High-altitude cerebral edema, which is swelling or edema of the brain, most often occurs at altitudes greater than 12,000 feet. Edema forms as a consequence of the body's decreased supply of oxygen, known as hypoxia. Signs and symptoms are similar to those of acute mountain sickness, plus an unusually severe and unrelenting headache, abnormal mental function, such as confusion, loss of memory, poor judgment, and hallucinations, and ataxia (poor coordination). If left untreated, a coma and death could occur. Early recognition is critical for saving someone who develops HACE. If someone has a severe chronic headache with confusion and/or ataxia, he or she must be treated for high-altitude cerebral edema—a true emergency— so descend immediately. If the victim is ataxic or confused, he or she will need help. If oxygen is available, administer it through a tight-fitting face mask at 4 to 6 liters per minute for fifteen minutes and then decrease its flow rate to 2 liters per minute. Continue using the oxygen for an additional twelve hours, if possible. Even if the victim recovers, he or she shouldn't return to the climb. If the victim is unconscious or has severe symptoms, try to obtain an air evacuation to the nearest hospital.

INFECTIONS FROM HANDLING FISH

Fish poisoning occurs when bacteria from the fish enter your system through cuts, scrapes, and other soft-tissue openings. Signs and symptoms of fish poisoning include swelling and redness at the site, fever, and chills. The best treatment is prevention. Keep hands clean and dry, and wash them thoroughly after handling fish. If an infection does occur, clean the site several times a day and apply a new clean, dry dressing each time. If you have antibiotics specific to cellulites, use them.

TICKS

To remove a tick, grasp the tick at the base of its body, where its mouth attaches to the skin, and apply gentle backward pressure until the tick releases its hold. If its head isn't removed, apply antibiotic ointment, bandage, and treat as any other open wound.

BEES OR WASPS

If stung by a bee or wasp, immediately remove the stinger by scraping the skin, at a 90-degree angle, with a knife or your fingernail. This will decrease the amount of venom that is absorbed into the skin. To relieve itching, apply cold compresses and/or a cool paste made of mud or ashes. To avoid infection, don't scratch the stinger site. If you carry a bee sting kit, be sure to review the procedures of its use before you leave. If someone has an allergic anaphylactic reaction, you must act quickly. Using the medications in the bee sting kit and following basic first aid principles will, in most cases, reverse the symptoms associated with this type of reaction.

MOSQUITOES

Use insect repellant and cover the body's exposed parts with clothing or mud to decrease the number of bites from this pesky insect.

FISH PUNCTURE WOUNDS

If you are not careful, the spines from certain fish can cause a painful puncture or cut that may lead to a soft-tissue infection. All punctures should be cleaned and treated with an antibiotic ointment and dressing. For poisonous marine life stings and puncture issues, see chapter 14.

SALTWATER BOILS

After a week or two in a life raft, you probably will develop saltwater boils on areas of your skin that are in constant contact with the wet floor of the raft. These include your buttocks, knees, elbows, and hands. Prevention is the key. Try to keep the raft floor dry, and cover your skin with clothes, oils, or barrier creams. If a boil occurs, avoid further contact with the raft floor, and keep the wound clean, dry, and exposed to the air.

SEASICKNESS

As a result of the raft's motion, seasickness can happen to anyone. Nausea and vomiting, which can lead to severe dehydration, are the most common symptoms. Once one person starts vomiting, others often follow. Treat seasickness by cleaning the vomit from the victim and the raft, and treat the sick person for shock. If seasickness pills are available, use them as soon as possible. Do not allow the victim to eat or drink until symptoms decrease or end and then make sure the victim has no more than 2 ounces of water every twenty minutes. To overcome seasickness, try to focus on the horizon. This may or may not work.

CONSTIPATION

Constipation is common in a survival setting. To treat, drink fluids and exercise. Laxatives are rarely needed and not recommended.

SURVIVAL STRESS

The effects of stress in a survival situation cannot be understated. To decrease the magnitude of stress, you must understand it and prevail over it. How much stress you experience will depend on the environment, your condition, and the availability of materials. The most important key to overcoming survival stress is the survivor's will or drive. While this is not something that can be taught, your will is directly affected by the amount of stress associated with a survival situation. When preparing for a trip, remember the six P's of survival: Proper prior preparation prevents poor performance. To further your chances of surviving, using my three-step approach to survival, keep a clear head and think logically, prioritize your needs, and improvise.

14

Dangerous Marine Life

I once read that you are safer in the water than on the nation's highways. However, driving down a crowded highway may seem like a pretty safe place when you are floating in the water on a moonless night.

> —*Aviation Survival Technician James Q. Lyon*
> *U.S. Coast Guard Helicopter Rescue Swimmer*

Although the chances of being stung or bit by a marine creature are fairly small, it still remains a threat. This chapter, while not all-inclusive, does outline a few of the various threats you might encounter at sea or along the shore.

MARINE CREATURES THAT BITE

SHARK
Sharks are perhaps the most successful sea predators that man should fear. With that said, realize that while shark attacks should be feared, they are unlikely to occur. A few sharks are known to get as big as 45 to 50 feet in length. Most live in shallow waters close to major continents or islands in

Shark

the temperate or tropical zones. Shark attacks are more likely to occur at dusk, during a shark's natural feeding time, near deep channels, in murky waters, and where animal products are dumped. If sharks approach close to your raft, hit them on the nose with your paddle, taking care not to lose or break the paddle.

Methods for reducing risk

Stay in the life raft.

Throw garbage, vomit, and even deceased individuals overboard at night.

Don't fish when sharks are present, and if one appears when a fish is on a line, cut it free.

Never clean fish in the water.

Shark bites produce a lot of tissue damage, and shock is sure to follow. To treat a bite, get the victim out of the water, immediately treat any potentially life-threatening injuries, treat for shock, clean the wound, and apply a dressing.

BARRACUDA

The barracuda is an aggressive carnivorous fish, and on rare occasions, it has been known to bite humans. These long fish can grow up to 6 feet in length and weigh as much as 80 pounds. Most live in shallow waters close to major continents or islands in tropical and subtropical zones. Barracuda attacks are more likely to occur at night, especially if you're using a light, which seems to attract them. If a barracuda approaches, it can usually be temporarily chased away, but it probably won't leave.

Methods for reducing risk

Stay in the life raft.

If you must get in the water, avoid colorful clothing, bright shiny objects, and lights.

Don't spear a barracuda as the risk of injury to you or your raft is too high.

Barracuda bites produce a lot of local tissue damage, and depending on the degree of the injury, shock may follow. To treat a bite, get the victim out of the water, treat for potentially life-threatening injuries, treat for shock, clean the wound, and apply a dressing.

EEL

Although the eel has been known to attack people, it rarely does so without provocation. Eels can grow up to 9 feet in length and 1 foot in diameter. Eels are bottom dwellers that stay in holes and crevices, under rocks, or in corals close to shore. These night feeders are common in tropical zones. If left alone, an eel will probably not bite you.

Eel bites produce a lot of local tissue damage, and depending on the degree of the injury, shock may follow. To treat a bite, get the victim out of the water, treat for potentially life-threatening injuries, treat for shock, clean the wound, and apply a dressing.

GROUPER (SEA BASS)

The grouper is a large carnivorous member of the sea bass family. Some groupers can get as big as 6 feet long and 500 pounds, and although they pose a small threat, these fish can inflict significant damage just due to their tremendous size. Historically, the greatest risk has been to fingers and toes. Fortunately, the fish will usually spit out the digit before completely severing it from your body. Groupers are abundant in tropical and subtropical zones.

Methods for reducing risk

Stay in the life raft.

If you must get in the water, make sure you have no fish products on you. If a grouper is spotted, don't dispute its territorial rights. Get out of the water.

Grouper bites produce a lot of local tissue damage, and depending on the degree of the injury, shock may follow. To treat a bite, get the victim out of the water, treat for potentially life-threatening injuries, treat for shock, clean the wound, and apply a dressing.

SEA SNAKE

A sea snake's venom is approximately two to ten times as toxic as a cobra's. A sea snake bite, however, doesn't always deliver toxin, and only about one quarter of people bitten ever develops symptoms. The snake's paddle-shaped tail distinguishes it from the land snake in the water. Most live in shallow waters close to major continents or islands in the temperate or tropical zones. Sea snakes appear to be curious and are attracted by fast-moving objects.

Methods for reducing risk

Do not handle snakes.

Shuffle your feet when walking along a muddy bottom.

Wear protective clothing while in the water.

Snake bites produce local bite marks. If symptoms develop, they will usually begin between ten minutes and two hours of receiving the bite. Symptoms may include anxiety, thick tongue, thirst, nausea, vomiting, generalized aches, eventual paralysis, muscle twitching and spasms, respiratory distress, and even cardiac failure. To treat, remove any surface venom you see, immobilize the patient and affected limb, provide reassurance, and perform CPR when necessary.

MARINE CREATURES THAT STING

There are several species of fish and invertebrate that sting using a venom apparatus often located in their fins or tentacles. Their venom can cause intense pain, and some are potentially fatal. Because it may be difficult to identify the species that stung you, a few general guidelines should be addressed.

UNIDENTIFIED STING

Most stings produce a localized pain that increases in intensity over a matter of minutes. Some stings become excruciating and may last for several hours. The sting site may look like a puncture wound with surrounding inflammation that often becomes pale and swollen with tissue pitting (you pushed down on the swollen area and an indent was left). The victim may become very anxious and even delirious. Fatigue, nausea, vomiting, and sweating may occur, and on rare occasions the stings, especially those of stonefish and stingrays, can lead to death.

If possible, treat an unidentified sting by immersing the affected area, usually a hand or foot, in hot water, but not too hot as to burn, for thirty minutes. This is thought to break down the venom. If you have a first aid kit with lidocaine (without epinephrine) or a similar product (and know how to use it) with a syringe and a needle, use it to anesthetize the area. Clean and wash the area, and remove any broken spines or their integuments. Perform CPR, if needed. Treat for shock, and slightly elevate the affected area.

STINGRAY

Stingrays live in shallow water, especially in the tropics and in temperate zones. All stingrays have the ray appearance, which is easily disguised when they bury themselves in the seabed. Most stings occur when the ray is stepped on, which causes it to react like a scorpion, bringing its tail up and forward to drive the tail spine into the victim. The venomous, barbed spine in a ray's tail can cause a severe or fatal injury.

Methods for reducing risk

> Shuffle your feet when walking in the water.
> Wearing rubber boots may help decrease the severity of a sting but will not stop it.

A stingray's sting may create deep and painful penetrating wounds. The pain increases over one to two hours and often subsides in six to ten hours but sometimes lasts for days. The wound will be pale with a wide bluish rim that encircles the wound, and secondary infection often follows these injuries. The victim may become very anxious and even delirious. Anorexia, nausea, vomiting, and excessive sweating and salivation are common systemic symptoms. Symptoms common to the wound site and the affected extremity include muscle cramps, tremors, and paralysis. In severe cases, palpitations, hypotension, cardiac irregularities, respiratory distress, and on occasion even death can occur. If possible, treat the sting by immersing the affected area, usually a hand or foot in hot water, but not so hot as to burn,

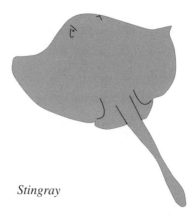

Stingray

for thirty minutes. This is thought to break down the venom. If you have a first aid kit with lidocaine (without epinephrine) or a similar product (and know how to use it) with a syringe and a needle, use it to anesthetize the area. Clean and wash the area, and remove any broken spines. Treat for shock, and slightly elevate the affected area. Perform CPR, if needed. Broad-spectrum antibiotic prophylaxis should be used.

STONEFISH

Stonefish live in shallow water, especially in the Pacific and Indian Oceans. With their subdued color and irregular shape, they easily camouflage when resting in mud, rock, or coral. Most stings occur when the stonefish is stepped on and its dorsal spine inflicts an extremely painful and potentially fatal wound.

Methods for reducing risk

Shuffle your feet when walking in the water.

Wear thick-soled shoes when in danger areas.

Be cautious when on coral reefs and while entering or leaving a boat.

A stonefish sting will cause immediate pain, which increases in severity within ten minutes. The affected wound and limb will become ischemic, cyanotic, swollen, hot, numb, and tender, and paralysis of the limb often occurs. The pain may last for several days. Stonefish stings often cause cardiovascular compromise and respiratory failure. The first concern for a victim will be to prevent drowning. If possible, treat the sting by immersing the affected area, usually a hand or foot, in hot water, but not too hot as to burn, for thirty minutes. This is thought to break down the venom. If you have a first aid kit with lidocaine (without epinephrine) or a similar product (and know how to use it) with a syringe and a needle, use it to anesthetize the area. Clean and wash the area, and remove any broken spines. Treat for shock, and slightly elevate the affected area. Perform CPR, if needed. Broad-spectrum antibiotic prophylaxis should be used.

JELLYFISH

The sting of a jellyfish is extremely painful but rarely lethal. Since it may be difficult to identify which jellyfish are dangerous and which are not, it is best to avoid all of them.

Methods for reducing risk

Do not touch a jellyfish.

Use protective clothing when in areas indigenous to jellyfish.

Don't enter the water where a jellyfish was recently spotted.

Depending on the type of jellyfish, the sting can range from a blistering rash to muscle cramps, chills, sweating, nausea, vomiting, paralysis, delirium, convulsions, and even death. The first concern for a victim of a jellyfish sting is to prevent drowning. As soon as possible, apply household vinegar, if available, over the adhering tentacles to inactivate their stinging cells. Do not apply alcohol to the tentacles as this may actually increase the amount of poison injected into the victim. You can use alcohol, however, on bare skin once the tentacles have been removed. Wearing gloves, remove the tentacles with an upward motion to prevent further skin contact. Oral antihistamines, narcotic pain medications, and local anesthetic will help. Treat for shock, and perform CPR, if needed.

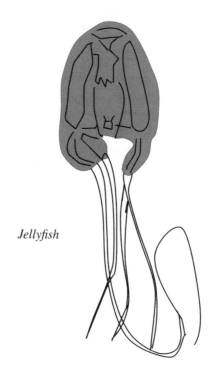

Jellyfish

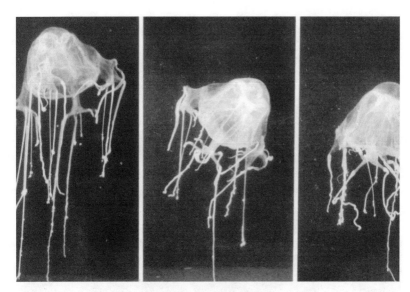

Jellyfish stings are extremely painful.

BLUE-RINGED OCTOPUS

This small octopus is located on the Great Barrier Reef off of eastern Australia. Grayish-white with gleaming blue ring-like markings, the octopus's toxin is considered more potent than that of any land animal, and bites often lead to death. The octopus is not aggressive unless provoked, and most bites occur when the octopus is stepped on or handled.

Methods for reducing risk

Avoid contact with this deadly octopus.

Be wary of empty shells and small openings that might provide a good home or hiding area.

Bites often go unnoticed, but within fifteen minutes, the site will become swollen and produce a blood blister appearance. Within minutes, the victim will often develop a painless paralysis. Abdominal numbness, nausea, vomiting, difficulty breathing, visual disturbances, weakness, and chest pain may occur. To treat, wash the toxin out of the bite, apply a pressure bandage, and immobilize the limb. If paralysis does occur, CPR may be necessary.

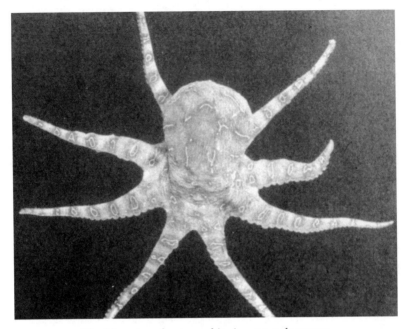

The blue-ringed octopus bite is extremely potent.

CONE SHELL

Cone shells live under rocks, inside coral reef crevices, and along rocky shores in tropical zones. They have a smooth cone-shaped shell that is long with a narrow opening at the base. The cone uses a harpoon (similar to hypodermic needles) that it can thrust into its victim injecting its venom.

Methods for reducing risk

Don't collect cone shells. A cone shell sting often produces immediate excruciating pain, which increases in severity within ten minutes. The affected wound and limb may become ischemic, cyanotic, swollen, hot, numb, and tender. Within minutes, the entire body, especially the lips and mouth, may feel numb. Muscular paralysis may develop and can vary from mild to full body. Respiratory paralysis and even cardiac death often occur. To treat, apply a pressure bandage, and immobilize the limb. If paralysis does occur, CPR may be necessary.

15

Kits

Survival kits do not need to be extravagant and can be put together quickly using everyday household items. With a little ingenuity and creative thinking you will find unlimited resources to meet your every need.

—*Aviation Survival Technician Jeff Danner*
U.S. Coast Guard Helicopter Rescue Swimmer

Prior knowledge and skill in the basic elements of survival is the key to ensuring a safe wilderness experience. In addition, in the event of a survival setting, proper preparation may reduce the amount of stress you experience and may save your life. An adequate abandon-ship bag, survival kit, and first aid kit will play an instrumental role in how you meet your needs.

ABANDON-SHIP BAG

It is doubtful that the contents in your raft or any kit you purchase will meet all your needs. For the best kit you could ever have, make it yourself! Many factors will influence what you put in your kit, including cost, storage space (in raft and on ship), the size of your crew, and where you're traveling.

Inflatable life rafts that are coast guard certified for ocean use will often include the following items. However, you should familiarize yourself with your life raft kit before you need it. An abandon-ship bag should be used to fill the voids left in your raft's survival kit.

285

THE RAFT KIT

- Heaving line: This buoyant heaving line, 100 feet long, with a small floating ring attached at one end is used to reach people who are in the water and need help getting to the raft.
- Knife: This knife is used to cut the painter and free the life raft from the larger disabled vessel. Its rounded tip helps prevent accidental damage to the raft.
- Paddles: Paddles are used to escape sinking vessels and for breaking surf. Otherwise, they are not used at open sea except as a shark club.
- Pump: The pump is used to inflate and adjust cell inflation as needed.
- Sea anchors: Often two sea anchors, which are attached to 50 feet of nylon, are provided. Usually one deploys when the raft inflates, and the other is a spare.
- Bailers: Bailers are used to ride the raft of water.
- Sponges: Used to dry the bottom of the raft, sponges play an important role in preventing saltwater sores and heat loss.
- First aid kit: Most rafts include a first aid kit. Take time to look it over and augment it as appropriate.
- Flashlight: A coast guard–approved flashlight with several spare batteries and bulbs should be provided. These flashlights are waterproof and have a blinker button for signaling.
- Signal mirror: A signal mirror is perhaps the most effective signal you'll have.
- Whistle: A whistle may be helpful up close, but wave and boat noises may make it ineffective.
- Parachute flares: Most kits contain two red rocket parachute flares, which keep the flare in the air longer and make it more likely to be seen by rescue.
- Handheld red flares: Many kits contain up to six handheld red flares, which can be used to attract rescue to your position.
- Provisions: Most kits have 1 pound of hard bread, packed in sealed containers, or an approved nutritional equivalent for the raft's size (number of people).
- Water: The kit will have water in quantities that range from 1 pint per person and up. The water is normally held in 4-ounce plastic pouches. (Four pouches make a pint.)

- Can openers: Sometimes, water and food rations will be in cans, and thus a can opener might be included.
- Drinking cup: A flexible drinking cup marked in ounces is provided.
- Fishing tackle kit: A small amount of fishing tackle is provided. Don't count on this being enough—augment it.
- Seasickness tablets: You will be happy to have these. Use them before it is too late.
- Repair kit: This kit is used to repair buoyancy tubes. Take the time to see if it includes patches, plugs, or clamps. If it doesn't have enough or any plugs and clamps, augment it.

ABANDON-SHIP BAG

When making an abandon-ship bag, take the time to review what your raft kit contains and build your bag based on this information and the five survival essentials.

1. Personal protection

    Clothing: Dry clothes, survival suits, etc.

    Shelter: Tarps, blankets, space blankets, etc.

    Fire: Only an issue on shore. Consider carrying a metal match, lighter, and tinder.

2. Signaling: EPIRB, VHF radio, signal mirror, flares and smoke devices, sea marker dye, etc. Be sure to carry fresh batteries as needed.

3. Sustenance

    Water: Four-ounce plastic water bottles, hand-powered reverse-osmosis water maker, solar stills, desalting kits, plastic sheets and tubing, water purification tablets, water storage containers, etc.

    Food: Freeze-dried foods, vitamins, fishing tackle and snare line, plankton net, etc.

4. Travel: Magnetic compass, watch, charts, tables related to navigation along with detailed instructions on use, calculator, paper, pencils, protractor, etc.

5. Health

    Psychological stress: Family photo, religious material, something to read, etc.

Traumatic injuries: A large yet varied dressing and bandage kit (adhesive and nonadhesive), medical tape, bee sting kit, broad-spectrum antibiotics, aspirin, narcotic pain pills, tincture of benzoin, Bactroban ointment (broad-spectrum antibiotic ointment), duct tape, etc.

Environmental injuries: Sunglasses, sunscreen, multivitamins, seasickness pills (transderm scop patch, acupressure, and relief bands), etc.

Other items to consider include flashlight, cup, plastic bags, pocketknife and sharpener, nonlubricated condoms (they will work for holding water!), scissors, tweezers, routine medications, moleskin, lip balm, extra sponges and bailers, light sticks, nylon string, hard rubber plugs (various sizes), hose clamps (various sizes), long needle-nose pliers, sewing kit, and aluminum foil.

16

Knots and Lashes

Whether it is seamanship, Boy Scouts, mountaineering, or river rafting, knowledge and mastery of basic knots is a must. Knots are used for many tasks, including food procurement, shelter construction, and improvising clothing. In the business of saving lives, a well-tied knot can be the difference between life and death.

> —*Aviation Survival Technician Chris Razoyk*
> *U.S. Coast Guard Helicopter Rescue Swimmer*

KNOTS

SQUARE KNOT

Square knot connects two ropes of equal diameter together.

DOUBLE SHEET BEND

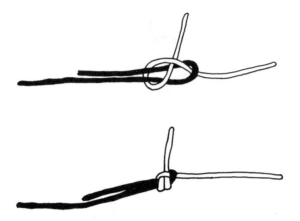

Double sheet bend connects two ropes of different diameters.

IMPROVED CLINCH KNOT

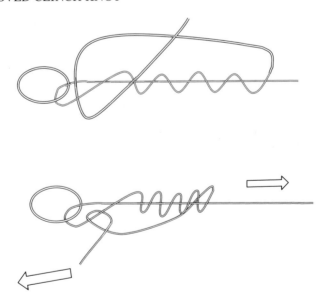

Improved clinch knot is used to attach a hook to a line.

OVERHAND FIXED LOOP

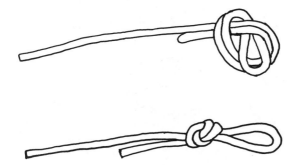

Overhand fixed loop has multiple uses in a survival setting.

BOWLINE

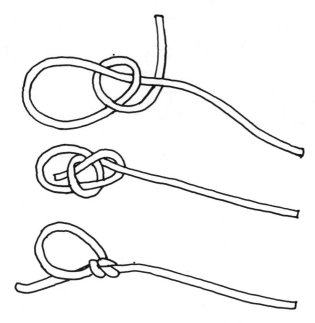

Unlike the overhand fixed loop, bowline is much easier to untie after you use it.

DOUBLE HALF HITCH

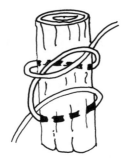

Double half hitch secures a line to a stationary object.

LASHES

SQUARE LASH

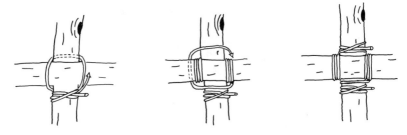

Square lash secures two perpendicular poles together.

SHEAR LASH

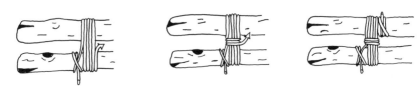

Shear lash attaches several parallel poles together.

17

Float Plan

A float plan should be completed and left with a reliable friend prior to your departure. If you fail to return as scheduled, your friend should notify the coast guard or other rescue organization. Remember that plans are not filed with the coast guard, so unless your friend notifies the USCG, a rescue mission will not be started. To avoid unnecessary searches, be sure to notify your friend of any delays in your plans and upon your return.

Person Reporting Overdue

Name _____ Phone_____

Address_____

Description of Boat

Name _____

Registration/Documentation No. _____ Length _____

Make_____ Type_____

Hull Color_____ Trim Color_____

Fuel Capacity_____ Engine Type_____ No. of Engines _____

Distinguishing Features _____

_____

Operator of Boat

Name _____

Age_____ Health _____

Phone _____

Address_____

Operator's Experience _____

Survival Equipment (provide numbers and check as appropriate)

____PFDs	____Flares	____Mirror	____Smoke
____Signals	____Flashlight	____Paddles	____Water
____Food	____EPIRB	____Anchor	____Raft or dinghy
____Others			

Marine Radio _____Yes _____No

Type _____ Frequency _____

Digital Selective Calling (DSC) _____Yes _____No

Trip Expectations

Depart from _____

Departure Date _____ Time _____

Going to _____

Arrival Date _____ Time _____

If operator has not arrived/returned by:

Date _____ Time _____

Call the coast guard or local authority at the following number:_____

Vehicle Description

License No._____ Make _____

Model _____ Color _____

Where is vehicle parked? _____

Persons on Board

Name	Age	Phone	Medical Conditions

Additional Information

Index

Page numbers in italics indicates illustrations, tables and charts.